LOW-FAT INGREDIENT SUBSTITUTIONS

Needed Ingredient	Substitutions
FATS AND OILS	
Butter or margarine	Reduced-calorie margarine or margarine made with canola, corn, peanut, safflower, or soybean oil; reduced-calorie stick margarine in baked products
Mayonnaise	Nonfat, reduced-fat, or low-fat mayonnaise
Oil	Safflower, soybean, corn, canola, or peanut oil in reduced amount
Salad dressing	Fat-free or oil-free dressing
Shortening	Soybean, corn, canola, or peanut oil in amount reduced by one-third
DAIRY PRODUCTS	
Cheeses: American, Cheddar, colby, Edam, or Swiss	Cheeses with 5 grams of fat or less per ounce like reduced-fat and part-skim cheeses
Cheese, cottage	Nonfat or 1% low-fat cottage cheese
Cheese, cream	Fat-free, ⅓-less-fat cheese, or tub-style light cream cheese
Cheese, ricotta	Nonfat, lite, or part-skim ricotta cheese
Cream, sour	Low-fat or nonfat sour cream; low-fat or nonfat yogurt
Cream, whipping	Chilled fat-free evaporated milk or fat-free half-and-half
Ice cream	Nonfat or low-fat frozen yogurt; nonfat or low-fat ice cream; sherbet; sorbet
Milk, whole	Fat-free, low-fat, or reduced-fat milk
MEATS, POULTRY, AND EGGS	
Bacon	Canadian bacon; turkey bacon; lean ham
Beef, ground	Extralean or ultralean ground beef; freshly ground raw turkey
Beef, lamb, pork, or veal	Chicken, turkey, or lean cuts of meat trimmed of all visible fat
Luncheon meat	Skinned, sliced turkey or chicken breast; lean ham; lean roast beef
Poultry	Skinned poultry
Tuna packed in oil	Tuna packed in water
Turkey, self-basting	Turkey basted with fat-free broth
Egg, whole	2 egg whites or ¼ cup fat-free egg substitute
MISCELLANEOUS	
Fudge sauce	Fat-free fudge sauce or chocolate syrup
Nuts	Reduce amount one-third to one-half, and toast
Soups, canned	98% fat-free or reduced-fat, reduced-sodium condensed cream soups

Sicilian Tuna With
Fettuccine, page 52

Chili-Crusted Flank Steak
Fajitas, page 107

Caramel Upside-Down
Pull-Apart Loaf, page 40

Passion Fruit
Sorbet, page 87

Weight Watchers® MAGAZINE

ANNUAL RECIPES *for* SUCCESS

2000

Oxmoor House®

WE'RE HERE FOR YOU!

We at Oxmoor House are dedicated to serving you with reliable information that expands your imagination and enriches your life. We welcome your comments and suggestions. Please write us at:

Oxmoor House, Inc.
Weight Watchers® Magazine Annual Recipes for Success
2100 Lakeshore Drive
Birmingham, AL 35209

To order additional publications,
    call 1-205-877-6560.

COVER: Fudgy Pie With Ice Cream, page 101
BACK COVER: Herb-Marinated Shrimp, page 108
            Turkey Burgers With Sweet Red Onion
            Relish, page 93

WEIGHT WATCHERS® MAGAZINE
Editor: Kate Greer
Executive Editor: Mary Kay Culpepper
Managing Editor: Kay Fuston
Art Director: Amy Heise
Senior Food Editor: Alyson M. Haynes
Assistant Food Editor: Regan M. Jones, R.D.
Copy Editor: Maria Parker Hopkins
Fitness/Health Editor: Kate Neale Cooper
Beauty/Fashion Editor: Melissa Bigner
Editorial Coordinator: Christine O'Connell
Assistant Editor: Kate McWhorter
Assistant Art Director: Craig Hyde
Photo Stylist: Rose Nguyen
Test Kitchens Director: Kathleen Royal Phillips
Assistant Test Kitchens Director: Gayle Hays Sadler
Test Kitchens Staff: Julie Christopher, Lorrie Hulston,
    Natalie E. King, Rebecca W. Mohr, Jan A. Smith,
    Kate M. Wheeler, R.D.

OXMOOR HOUSE, INC.
Editor-in-Chief: Nancy Fitzpatrick Wyatt
Senior Foods Editor: Katherine M. Eakin
Senior Editor, Copy and Homes: Olivia Kindig Wells
Art Director: James Boone

WEIGHT WATCHERS® MAGAZINE ANNUAL
RECIPES FOR SUCCESS 2000
Editor: Patricia Wilens
Copy Editor: Donna Baldone
Editorial Assistant: Heather Averett
Associate Art Director: Cynthia R. Cooper
Designers: Clare Minges, Emily Albright Parrish
Contributing Indexer: Mary Ann Laurens
Director, Production and Distribution: Phillip Lee
Associate Production Managers: James McDaniel,
    Vanessa Cobbs Richardson
Production Assistant: Faye Porter Bonner

CONTENTS

Welcome

Readers often call or write us for copies of recipes from earlier magazines. Thus was born the idea for this book—a collection of all recipes that appeared in the 1999 issues of *Weight Watchers* Magazine. No more lost clippings and cut-apart issues. And we include nutrition information, tips on how to eat wisely, and popular Success stories to inspire anyone wanting to lose weight effectively. So this is a cookbook-plus.

Despite press reports that Americans subsist on take-out and restaurant meals, we found that our readers cook the main meal three to five nights a week; even more do so on a weekend. That's what 80% of the respondents to an April 1999 questionnaire told us. What's more, 90.6% consider themselves skilled or average cooks, but with little time. They prefer recipes with a limited number of ingredients and they want lightened recipes for delicious foods.

Above all, what they want is what the magazine serves up every month. Recipe developers work with our mandate that recipes should be wonderfully tasty and yet use as few ingredients and methods as possible. Moreover, recipes must be family-friendly dishes that are reliable, satisfying, and healthy. And low in **POINTS**®.

That reliability is important. When you spend time, money, and effort to create a meal, you should feel secure that the recipe is goof-proof. Our test kitchens prepare each recipe just as *you* would, with regular kitchen equipment. The dish is then evaluated by a taste-testing panel. Some recipes sail through, while others may be adjusted and retested several times. So you can have confidence in every recipe in this book.

Our year included awards and other recognition that make us very proud. But real satisfaction comes from serving our readers with useful information, helpful advice, and the best recipes you'll find anywhere. I hope you enjoy this book and will let me know what you think of it. Write to me at 2100 Lakeshore Drive, Birmingham, AL 35209, or E-mail kate_greer@spc.com.

Kate Greer

Editor, *Weight Watchers* Magazine

Our Favorite Recipes

All the recipes in *Weight Watchers* Magazine are terrific. But some *really* take the cake. After a year of taste-testing every recipe, magazine staff members chose their personal favorites. In this subjective and unscientific poll, several recipes earned multiple votes. We've listed the top three vote-getters first and the remaining favorites in no particular order. We're pleased to share with you our selections for the yummiest recipes of 1999.

CURRIED CHICKPEAS IN COCONUT-CILANTRO BROTH (PAGE 78). This unusual blend of flavors is the number one pick of food editors Alyson Haynes and Regan Jones. Alyson says this vegetarian delight is easy to make and reheats nicely, so she can make a batch in the evening to bring for lunch the next day.

CRAB QUESADILLAS WITH POBLANO CREAM (PAGE 34). The top choice of Managing Editor Kay Fuston and Copy Editor Maria Hopkins is a delectable combination of shellfish, cheese, and chiles. Loaded with calcium, it's a mouthwatering family favorite.

PESTO PIZZA WITH SHRIMP, ASPARAGUS, AND PROSCIUTTO (PAGE 123). Editor Kate Greer was among those casting votes for this savory concoction. You can keep refrigerated pizza crust dough and prepared pesto on hand to support fresh shrimp and asparagus in season.

THAI CHILI WITH SHRIMP (PAGE 20). Ginger, soy sauce, coconut milk, and cilantro lend an exotic flavor to this satisfying stew. This is quick and easy weeknight fare that's sure to please.

WARM BITTERSWEET CHOCOLATE-RUM TORTE (PAGE 29). A slice of this chocolate treat is pure decadence, but it's lightened to make it guilt-free. The torte comes out of the oven puffed like a soufflé, but cools to a dense, fudgy texture with a crackled, crunchy top.

TORTILLA CHILE SOUP (PAGE 35). This hearty soup is a man-pleasing union of chicken, strips of corn tortillas, beans, and chiles. Served with a dollop of sour cream and a sprinkling of Cheddar, it's a meal in itself.

MRS. PARKER'S CORN-AND-RICE CASSEROLE (PAGE 64). A rich cheesy flavor makes this a family favorite. Serve it as a side dish or double the serving size for a filling meatless main dish.

ROASTED ASPARAGUS-AND-GOAT CHEESE CROSTINI (PAGE 74). These "little toasts" are a satisfying, low-**POINTS** snack or appetizer. The oven-baked asparagus is the perfect complement to tangy goat cheese.

PLUM COBBLER (PAGE 120). Make the most of summer produce with this easy-to-fix treat. Just add slices of juicy, ripe plums to pantry staples and bake. A wonderful potluck dessert, this cobbler is good served warm or at room temperature.

BRAISED BEEF WITH PRUNES AND CARAMELIZED ONIONS (PAGE 138). Try this succulent dish to experience the ease of braising, the one-pot method that steams and simmers meat to tender, juicy perfection. This dish makes its own sauce that goes well with noodles for a hearty meal.

FALL VEGETABLE BRAISE WITH WHITE BEANS (PAGE 139). Mix a bounty of autumn vegetables with a flavorful sauce for a terrific meatless main dish. Beans and a sprinkling of cheese make the meal a good source of protein—just the thing to take the chill off cool autumn nights.

ENCHILADAS SUIZAS (PAGE 150). Put new life in your holiday leftovers with this variation on a Mexcian specialty. These enchiladas are a quick-fix meal that blends piquant salsa and jalapeño pepper with luscious sour cream—a taste sensation.

About Our Recipes

Here are some guidelines that *Weight Watchers* Magazine adheres to regarding our recipes. Follow our suggestions for nutritional accuracy.

• When preparing a recipe that yields more than one serving, mix the ingredients well, and divide the mixture (both liquids and solids) evenly.

• Unless otherwise indicated, servings of meat, fish, and poultry refer to cooked, skinned, and boned.

• Recipes give approximate nutritional information, including CAL (calories), PRO (protein), FAT (total fat), SAT (saturated fat), CARB (carbohydrate), FIB (dietary fiber), CHOL (cholesterol), IRON (iron), SOD (sodium), and CALC (calcium). Measurements are abbreviated as follows: g (grams), mg (milligrams).

• Some recipes call for egg whites at room temperature. Do not leave eggs sitting out for long periods of time. A quick way to bring an egg to room temperature is to let it stand in warm water for approximately 15 minutes.

• Recipes include **POINTS**® based on Weight Watchers International's *1•2•3 Success*® Weight Loss Plan. **POINTS** are calculated from a formula based on calories, fat, and fiber that assigns higher points to higher calorie, higher fat foods. Based on your present weight, you are allowed a certain number of **POINTS** per day.
NOTE: Because data on fat distribution are not available for some processed foods, these breakdowns should be considered approximate.

• Recipes now include diabetic exchanges, which have been calculated from the *Exchange List for Meal Planning* developed by The American Dietetic Association and the American Diabetes Association. The exchange information is designated as follows: starch, fruit, skim milk (sk milk), low-fat milk (l-f milk), whole milk (wh milk), vegetable (veg), very lean meat, lean meat, medium-fat meat (med-fat meat), high-fat meat (hi-fat meat), and fat. Foods within the same category can be substituted: for example, ½ cup cereal for 1 slice of bread.

• In the 5 Ingredients columns, recipes contain five ingredients or less, excluding water, salt, pepper, and cooking spray.

• The recipes shown in our photos may vary as to the number of servings pictured.

January/February

A Healthy Head Start

Five low-calorie menus with 10 **POINTS** or fewer are the perfect beginning to a happy New Year.

Making New Year's resolutions was first practiced by Babylonians 4,000 years ago. The resolution they made most often was to return borrowed tools. Today's number one resolution is to eat more healthfully and lose weight. We know it's tough to keep such lofty goals in mind, so we created five complete menus with 10 **POINTS** or fewer to get you started. And if you still have the Smiths' lawn mower in your garage, be sure to return it with a full tank of gas.

CHICKEN-BLUE CHEESE SALAD WITH WARM BACON VINAIGRETTE

(pictured on page 23)

Assemble the salad before you make the vinaigrette, and then pour the warm vinaigrette over the salad.

1 cup dry white wine
1 (14¼-ounce) can fat-free chicken broth
1 pound skinned, boned chicken breasts
12 cups mixed baby salad greens
1 medium-size red Bartlett pear, cored and cut into ½-inch-thick slices
1 medium-size green Bartlett pear, cored and cut into ½-inch-thick slices
Warm Bacon Vinaigrette
¾ cup (3 ounces) crumbled blue cheese

1. Bring wine and broth to a boil in a large skillet. Add chicken breasts; cover, reduce heat, and simmer 15 minutes or until done. Remove chicken with a slotted spoon; discard wine mixture. Cut

chicken diagonally into thin slices.
2. Combine chicken, salad greens, and pear slices in a large bowl. Drizzle Warm Bacon Vinaigrette over salad, and toss gently. Sprinkle with blue cheese. YIELD: 6 servings (serving size: 2 cups salad greens, about 3 ounces chicken, 4 pear slices, ½ ounce blue cheese, and about 2½ tablespoons vinaigrette).

POINTS: 5; **EXCHANGES:** 3 Very Lean Meat, 2 Veg, ½ Fruit, 1 Fat; **PER SERVING:** CAL 237 (33% from fat); PRO 24.4g; FAT 8.6g (sat 3.8g); CARB 15.5g; FIB 3.5g; CHOL 67mg; IRON 2.2mg; SOD 572mg; CALC 137mg

---

Menu One

Serves 6

Chicken-Blue Cheese Salad With Warm Bacon Vinaigrette

sesame breadsticks

Light Vanilla Crème Brûlée

Note: Serve 2 (8-inch) sesame breadsticks per person. We used Alessi brand.

Per Serving: *POINTS* 9; Calories 437 (24% from fat); Fat 11.6g; Fiber 4.5g

---

WARM BACON VINAIGRETTE:

Cooking spray
⅓ cup chopped red onion
3 turkey-bacon slices, chopped
½ cup fat-free chicken broth
⅓ cup cider vinegar
2 tablespoons brown sugar
½ teaspoon salt
¼ teaspoon dry mustard
¼ teaspoon celery seeds
¼ teaspoon pepper

1. Coat a nonstick skillet with cooking spray, and place over medium-high heat until hot. Add chopped onion and bacon, and sauté 10 minutes or until onion is tender and bacon is browned. Remove skillet from heat, and add chicken broth and remaining ingredients, stirring until sugar dissolves. YIELD: 1 cup.

LIGHT VANILLA CRÈME BRÛLÉE

The longer the vanilla bean stands in milk, the more the dessert tastes like vanilla.

1 (12-ounce) can evaporated skim milk
½ cup 1% low-fat milk
1 (2-inch) piece vanilla bean, split lengthwise
⅓ cup sugar
⅛ teaspoon salt
2 large eggs, lightly beaten
2 large egg whites, lightly beaten
3 tablespoons brown sugar

1. Preheat oven to 325°.
2. Combine milks in a medium bowl. Scrape seeds from vanilla bean; add seeds and bean to milks.

Cover and let milk mixture stand in refrigerator at least 10 minutes. Discard vanilla bean.

3. Add ⅓ cup sugar and next 3 ingredients to milk mixture; beat at medium speed of a mixer 1 minute. Pour evenly into 6 (6-ounce) ramekins or custard cups. Place ramekins in a 13- x 9-inch baking pan; add hot water to pan to depth of 1 inch.

4. Bake at 325° for 45 minutes or until knife inserted near center comes out clean. Remove cups from pan; let cool on a wire rack. Cover and chill at least 3 hours.

5. Sprinkle 1½ teaspoons brown sugar over each serving. Place ramekins on a baking sheet; broil 2 minutes or until brown sugar melts. Serve immediately. YIELD: 6 servings.

NOTE: You may substitute 1½ teaspoons vanilla extract for vanilla bean, if desired. Simply add extract to milk mixture and proceed to Step 3 of recipe.

POINTS: 3; EXCHANGES: 1 Starch, ½ Sk Milk, ½ Lean Meat; PER SERVING: CAL 145 (12% from fat); PRO 8.4g; FAT 2g (sat 0.7g); CARB 23.5g; FIB 0g; CHOL 74mg; IRON 0.5mg; SOD 168mg; CALC 210mg

---

Menu Two

Serves 8

⌇

Maple-Mustard Pork Roast

Creamed Spiced Rutabaga

steamed green beans

Note: Serve about 1 cup steamed green beans per person.

⌇

Per Serving: *POINTS* 9; Calories 422 (28% from fat); Fat 13.2g; Fiber 5.2g

---

MAPLE-MUSTARD PORK ROAST

(pictured on page 69)

1 (2½-pound) lean, boned pork loin roast
1½ tablespoons Dijon mustard
2 teaspoons light maple-flavored syrup
1¼ cups fresh whole-wheat breadcrumbs
1 tablespoon dried parsley
2 teaspoons cracked pepper
½ teaspoon dried marjoram
¼ teaspoon salt
⅛ teaspoon garlic powder
Cooking spray
Parsley sprigs (optional)
Maple-Mustard Sauce

1. Preheat oven to 325°.

2. Trim fat from pork loin roast. Combine mustard and syrup, and spread evenly over roast. Combine breadcrumbs and next 5 ingredients; press into mustard mixture, coating roast with crumb mixture.

3. Place roast on a broiler pan coated with cooking spray, and

insert meat thermometer into thickest portion of roast.

4. Bake at 325° for 1½ hours. Cover loosely with foil to prevent crumb mixture from burning; bake an additional 30 minutes or until meat thermometer registers 160° (slightly pink).

5. Remove from oven; uncover and let stand 10 minutes before slicing. Garnish with parsley sprigs, if desired. Serve with Maple-Mustard Sauce. YIELD: 10 servings (serving size: 3 ounces meat and 2 tablespoons sauce).

POINTS: 5; EXCHANGES: 3½ Lean Meat, ½ Starch; PER SERVING: CAL 222 (35% from fat); PRO 27.2g; FAT 8.7g (sat 2.9g); CARB 6.6g; FIB 0.3g; CHOL 72mg; IRON 1.4mg; SOD 398mg; CALC 69mg

MAPLE-MUSTARD SAUCE:
1½ tablespoons all-purpose flour
¾ cup evaporated skim milk
½ cup fat-free chicken broth
2 tablespoons Dijon mustard
1 tablespoon light maple-flavored syrup
¼ teaspoon salt
¼ teaspoon pepper

1. Place flour in a medium saucepan. Gradually add milk and chicken broth, stirring with a whisk until blended. Stir in mustard and remaining ingredients. Place over medium heat; cook 10 minutes or until thick and bubbly, stirring constantly. YIELD: 1¼ cups.

CREAMED SPICED RUTABAGA

(pictured on page 69)

Rutabaga tastes similar to cabbage and turnips. Select those that are smooth, firm, and heavy for their size.

  6 cups peeled, cubed rutabaga (about 1½ pounds)

  4 cups peeled, cubed Yukon gold or baking potato (about 1 pound)

  ¼ cup evaporated skim milk

  2 tablespoons stick margarine

1½ tablespoons brown sugar

  ½ teaspoon salt

  ¼ teaspoon ground allspice

  ¼ teaspoon ground nutmeg

Additional ground nutmeg (optional)

1. Place rutabaga in a large Dutch oven, and cover with water; bring to a boil. Reduce heat, and simmer 15 minutes. Add cubed potato, and bring to a boil. Reduce heat, and simmer an additional 15 minutes or until rutabaga and potato are tender.
2. Drain and return rutabaga-potato mixture to pan. Add milk and next 5 ingredients; beat at medium speed of a mixer until smooth. Spoon into serving bowl; sprinkle with additional nutmeg, if desired.
YIELD: 8 servings (serving size: 1 cup).
NOTE: For a savory alternative to this slightly sweet side dish, omit sugar, allspice, and nutmeg. Substitute ½ teaspoon dried marjoram and ½ teaspoon black pepper.

POINTS: 3; EXCHANGES: 1 Starch, 1 Veg, ½ Fat; PER SERVING: CAL 136 (21% from fat); PRO 3.4g; FAT 3.2g (sat 0.6g); CARB 24.7g; FIB 2.4g; CHOL 0mg; IRON 1.2mg; SOD 215mg; CALC 81mg

---

Menu Three

Serves 5

⌒⌒⌒

Mediterranean Vegetable Pasta

mixed greens with fat-free balsamic vinaigrette

Toasted Pecan Biscotti

Note: Serve 1½ cups greens and 1½ tablespoons balsamic vinaigrette per person.

⌒⌒⌒

Per Serving: *POINTS* 9; Calories 490 (12% from fat); Fat 6.6g; Fiber 6.6g

---

MEDITERRANEAN VEGETABLE PASTA

(pictured on page 114)

Olive oil-flavored cooking spray

  3 cups cubed eggplant

  1 cup sliced fresh mushrooms

  ¾ cup coarsely chopped onion

  1 medium zucchini, quartered lengthwise and cut into 1-inch pieces

  1 small green bell pepper, coarsely chopped

  1 garlic clove, minced

  1 (14.5-ounce) can no-salt-added stewed tomatoes, undrained

  1 (15-ounce) can chickpeas (garbanzo beans), drained

  2 tablespoons dry red wine

  2 tablespoons capers

  ½ teaspoon dried rosemary, crushed

  ¼ teaspoon salt

  ¼ teaspoon pepper

  4 cups hot cooked penne, cooked without salt or fat (about 3 cups uncooked tubular pasta)

  ⅓ cup (1⅓ ounces) finely grated fresh Asiago or Parmesan cheese

1. Coat a Dutch oven with cooking spray; place over medium-high heat until hot. Add eggplant and next 5 ingredients; sauté 7 minutes or until crisp-tender. Stir in tomatoes and next 6 ingredients. Bring to a boil; cover, reduce heat, and simmer 8 minutes or until vegetables are tender. Spoon vegetable mixture over pasta, and sprinkle with cheese.
YIELD: 5 servings (serving size: 1 cup vegetable mixture, about ¾ cup pasta, and 1 tablespoon cheese).

POINTS: 7; EXCHANGES: 4 Starch, 1 Veg, ½ Lean Meat; PER SERVING: CAL 371 (11% from fat); PRO 16.8g; FAT 4.5g (sat 1.5g); CARB 67.6g; FIB 5.4g; CHOL 5mg; IRON 5.1mg; SOD 636mg; CALC 177mg

TOASTED PECAN BISCOTTI

  2 cups all-purpose flour

  ¾ cup sugar

  ⅓ cup chopped pecans, toasted

  2 teaspoons grated orange rind

  ¾ teaspoon ground cinnamon

  ½ teaspoon baking powder

  ½ teaspoon baking soda

  ½ teaspoon salt

  2 large eggs, lightly beaten

  1 large egg white

  1 teaspoon vanilla extract

Cooking spray

1. Preheat oven to 325°.
2. Combine first 8 ingredients in a bowl. Add eggs, egg white, and vanilla to flour mixture; stir just until blended.
3. Turn dough out onto a floured surface; divide in half. Shape each half into an 8-inch-long log. Place logs on a baking sheet coated with cooking spray; flatten to ¾-inch thickness.

4. Bake at 325° for 30 minutes. Remove from oven; reduce oven temperature to 300°. Place logs on a wire rack; let cool 10 minutes. Cut each log diagonally into 12 (½-inch-thick) slices. Place cut sides down on baking sheet.

5. Bake at 300° for 20 minutes. Turn cookies over; bake an additional 10 minutes (cookies will be slightly soft but will harden as they cool). Let cool on wire racks. YIELD: 2 dozen (serving size: 1 cookie).

POINTS: 2; EXCHANGES: 1 Starch; PER SERVING: CAL 78 (18% from fat); PRO 1.8g; FAT 1.6g (sat 0.2g); CARB 14.1g; FIB 0.4g; CHOL 18mg; IRON 0.6mg; SOD 80mg; CALC 9mg

ITALIAN BEEF-AND-POTATO CASSEROLE

1 pound ground chuck
1 cup chopped onion
1 (8-ounce) package presliced
   fresh mushrooms
2 garlic cloves, minced
1 (27.5-ounce) jar fat-free chunky
   mushroom and garlic pasta
   sauce (such as Ragu Light)
1 (10-ounce) package frozen
   chopped spinach, thawed,
   drained, and squeezed dry
¼ cup water
¼ teaspoon fennel seeds, crushed
¼ teaspoon salt
¼ teaspoon pepper
Butter-flavored cooking spray
4 medium baking potatoes, peeled
   and cut into ¼-inch slices
   (about 2 pounds)
½ cup (2 ounces) finely grated
   fresh Parmesan cheese

1. Preheat oven to 350°.

2. Combine first 4 ingredients in a nonstick skillet; cook over medium heat until beef is browned, stirring to crumble. Drain well; return to skillet. Add pasta sauce and next 5 ingredients; bring to a boil. Reduce heat; simmer 5 minutes.

3. Spread half of beef mixture in a 13- x 9-inch baking dish coated with cooking spray. Arrange half of potato slices over mixture, slightly overlapping slices. Repeat with remaining beef mixture and potato slices, ending with potato slices. Coat with cooking spray. Cover and bake at 350° for 30 minutes. Uncover; bake 20 minutes or until golden. Top with cheese; bake an additional 10 minutes. Let stand 10 minutes before serving. YIELD: 8 servings.

POINTS: 6; EXCHANGES: 2 Starch, 1½ Med-fat Meat, 1 Veg; PER SERVING: CAL 300 (30% from fat); PRO 17.8g; FAT 10g (sat 4.3g); CARB 33.1g; FIB 5.5g; CHOL 38mg; IRON 4mg; SOD 528mg; CALC 162mg

---

Menu Four

Serves 8

⌘

Italian Beef-and-Potato
Casserole

steamed broccoli

Apple-Pie Sundaes

Note: Serve 1 cup steamed
broccoli per person.

⌘

Per Serving: *POINTS* 10; Calories
522 (25% from fat); Fat 14.7g;
Fiber 10.5g

APPLE-PIE SUNDAES

1 tablespoon water
2 teaspoons cornstarch
2 cups peeled, sliced cooking
   apple
1 cup apple juice
2 tablespoons brown sugar
2 teaspoons stick margarine
1 teaspoon lemon juice
¼ teaspoon apple-pie spice
Dash of salt
4 cups vanilla low-fat ice cream
¾ cup low-fat granola with raisins
   or 4 reduced-fat oatmeal-raisin
   cookies (such as SnackWells),
   crushed

1. Combine water and cornstarch in a small bowl; stir well, and set aside.

2. Combine sliced apple and juice in a medium saucepan; bring mixture to a boil. Reduce heat, and simmer, uncovered, 2 minutes. Stir in sugar and next 4 ingredients. Add cornstarch mixture, and stir well. Cook over medium heat until thick, stirring constantly. Remove from heat; let cool slightly.

3. Spoon ½ cup ice cream into each of 8 individual dessert dishes; top each with ¼ cup apple mixture and 1½ tablespoons low-fat granola. Serve immediately. YIELD: 8 servings.

POINTS: 4; EXCHANGES: 1 Starch, 1 Fruit, 1 Fat; PER SERVING: CAL 180 (22% from fat); PRO 2.8g; FAT 4.5g (sat 2.3g); CARB 32.8g; FIB 1.2g; CHOL 20mg; IRON 0.3mg; SOD 96mg; CALC 69mg

GLAZED SHRIMP KABOBS

1½ pounds unpeeled large fresh shrimp
 2 cups fresh pineapple chunks
⅓ cup no-sugar-added all-fruit apricot spread
 1 tablespoon rice vinegar
 1 tablespoon low-salt soy sauce
 1 teaspoon bottled minced ginger
 1 teaspoon dark sesame oil
Cooking spray

1. Peel and devein shrimp, leaving tails intact, if desired. Thread shrimp and pineapple alternately onto 8 (12-inch) skewers; set aside.
2. Spoon apricot spread into a medium bowl, and chop any large chunks of apricot, if desired. Add rice vinegar and next 3 ingredients, and stir well. Divide apricot mixture in half; reserve half of mixture.
3. Place kabobs on a broiler pan coated with cooking spray. Brush kabobs with apricot mixture; broil 3 minutes. Turn kabobs over, and brush with apricot mixture. Broil an additional 3 minutes or until done.

Brush with reserved apricot mixture before serving. YIELD: 4 servings (serving size: 2 kabobs).
NOTE: Substitute one 20-ounce can pineapple chunks in juice, drained, for fresh pineapple, if desired.

POINTS: 4; EXCHANGES: 3 Very Lean Meat, 1½ Fruit; PER SERVING: CAL 201 (11% from fat); PRO 20.5g; FAT 2.4g (sat 0.5g); CARB 23.6g; FIB 0.6g; CHOL 187mg; IRON 3.5mg; SOD 313mg; CALC 56mg

HOISIN SNOW PEAS AND PEPPERS

 1 cup fat-free chicken broth
 2 tablespoons hoisin sauce
1½ tablespoons dry sherry
 2 teaspoons cornstarch
Cooking spray
 1 teaspoon peanut or vegetable oil
 3 cups fresh snow peas, trimmed
 1 cup red bell pepper strips
 2 teaspoons finely chopped unsalted, dry-roasted peanuts

1. Combine first 4 ingredients in a small bowl; stir well, and set aside.
2. Coat a large nonstick skillet with cooking spray; add peanut oil, and place over medium-high heat until hot. Add snow peas and bell pepper; sauté 3 minutes or until vegetables are crisp-tender. Add broth mixture, and cook 2 minutes or until mixture is thick, stirring constantly. Sprinkle with peanuts. YIELD: 4 servings (serving size: 1 cup vegetables and ½ teaspoon peanuts).

POINTS: 2; EXCHANGES: 1 Veg, ½ Starch, ½ Fat; PER SERVING: CAL 95 (26% from fat); PRO 4.8g; FAT 2.7g (sat 0.5g); CARB 12.8g; FIB 2.6g; CHOL 6.3mg; IRON 2mg; SOD 116mg; CALC 37mg

GOODS

Freeze Frame

Your freezer is the first step to simplifying supper.

You leave work planning to go to the market. But you get home and you've forgotten to stop. Other times, you're too tired to make a meal. Until recently, either scenario meant a date with pizza delivery. But with a stocked freezer, those days are over. Here are five cool ways to whip up a quick dinner, full of flavor. Let's hope the pizza guy doesn't get lonely.

PESTO, PRESTO. The next time you make pesto, make extra. Use an ice cube tray to freeze the pesto in 1-tablespoon-size amounts. Pop the frozen cubes into a zip-top plastic bag. They will keep in the freezer several months. Use the sauce on pizza, over fish, or tossed with hot pasta and cannellini beans.

SAVOR THE FLAVOR. Roasted garlic imparts garlic's pungent flavor with none of its bite. To save roasting time, try this with several heads of garlic: Remove the papery skins, and wrap each head separately in foil. Bake at 350° for 1 hour. Let the garlic cool; then carefully separate (but don't peel) the cloves. Toss the cloves into a zip-top plastic bag and freeze. When you need them, they just take a few seconds to thaw in the microwave. Squeeze the cloves to extract the roasted pulp and use it to add flavor to everything from pasta and pizza to dips and marinades.

WASTE NOT, WANT NOT.
A recipe calls for a tablespoon of tomato paste, which leaves you with nearly a full can left over. Sound familiar? Here's a simple solution. Place a can of tomato paste in the freezer for a few hours, and then run it under warm water. Open both ends, push out the paste, and freeze it in a zip-top plastic bag. Whenever you need tomato paste, just slice off a tablespoon or two of the frozen paste. Return the remaining paste to the freezer.

GOOD THINGS IN SMALL PACKAGES. Casseroles don't have to be time-consuming. Make a large casserole recipe that freezes well, and spoon it into individual containers coated with cooking spray; then freeze. Flip out mini casseroles into heavy-duty, zip-top plastic bags. (You may need to dip the bottoms in warm water for a minute.) To serve, slip the casserole back into its dish, thaw, and bake according to recipe directions. (Adjust baking time since these are smaller casseroles than your recipe makes.)

TEMPTATION, THY NAME IS COOKIE. Some cookie recipes freeze quite well. Just roll the dough into a log, wrap in wax paper, and freeze in a zip-top plastic bag. Slice off a cookie or two, and bake as needed (or wanted) for a quick dessert. You can do the same thing with store-bought cookie dough—just be sure to select a brand that's low fat.

Endless Summer

Put the freeze on winter blues by harvesting the flavor of summer from your freezer.

By January you'd love to have a reason to don shorts, even if that means baring winter-pale skin. We have no pull with Mother Nature, but we do have some ideas for bringing a taste of summer to your table. Use frozen summer produce, which is just as nutritious as the fresh variety because it's packaged within six hours of harvest. Just turn up the heat, pull on your shorts, and start cooking.

CINNAMON-SPICED PEACHES

(pictured on page 68)

Be sure to use sweetened dried cranberries. Unsweetened ones are too tart for this dish.

½ (16-ounce) package frozen sliced peaches, thawed (about 2 cups)
¼ cup sweetened dried cranberries (such as Craisins)
¼ cup peach nectar
3 tablespoons dark brown sugar
½ teaspoon ground cinnamon

1. Combine all ingredients in a medium nonstick skillet; stir well. Cover and cook over medium heat 10 minutes or until peaches are tender. Serve as a fruit side dish; a sauce for fat-free pound cake, angel food cake, or vanilla ice cream; or with ham or roast pork. YIELD: 5 servings (serving size: ¼ cup).

POINTS: 1; *EXCHANGES:* 1 Fruit;
PER SERVING: CAL 67 (1% from fat); PRO 0.4g; FAT 0.1g (sat 0g); CARB 17.2g; FIB 1.1g; CHOL 0mg; IRON 0.3mg; SOD 3mg; CALC 10mg

WILD RICE SALAD WITH PEAS

(pictured on page 22)

Serve this colorful rice salad at room temperature alongside roast turkey, chicken, or pork.

1 (6.2-ounce) package fast-cooking long-grain-and-wild rice mix (such as Uncle Ben's)
1 (10-ounce) package frozen green peas, thawed
⅔ cup chopped red bell pepper
½ cup sliced almonds, toasted
⅓ cup teriyaki sauce

1. Cook rice mix according to package directions, omitting seasoning packet and fat. Reserve seasoning packet for another use.
2. Combine rice mix, peas, bell pepper, almonds, and teriyaki sauce in a large bowl. Stir well, and let cool. Serve at room temperature. YIELD: 6 servings (serving size: 1 cup).

POINTS: 4; *EXCHANGES:* 2 Starch, 1 Fat;
PER SERVING: CAL 203 (20% from fat); PRO 7.1g; FAT 4.6g (sat 0.5g); CARB 33.7g; FIB 3.6g; CHOL 0mg; IRON 2.4mg; SOD 616mg; CALC 43mg

BLACK-EYED
PEA AND BASIL SALAD

Full of fiber and good luck but practically fat free, this salad is a great way to start the New Year.

1 (10-ounce) package frozen black-eyed peas (about 2 cups)
1¼ cups chopped plum tomato (about ¾ pound)
⅓ cup fat-free Caesar Italian dressing (such as Kraft)
¼ cup finely chopped fresh parsley
2 teaspoons dried basil
¼ teaspoon salt

1. Combine 1½ cups water and black-eyed peas in a medium saucepan; bring to a boil. Cover, reduce heat, and simmer 30 minutes or until peas are just tender (do not overcook). Drain; let cool.
2. Combine black-eyed peas, chopped tomato, and remaining ingredients in a medium bowl; toss well. Serve salad chilled or at room temperature. YIELD: 3 servings (serving size: 1 cup).
NOTE: Plum tomatoes have more flavor during the winter season and have considerably fewer seeds to water down the salad. If you use regular tomatoes, be sure to seed the tomatoes before chopping.

POINTS: 3; **EXCHANGES:** 2 Starch, ½ Very Lean Meat; **PER SERVING:** CAL 159 (5% from fat); PRO 9.4g; FAT 0.9g (sat 0.2g); CARB 29.7g; FIB 2.8g; CHOL 0mg; IRON 3.2mg; SOD 468mg; CALC 51mg

TENDER PEAR CAKE
WITH RASPBERRIES

1 (15¼-ounce) can pear halves in heavy syrup, undrained
1 (18-ounce) package white cake mix (such as Betty Crocker SuperMoist)
3 large egg whites
Cooking spray
1 (10-ounce) package frozen raspberries in syrup, thawed and undrained
2 teaspoons cornstarch

1. Preheat oven to 350°.
2. Drain pear halves, reserving heavy syrup. Place pear halves in a medium bowl; mash with a fork or potato masher. Add water to reserved syrup to measure 1¼ cups; add syrup mixture to mashed pears. Add cake mix and egg whites to pear mixture, and beat at medium speed of a mixer 2 minutes.
3. Pour batter into a 13- x 9-inch baking pan coated with cooking spray. Bake at 350° for 24 minutes or until a wooden pick inserted in center comes out clean. Let cool completely in pan on a wire rack.
4. Combine raspberries in syrup and cornstarch in a medium saucepan; stir until mixture is well blended. Cook over medium heat 30 seconds or until mixture is thick, stirring constantly. Serve warm raspberry sauce with pear cake. YIELD: 16 servings (serving size: 1 slice cake and 1 tablespoon raspberry sauce).

POINTS: 4; **EXCHANGES:** 1 Fruit, 1 Starch, ½ Fat; **PER SERVING:** CAL 173 (14% from fat); PRO 2.2g; FAT 2.7g (sat 1.1g); CARB 34.6g; FIB 0.8g; CHOL 0mg; IRON 0.5mg; SOD 222mg; CALC 45mg

BUTTERY HERBED
GREEN BEANS

(pictured on page 22)

Substitute other dried herbs such as oregano, basil, or thyme for the tarragon, if desired.

2 (9-ounce) packages frozen whole green beans (about 5 cups)
2 teaspoons stick margarine
2 tablespoons finely chopped fresh parsley
2 teaspoons cider or balsamic vinegar
½ teaspoon salt
½ teaspoon dried tarragon
Parsley sprigs (optional)

1. Bring ½ cup water to a boil over high heat in a large nonstick skillet; add green beans. Cover and cook 8 minutes or until beans are crisp-tender; drain.
2. Combine beans and margarine in skillet; cook over low heat until margarine melts. Add chopped parsley, vinegar, salt, and tarragon; toss well. Garnish with parsley, if desired. YIELD: 3 servings (serving size: 1 cup).

POINTS: 1; **EXCHANGES:** 2 Veg, ½ Fat; **PER SERVING:** CAL 80 (32% from fat); PRO 3.0g; FAT 2.9g (sat 0.6g); CARB 13.3g; FIB 4.9g; CHOL 0mg; IRON 1.7mg; SOD 231mg; CALC 78mg

Cowboy Comfort

Those cattlemen had the right idea, but it's time to break with tradition by changing your chili.

Like the cowboys who invented it, chili has come a long way since pioneer days. People in places those cowboys never heard of are reinventing chili and creating Caribbean, Mexican, even Thai versions of America's native stew. The only thing holding you back is tradition.

BLACK-EYED PEA AND CHUTNEY CHILI

(pictured on page 110)

1 pound lean ground pork
1¼ cups chopped red onion
1¼ cups chopped green bell pepper
½ cup hot mango chutney
¼ cup low-salt soy sauce
½ teaspoon ground allspice
2 (14½-ounce) cans diced tomatoes with garlic and onion, undrained
1 (15.8-ounce) can black-eyed peas, rinsed and drained
3 cups hot cooked instant brown rice, cooked without salt or fat

1. Cook pork in skillet over medium-high heat until browned, stirring to crumble. Drain in colander; set aside.
2. Add onion and next 4 ingredients to skillet; cook over medium heat 7 minutes, stirring occasionally. Add tomatoes; bring to a boil. Cover, reduce heat, and simmer 5 minutes. Add pork and peas; cover and cook until thoroughly heated. Serve over rice. YIELD: 6 servings (serving size: 1 cup chili and ½ cup rice).

POINTS: 9; **EXCHANGES:** 3½ Starch, 1 Hi-fat Meat, 2 Veg; **PER SERVING:** CAL 445 (21% from fat); PRO 23.4g; FAT 10.3g (sat 3g); CARB 62.6g; FIB 6g; CHOL 54mg; IRON 1.5mg; SOD 1,339mg; CALC 42mg

MEXICAN GREEN CHILI

Serve this chili with flour tortillas.

1½ pounds lean top round steak, cut into 1-inch pieces
1 (16-ounce) jar tomatillo salsa (such as Jardine's)
1 (14½-ounce) can Mexican-style stewed tomatoes with garlic, cumin, and jalapeños, undrained and chopped
1 (14¼-ounce) can fat-free beef broth
2 (4.5-ounce) cans chopped green chiles, undrained
1 cup chopped onion
2 teaspoons ground cumin
1 teaspoon freshly ground pepper
2 teaspoons bottled minced garlic
2 teaspoons chili oil

1. Combine all ingredients in a 5-quart electric slow cooker; stir well. Cover; cook on low-heat setting 8 hours. YIELD: 9 servings (serving size: 1 cup).

POINTS: 3; **EXCHANGES:** 2 Lean Meat, 2 Veg; **PER SERVING:** CAL 156 (24% from fat); PRO 19.3g; FAT 4.2g (sat 1.3g); CARB 8.7g; FIB 1g; CHOL 43mg; IRON 2.1mg; SOD 675mg; CALC 52mg

CARIBBEAN BLACK BEAN CHILI

2 teaspoons olive oil, divided
1 pound skinned, boned chicken breasts, cut into ½-inch pieces
¼ cup sliced shallots
2 tablespoons seeded, minced jalapeño pepper
1 tablespoon bottled chopped ginger
2 teaspoons bottled minced garlic
1 cup fresh orange juice
¾ teaspoon dried thyme
½ teaspoon ground allspice
3 (14.5-ounce) cans diced tomatoes, undrained
1 (15-ounce) can black beans, rinsed and drained
1 (11-ounce) can vacuum-packed whole-kernel corn, drained

1. Heat 1 teaspoon oil in a large Dutch oven over medium-high heat. Add chicken; sauté 6 minutes or until browned. Remove chicken from pan, and set aside.
2. Heat remaining oil in pan over medium heat. Add shallots and next 3 ingredients; sauté 3 minutes. Add orange juice and next 3 ingredients; bring to a boil. Reduce heat; simmer, uncovered, 8 minutes. Stir in chicken, beans, and corn; cook until thoroughly heated. YIELD: 9 servings (serving size: 1 cup).
NOTE: You can use fresh minced garlic and ginger, but bottled products save time on preparation.

POINTS: 4; **EXCHANGES:** 1½ Very Lean Meat, 1 Veg, 1½ Starch; **PER SERVING:** CAL 194 (14% from fat); PRO 16.9g; FAT 3g (sat 0.6g); CARB 28.4g; FIB 3.1g; CHOL 32mg; IRON 2.4mg; SOD 685mg; CALC 41mg

THAI CHILI WITH SHRIMP

(pictured on page 28)

1 (14-ounce) can light coconut
milk
1½ tablespoons bottled chopped
ginger
1 tablespoon chili paste with garlic
2 pounds medium-size fresh
shrimp, peeled
2 tablespoons all-purpose flour
3 tablespoons low-salt soy sauce
1 (14.5-ounce) can diced
tomatoes, undrained
½ cup sliced green onions
2 tablespoons fresh lime juice
½ teaspoon brown sugar
1½ cups sliced fresh shiitake or
oyster mushroom caps
7 teaspoons chopped fresh cilantro

1. Combine first 3 ingredients in a
saucepan, and bring mixture to a
boil. Add shrimp; reduce heat, and
simmer 3 minutes or until done.
Remove shrimp with slotted spoon.
2. Combine flour and soy sauce in a
small bowl, and stir with a whisk;
add to coconut milk mixture. Add
tomatoes and next 3 ingredients;
bring to a boil, stirring constantly.
Reduce heat; simmer 5 minutes or
until mixture is slightly thick, stirring occasionally. Stir in mushrooms;
cook 2 minutes. Return shrimp to
pan, and cook until thoroughly
heated. Ladle into bowls, and sprinkle with cilantro. YIELD: 7 servings
(serving size: 1 cup chili and 1 teaspoon cilantro.)

POINTS: 4; **EXCHANGES:** 2½ Very Lean Meat,
2 Veg, 1 Fat; **PER SERVING:** CAL 168
(26% from fat); PRO 20.9g; FAT 4.8g (sat 2.3g);
CARB 9.1g; FIB 1g; CHOL 148mg;
IRON 3.4mg; SOD 573mg; CALC 78mg

RED CHIPOTLE CHILI WITH LAMB

1½ pounds lean, boned leg of lamb
2 teaspoons olive oil
2 (14½-ounce) cans Mexican-
style stewed tomatoes with
garlic, cumin, and jalapeños,
undrained
¼ cup all-purpose flour
1 (15-ounce) can kidney beans,
drained
1 (12-ounce) bottle Mexican
dark beer (such as Dos Equis)
1 teaspoon dried thyme
1 teaspoon freshly ground pepper
2 teaspoons bottled minced garlic
2 to 4 chipotle chiles in adobo
sauce, chopped
4 cups hot cooked couscous,
cooked without salt or fat

1. Trim fat from leg of lamb, and cut
lamb into bite-size pieces. Heat olive
oil in a large nonstick skillet over
medium-high heat. Add lamb pieces,
browning on all sides. Drain well,
and set aside.
2. Drain tomatoes, reserving juice.
Place flour in a small bowl; gradually
add reserved tomato juice, stirring
with a whisk until blended.
3. Place lamb, tomatoes, flour mixture, beans, and next 5 ingredients in
a 5-quart electric slow cooker.
Cover; cook on low-heat setting 8
hours. Serve over couscous. YIELD:
8 servings (serving size: 1 cup chili
and ½ cup couscous).

POINTS: 6; **EXCHANGES:** 2½ Starch,
1 Lean Meat, 1 Very Lean Meat, 1 Veg;
PER SERVING: CAL 307 (17% from fat);
PRO 22.8g; FAT 5.8g (sat 1.6g); CARB 42.2g;
FIB 4.3g; CHOL 46mg; IRON 3.2mg;
SOD 500mg; CALC 39mg

MEDITERRANEAN CHILI BLANCO

2 fresh poblano chiles
2 (16-ounce) cans cannellini
beans, drained and divided
4 ounces (about ¾ cup) ⅓-less-
fat cream cheese (Neufchâtel),
softened
2 teaspoons olive oil
1 cup chopped onion
1 cup chopped red bell pepper
1 (14½-ounce) can vegetable
broth (such as Swanson's)
2 teaspoons ground cumin
1 teaspoon ground coriander
⅓ cup chopped plum tomato

1. Place chiles on foil-lined baking
sheet; broil 10 minutes or until
blackened, turning occasionally. Place
chiles in a zip-top plastic bag; seal
and let stand 15 minutes. Peel chiles;
cut in half lengthwise. Discard stems,
seeds, and membranes.
2. In processor, process chiles, half of
beans, and cheese until smooth.
3. Heat oil in a nonstick skillet over
medium-high heat. Add onion and
bell pepper; sauté 5 minutes or until
tender. Add broth, cumin, and coriander; bring to a boil. Reduce heat;
simmer 5 minutes. Add bean mixture
and remaining beans; cook until
thoroughly heated. Ladle into individual bowls, sprinkle with chopped
tomato. YIELD: 5 servings (serving size:
1 cup chili and 1 tablespoon tomato).
NOTE: Substitute 2 (4.5-ounce) cans
chopped green chiles, undrained, for
fresh poblano chiles.

POINTS: 4; **EXCHANGES:** 2 Starch, 1 Veg,
1 Very Lean Meat, 1 Fat; **PER SERVING:**
CAL 256 (28% from fat); PRO 13.3g; FAT 8g (sat
3.7g); CARB 34.1g; FIB 7.3g; CHOL 17mg;
IRON 3.9mg; SOD 969mg; CALC 94mg

Up to the Challenge

KAREN COLLINS • **HEIGHT** 5'2" • **BEFORE** 200 LBS. • **AFTER** 120 LBS.

Proudest Moment: Walking into a plus-size clothing store out of habit, and then realizing her mistake.

Karen Collins expected support when she joined Weight Watchers in 1994; instead, she got a challenge. When Karen and her sisters arrived at their first meeting, Karen's mind was on the restaurant next door. "I was thinking, 'Another diet? I'm over this,'" she recalls.

Karen's indifference was so obvious that the instructor, Leeann, suggested she wasn't ready for the program and might want to return another time. Karen says, "If you want me to do something, tell me I can't."

Karen gained weight in her twenties, when restaurant lunches with coworkers were routine. Between all-you-can-eat buffets and "super-size" portions, moderation was not a popular concept. "I look at those plates now and I can't believe it," Karen says.

With a sore back and other weight-related ailments, Karen realized she was compromising her health. "Everything hurt on me," she says. At age 33, Karen adopted Cody, who gave her incentive to take care of herself. "I want to be around for him, so I had a mission."

Leeann's challenge was the push Karen needed. She returned for her next meeting 4 pounds lighter. Soon she was dropping a size a month. The key, Karen found, was not to eliminate high-fat foods altogether, but rather to eat all foods in moderation. "I could

eat a bucket of diet food and still open the cabinet because I wasn't satisfied," she says.

An instructor suggested that Karen could still enjoy fast food, but in small portions, such as a kids meal instead of a value meal, or a bag-lunch portion of chips instead of a family-size bag. She could satisfy cravings without sacrificing goals. "At meetings, I learned all kinds of tricks," Karen explains, "but it's really about moderation."

And it's about exercise. Karen began walking, and it wasn't long before she saw results. "The more I walked, the bigger the weight loss, even though I was eating the same," she says. She tapped a spring of new energy. "I'd walk a mile, and then I'd come back in and still be hyped up," recalls Karen. She often headed back for another mile or climbed on her treadmill to continue the workout indoors.

By the time she reached her goal weight of 120 pounds, Karen says, her life had changed. "Even my sales ability improved," she says. But the best reward is being with Cody. "It's wonderful. I play with him and Rollerblade and bike, and it's giving him a great life."

"At meetings, I learned all kinds of tricks, but it's really about moderation."

Wild Rice Salad With Peas, page 17

Sweet Onions With Pistachios, page 76

Buttery Herbed Green Beans, page 18

Chicken-Blue Cheese Salad With Warm Bacon Vinaigrette, page 12

Orange-Hoisin Shrimp Stir-Fry, page 59

Marinated Broccoli-Corn Salad, page 51

Mango Mousse
With Raspberry Sauce, page 100

Dijon Pot Roast
and Vegetables, page 51

Spinach-and-Caramelized
Onion Pizza, page 36

Stuffed Sweet Potatoes, page 37

27

Warm Bittersweet
Chocolate-Rum Torte, at right

Thai Chili With Shrimp,
page 20

Bittersweet Surrender

Say "Be mine" with a decadent dessert—the answer will surely be "Yes!"

Only one day a year is officially dedicated to celebrating love. Valentine's Day is about being completely smitten with someone, someone you want to spoil. Do it with this rich torte, which we lightened for Dorothy "Dot" Ramsay of McKenzie, Tennessee. As Dot's husband knows, this homemade dessert says "I love you."

WARM BITTERSWEET CHOCOLATE-RUM TORTE

(pictured at left)

Cooking spray
1 (3-ounce) bar premium bittersweet chocolate (such as Lindt Swiss)
½ cup sugar
3½ tablespoons unsalted butter, softened
1 teaspoon vanilla extract
1 large egg
¼ cup skim milk
2 tablespoons dark rum
¼ cup Dutch process cocoa
2 tablespoons all-purpose flour
4 large egg whites at room temperature
¼ teaspoon cream of tartar
¼ cup sugar
Vanilla-Rum Custard Sauce
2 tablespoons powdered sugar
24 fresh raspberries

1. Preheat oven to 300°.
2. Coat bottom and sides of an 8-inch springform pan with cooking spray. Set aside.
3. Break chocolate into small pieces; place in a microwave-safe bowl. Microwave at MEDIUM (50% power) 2 minutes or until softened,

stirring until smooth. Set aside.
4. Combine ½ cup sugar and butter; beat at medium speed of a mixer until well blended (about 3 minutes). Add vanilla and egg; beat 1 minute. Add milk and rum; beat well (mixture will appear curdled). Add melted chocolate; beat just until blended. Add cocoa and flour; beat at low speed just until blended.
5. Using clean, dry beaters, beat egg whites and cream of tartar at high speed until foamy. Add ¼ cup sugar, 1 tablespoon at a time, beating until stiff peaks form. Stir ¼ of egg white mixture into batter; gently fold in remaining egg white mixture. Spoon batter into prepared pan.
6. Bake at 300° for 45 minutes or until a wooden pick inserted in center comes out slightly wet and with a few crumbs on it. Remove torte from oven; immediately run tip of a

small knife around edge of torte. Let cool (torte will rise to top of pan while baking, but will sink while it cools). Remove sides of springform pan; cut torte with a sharp knife rinsed in hot water.
7. Spoon ¼ cup Vanilla-Rum Custard Sauce onto each of 8 dessert plates; top each with a slice of torte. Sift powdered sugar over each serving; garnish with raspberries. YIELD: 8 servings (serving size: 1 slice torte, ¼ cup sauce, and 3 raspberries).
NOTE: Torte is excellent served warm, at room temperature, or chilled.

POINTS: 7; **EXCHANGES:** 3 Starch, 1½ Fat; **PER SERVING:** CAL 296 (30% from fat); PRO 8.1g; FAT 10g (sat 5.7g); CARB 44.4g; FIB 0.6g; CHOL 70mg; IRON 1.2mg; SOD 133mg; CALC 159mg

VANILLA-RUM CUSTARD SAUCE:

1 cup skim milk
1 cup evaporated skim milk
¼ cup sugar
1 large egg yolk
4 teaspoons cornstarch
⅛ teaspoon salt
2 tablespoons dark rum
2 teaspoons vanilla extract

1. Combine milks in a medium saucepan; cook over medium heat until hot (do not boil).

(continued)

Before		After	
Serving Size	1 slice and ¼ cup sauce	Serving Size	1 slice, ¼ cup sauce, and 3 raspberries
Calories	505	Calories	296
Fat	32.5g	Fat	10g
Percentage of Calories from Fat	58%	Percentage of Calories from Fat	30%
Cholesterol	327mg	Cholesterol	70mg
Sodium	155mg	Sodium	133mg

2. Combine sugar and egg yolk in a bowl; stir well. Add cornstarch and salt; stir until well blended (mixture will be thick). Gradually add hot milk to egg yolk mixture, stirring constantly with a whisk. Return mixture to pan. Cook over medium heat 4 minutes or until thick, stirring constantly. Remove from heat; stir in rum and vanilla. Pour into a bowl; cover surface of custard with plastic wrap. Chill. Stir well with a whisk before serving. YIELD: 2 cups.

VARIATION

WARM BITTERSWEET CHOCOLATE-KAHLÚA TORTE: Prepare as directed for Warm Bittersweet Chocolate-Rum Torte, using 2 tablespoons Kahlúa instead of rum. Dissolve 1 tablespoon instant espresso granules or 2 tablespoons instant coffee granules in ¼ cup skim milk before adding to torte batter. Substitute 2 tablespoons Kahlúa for rum in custard sauce.

POINTS: 7; **EXCHANGES:** 3 Starch, 1½ Fat;
PER SERVING: CAL 299 (30% from fat);
PRO 8.1g; FAT 10g (sat 5.7g); CARB 45.1g;
FIB 0.7g; CHOL 70mg; IRON 1.2mg;
SOD 133mg; CALC 159mg

Light Tricks

- Decreased amount of chocolate, butter, and eggs in the torte.
- Reduced number of egg yolks in the sauce.
- Used skim milk instead of half-and-half, and evaporated skim milk instead of regular evaporated milk in the sauce.

EATING

Light in the Fast Lane

Fast-food restaurants push value meals over healthful ones, but they do have a lighter side.

Even though many of us heed the warnings of health professionals to shun cheeseburgers and French fries, let's face it, fast food is still attractive. It's convenient, economical, and fast. One-quarter of us eat in fast-food restaurants daily, but unfortunately the trend at these restaurants isn't toward healthful fare.

Consumer Reports laments "these are lean times for finding fast-food that is low in fat and calories."

BUCKING THE TREND. "Fast-food is a business," says Jennifer Nelson, M.S., R.D., director of clinical dietetics at the Mayo Clinic. "The customer is the driving source, so restaurants are only as responsive as we are responsible. Some years ago, we saw a trend toward lower fat, more healthful foods. Now the trend is comfort food and value."

Chains increase the attractiveness of high-profit-margin items by "supersizing" French fries and bundling burgers, fries, and soft drinks into low-priced value meals. Customers are taking the bait despite the nutritional drawbacks.

SEEK AND YOU SHALL FIND. If you work at it, you can find more healthful choices. The Subway chain actively promotes the health benefits of its menu, which has "seven for 6"—seven sandwiches, each with less than 6 grams of fat—along with light salad dressings, veggie burgers, veggie sandwiches, baked potato chips, pretzels, and the new low-fat WOW! chips.

"You *can* get healthful food at fast-food restaurants," says Joanne Larsen, a Minneapolis-based dietitian. She offers the following advice: First, choose a chain that offers as much variety as possible (are grains, fruits and vegetables, and low-fat dairy represented?) and cooking methods (can you order an item grilled or broiled instead of fried?).
SLOW DOWN. "Take time to read the menu. Take time when you order your food. And take time when you eat," says Larsen.
ASK FOR IT. Don't assume a restaurant won't oblige a special order. Some foods can be healthful if you order them made to your specifications. Ask for the dressing on the side or if they can leave off the cheese. An added bonus to this trick: If they make it special, you know it's fresh.
SELECT SIMPLE FOODS. The fewer the toppings, breading, dressings, croutons, and other add-ons, the better. Plain items are lower in fat and calories. "If you drink milk, you don't need the 100 calories a slice of cheese adds on a burger," says Larsen.
PORTION CONTROL. "Cut the burger in half or share it with a friend," suggests Nelson. "As soon as I get my meal, I ask for a take-home container." Put your waistline before your budget; smaller sandwiches are the better nutritional choice, even if you pay a few more pennies.

March

Mexican Dishes

Break out the Fiesta Ware and enjoy these lightened festive favorites at home in the company of friends. These recipes give us more reasons than ever to love Mexican food.

LIGHT GUACAMOLE

(pictured on page 110)

Tomatillo salsa also may be labeled salsa verde. We used Herdez brand.

1 large Anaheim chile (about 3 ounces)
2 green onions, cut into 2-inch pieces
2 garlic cloves, peeled and halved
2 large plum tomatoes (about 6 ounces), quartered
¾ cup peeled diced avocado (about 1 small)
½ cup tomatillo salsa
¼ cup cilantro sprigs
2 tablespoons fresh lemon or lime juice
½ teaspoon ground cumin
¼ teaspoon salt
Lime slices (optional)

1. Cut chile in half lengthwise; discard stem, seeds, and membranes. Place chile, green onions, and garlic in a food processor; pulse 5 times or until coarsely chopped. Add tomato and next 6 ingredients; pulse 10 times until blended (mixture should be chunky). Spoon into a bowl; garnish with lime slices, if desired. YIELD: 2 cups (serving size: ¼ cup).

POINTS: 1; EXCHANGES: 1 Veg, ½ Fat; PER SERVING: CAL 40 (52% from fat); PRO 0.8g; FAT 2.3g (sat 0.4g); CARB 4.3g; FIB 1.3g; CHOL 0mg; IRON 0.9mg; SOD 79mg; CALC 12mg

RED SNAPPER VERACRUZ

While the fish bakes, prepare the vegetable topping. Dinner will be ready in about 30 minutes.

4 (6-ounce) red snapper fillets
Olive oil-flavored cooking spray
½ cup fresh orange juice, divided
2 teaspoons olive oil, divided
½ teaspoon salt
1 (10-ounce) can diced tomatoes and green chiles (such as Rotel), undrained
1 large green bell pepper, cut into thin strips
1 small red onion, cut into thin strips
2 teaspoons bottled minced garlic
¼ cup sliced pitted green olives
1 tablespoon minced fresh cilantro
1 tablespoon capers
1 tablespoon caper juice

1. Preheat oven to 350°.
2. Place fillets in a 13- x 9-inch baking dish coated with cooking spray. Combine 2 tablespoons orange juice and 1 teaspoon olive oil; pour over fillets, and sprinkle with salt. Bake at 350° for 20 minutes or until fish flakes easily when tested with a fork.
3. Drain tomatoes, reserving ¼ cup juice; set both aside. Coat a large nonstick skillet with cooking spray; add remaining 1 teaspoon oil, and place over medium-high heat until hot. Add bell pepper, onion, and garlic; sauté 7 minutes. Add remaining 6 tablespoons orange juice, tomatoes, reserved ¼ cup tomato juice, olives, and next 3 ingredients; cook until thoroughly heated. Spoon ½ cup vegetable mixture over each fillet. YIELD: 4 servings.

POINTS: 5; EXCHANGES: 4 Very Lean Meat, 2½ Veg, 1 Fat; PER SERVING: CAL 247 (20% from fat); PRO 35g; FAT 5.5g (sat 0.9g); CARB 12.6g; FIB 2.4g; CHOL 60mg; IRON 1.7mg; SOD 994mg; CALC 125mg

CHIPOTLE CHILE PIE

Frozen chopped onion and frozen green bell pepper can be substituted for fresh, if desired.

1 pound ground round
1 cup chopped onion
1 cup chopped green bell pepper
1 (10-ounce) can enchilada sauce
1 cup frozen shoepeg white corn, thawed
1 cup (4 ounces) shredded reduced-fat sharp cheddar cheese
1 cup chipotle chile salsa (such as Jardine's)
⅔ cup white cornmeal (not self-rising cornmeal or cornmeal mix)
1 tablespoon all-purpose flour
1 teaspoon baking powder
½ teaspoon salt
¼ cup skim milk
3 tablespoons chipotle chile salsa
1 large egg

1. Preheat oven to 400°.
2. Cook first 3 ingredients in a 9-inch cast-iron skillet over medium-high heat until beef is browned, stirring to crumble. Drain well, and return beef mixture to pan. Stir in enchilada sauce and next 3 ingredients. Remove from heat; set aside.

3. Combine cornmeal and next 3 ingredients in a bowl; make a well in center of mixture. Combine milk, 3 tablespoons salsa, and egg; stir well. Add milk mixture to dry ingredients, stirring just until moist. Spoon batter over beef mixture in skillet, spreading batter evenly to edges of skillet (batter will be thin). Bake at 400° for 22 minutes or until cornbread is golden. Let stand 5 minutes before serving. YIELD: 6 servings.

NOTE: If chipotle chile salsa is not available in your area, stir 1 tablespoon chopped, drained canned chipotle chile and ¼ teaspoon sugar into 1 cup plus 2 tablespoons of a basic salsa like Old El Paso.

POINTS: 7; EXCHANGES: 2 Starch, 2 Med-fat Meat; PER SERVING: CAL 303 (31% from fat); PRO 22.3g; FAT 10.4g (sat 1.3g); CARB 31g; FIB 1.9g; CHOL 83mg; IRON 3.6mg; SOD 594mg; CALC 168mg

MARGARITA PORK WITH BLACK BEAN SALSA

⅓ cup fresh lime juice
⅓ cup tequila
2 tablespoons brown sugar
2 teaspoons bottled minced roasted garlic
2 teaspoons low-salt soy sauce
1 dried New Mexican chile
1 (1-pound) pork tenderloin
1 (10-ounce) package saffron rice mix (such as Mahatma)
Cooking spray
1 cup chopped red bell pepper
1 cup chopped tomato
1 (15-ounce) can black beans, drained

1. Combine first 5 ingredients; stir well, and set aside. Remove and discard stem and seeds from chile, keeping chile intact.
2. Place a small skillet over medium-high heat until hot. Add chile, and cook 1 minute on each side or until chile is blackened. Add lime juice mixture, and remove from heat. Cover and let cool. Place chile mixture in a food processor, and process until smooth.
3. Trim fat from pork tenderloin. Combine pork and chile mixture in a large zip-top plastic bag; seal bag. Marinate in refrigerator 2 hours, turning bag occasionally.
4. Prepare rice mix according to package directions, omitting fat. Set aside, and keep warm.
5. Prepare grill. Remove pork from bag, reserving marinade. Place pork on prepared grill rack coated with cooking spray; cover and grill 20 minutes or until instant-read thermometer registers 160° (slightly pink), turning pork occasionally. Let stand 10 minutes, and cut into ¼-inch-thick slices.
6. Combine reserved marinade and bell pepper in a large skillet; bring to a boil. Reduce heat, and simmer 5 minutes. Stir in tomato and black beans; cook until thoroughly heated. Spoon ⅔ cup prepared rice onto each of 6 plates, and top evenly with pork slices. Spoon about ½ cup bean mixture over pork and rice. YIELD: 6 servings.

POINTS: 7; EXCHANGES: 3½ Starch, 2 Very Lean Meat, ½ Veg; PER SERVING: CAL 355 (9% from fat); PRO 25g; FAT 3.4g (sat 1.1g); CARB 56g; FIB 3.5g; CHOL 53mg; IRON 4.1mg; SOD 1036mg; CALC 63mg

MANGOES AND CREAM

(pictured on page 46)

This cool and creamy treat soothes the palette after a piquant meal. Substitute pineapple or orange juice for the nectar, if desired.

2½ cups peeled chopped mango (about 2 large)
¾ cup evaporated skim milk
½ cup sugar
½ cup pear-and-passion fruit nectar

1. Place all ingredients in a food processor. Process until smooth.
2. Pour mixture into freezer can of an ice cream freezer; freeze according to manufacturer's instructions. Spoon ice cream into a freezer-safe container; cover and freeze 2 hours or until firm. YIELD: 8 servings (serving size: ½ cup).

NOTE: If you prefer not to use an ice cream freezer, simply pour puréed mango mixture into an 8-inch square baking pan; cover and freeze 4 hours or until firm. Break mixture into small chunks. Place half of frozen chunks in a food processor, and process until smooth. Return mixture to baking pan. Repeat procedure with remaining half of frozen chunks. Cover and freeze puréed mixture an additional 4 hours or until firm.

POINTS: 2; EXCHANGES: 1½ Fruit, ½ Starch; PER SERVING: CAL 116 (4% from fat); PRO 1.7g; FAT 0.5g (sat 0g); CARB 27.3g; FIB 1g; CHOL 4mg; IRON 0mg; SOD 31mg; CALC 68mg

CRAB QUESADILLAS WITH POBLANO CREAM

(pictured on page 46)

Each quesadilla has as much calcium as one glass of milk.

2 fresh poblano chiles (about ½ pound)
3 ounces Neufchâtel cheese or light cream cheese (about ⅓ cup), softened
¼ cup low-fat sour cream
1 tablespoon fresh lime juice
1 teaspoon bottled minced roasted garlic
1 pound lump crabmeat, shell pieces removed
1¼ cups (5 ounces) shredded reduced-fat Monterey Jack cheese
½ cup sliced green onions
1 teaspoon ground coriander
¼ teaspoon salt
6 (8-inch) fat-free flour tortillas
Butter-flavored cooking spray
1½ cups chopped tomato

1. Cut chiles in half lengthwise, and discard stems, seeds, and membranes. Place chile halves, skin side up, on a foil-lined baking sheet, and flatten with hand. Broil 15 minutes or until chiles are blackened. Place in a zip-top plastic bag; seal bag, and let stand 5 minutes. Peel chiles.
2. Place roasted chiles, Neufchâtel cheese, and next 3 ingredients in a food processor; process until smooth, scraping sides of processor bowl twice. Reserve 6 tablespoons Poblano Cream to top quesadillas.
3. Combine remaining Poblano Cream, crabmeat, and next 4 ingredients in a bowl; stir until blended.

Spread about ½ cup crab mixture over half of 1 tortilla; fold tortilla in half to cover filling. Repeat procedure with remaining crab mixture and tortillas. Cover quesadillas with a slightly damp towel to keep them from drying out.
4. Coat a large nonstick skillet with cooking spray, and place over medium heat until hot. Add 2 quesadillas, and cook 2 minutes on each side or until browned. Remove quesadillas from skillet; set aside, and keep warm. Repeat procedure with remaining quesadillas.
5. Cut each quesadilla in half. Top each serving with ¼ cup chopped tomato and 1 tablespoon reserved Poblano Cream. YIELD: 6 servings.
NOTE: For Shrimp Quesadillas, substitute 1 pound cooked peeled medium shrimp, coarsely chopped, for crabmeat.

POINTS: 7; **EXCHANGES:** 3 Very Lean Meat, 2 Starch, 1½ Fat; **PER SERVING:** CAL 337 (29% from fat); PRO 28.3g; FAT 10.7g (sat 5.7g); CARB 32g; FIB 2.4g; CHOL 106mg; IRON 2.7mg; SOD 770mg; CALC 306mg

LIME FLAN

Look for sweetened lime juice in the store with cocktail beverage mixes.

½ cup sweetened lime juice (such as Rose's)
1 lime
1½ cups water
1 (14-ounce) can fat-free sweetened condensed skim milk
1 vanilla bean, split lengthwise
1 (8-ounce) carton egg substitute
¼ teaspoon salt
3 large egg yolks
Fresh lime zest (optional)

1. Preheat oven to 325°.
2. Place lime juice in a heavy saucepan over medium heat, and cook 6 minutes or until golden, stirring constantly. Immediately pour into 8 (6-ounce) custard cups, tipping quickly until caramelized juice coats bottoms of cups; set aside.
3. Remove rind from lime in large strips, using a vegetable peeler or paring knife (do not remove the bitter white pith). Reserve lime for another use.
4. Combine lime rind strips, water, condensed milk, and vanilla bean in a saucepan; bring to a boil, stirring frequently. Reduce heat, and simmer 5 minutes, stirring occasionally. Discard rind strips and vanilla bean.
5. Combine egg substitute, salt, and egg yolks; stir well. Gradually add 1 cup hot milk mixture to egg mixture, stirring constantly with a whisk. Return mixture to pan, stirring constantly. Divide mixture evenly among prepared custard cups. Place cups in 2 (8-inch) square baking pans; add hot water to pans to a depth of 1 inch. Bake at 325° for 35 minutes or until a knife inserted in center comes out clean. Remove cups from pans; discard water. Let custards cool completely on a wire rack. Cover and chill at least 4 hours.
6. Loosen edges of custards with a knife or rubber spatula. Place a dessert plate, upside down, on top of each cup; invert custards onto plates. Drizzle any remaining caramelized syrup over custard. Garnish with lime zest, if desired. YIELD: 8 servings.

POINTS: 4; **EXCHANGES:** 2½ Starch; **PER SERVING:** CAL 205 (9% from fat); PRO 7.8g; FAT 2g (sat 0.6g); CARB 36.6g; FIB 0g; CHOL 86mg; IRON 0.8mg; SOD 98mg; CALC 144mg

PORTOBELLO MUSHROOM FAJITAS WITH CILANTRO SAUCE

1½ medium-size yellow bell
    peppers (about 8 ounces)
½ cup cilantro sprigs
4 ounces Neufchâtel cheese or
    light cream cheese (about ½
    cup)
¼ cup tomatillo salsa
1 medium-size red bell pepper
    (about 6 ounces), cut into strips
1 medium-size red onion (about
    8 ounces), thinly sliced
2 (6-ounce) packages portobello
    mushroom slices
2 teaspoons ground cumin
2 teaspoons chili powder
¼ teaspoon adobo seasoning with
    pepper
2 teaspoons olive oil
6 (8-inch) fat-free flour tortillas

1. Place 1 yellow bell pepper half,
cilantro, cheese, and salsa in a food
processor; process until smooth. Set
cilantro sauce aside.
2. Cut remaining yellow bell pepper
into strips. Combine yellow and red
pepper strips, onion, and mushrooms
in a bowl. Sprinkle with cumin, chili
powder, and adobo seasoning; toss
vegetables gently to coat.
3. Heat oil in a large nonstick skillet
over medium-high heat. Add vegetable mixture, and sauté 8 minutes
or until crisp-tender. Remove from
heat, and set aside.
4. Heat tortillas according to package directions. Spread 2 tablespoons
cilantro sauce over each tortilla.
Divide vegetable mixture evenly
among tortillas; roll up. Spoon 1
tablespoon cilantro sauce over each
fajita. YIELD: 6 servings.

NOTE: Substitute 2 fresh tomatillos
for the tomatillo salsa, if desired.
Remove husks from tomatillos, and
cut into wedges. Add to food
processor as directed for salsa.

POINTS: 4; **EXCHANGES:** 4 Veg, 1 Starch,
1 Fat; **PER SERVING:** CAL 225 (27% from fat);
PRO 7.3g; FAT 6.8g (sat 3.1g); CARB 34.8g;
FIB 3.9g; CHOL 14.3mg; IRON 3.7mg;
SOD 594mg; CALC 41mg

TORTILLA CHILE SOUP

5 (6-inch) corn tortillas, cut into
    thin strips
1½ pounds skinned, boned chicken
    breasts
1 (15.5-ounce) can cannellini
    beans or other white beans,
    undrained
1 (14.5-ounce) can Mexican-style
    stewed tomatoes with garlic,
    cumin, and jalapeños, undrained
1 (14¼-ounce) can fat-free
    chicken broth
3 (4.5-ounce) cans chopped green
    chiles, undrained
¼ cup fresh lime juice
2 teaspoons bottled minced garlic
¾ teaspoon ground cumin
½ teaspoon dried oregano
⅔ cup low-fat sour cream
⅔ cup (2⅔ ounces) shredded
    reduced-fat sharp cheddar cheese

1. Preheat oven to 375°.
2. Spread tortilla strips on a baking
sheet. Bake at 375° for 6 minutes or
until toasted, stirring after 3 minutes. Set aside.
3. Combine chicken and next 8
ingredients in a large Dutch oven;
bring to a boil. Cover, reduce heat,
and simmer 20 minutes or until
chicken is done.

4. Remove chicken from pan with
tongs or a slotted spoon. Let cool
slightly; shred chicken with 2 forks.
Return shredded chicken to pan; stir
well. Cook until thoroughly heated.
Ladle soup into bowls; top with sour
cream, cheese, and tortilla strips.
YIELD: 10 servings (serving size: 1 cup
soup, 1 tablespoon sour cream, 1
tablespoon cheddar cheese, and one-
fifth of tortilla strips).

POINTS: 5; **EXCHANGES:** 3 Very Lean Meat,
1½ Starch; **PER SERVING:** CAL 235
(19% from fat); PRO 23.8g; FAT 4.9g (sat 2.3g);
CARB 24g; FIB 3.5g; CHOL 51mg;
IRON 2.4mg; SOD 721mg; CALC 143mg

GRILLED MEXICAN PIZZAS

With more than 240 milligrams of
calcium per serving, this recipe is a
great way to get more in your diet.

2 medium leeks (about 1 pound)
2 fresh poblano chiles (about ½
    pound)
¼ teaspoon adobo seasoning with
    pepper
2 (6-ounce) filet mignon steaks
Cooking spray
½ cup fire-roasted garlic salsa
    (such as Green Mountain
    Gringo)
⅓ cup tomato chutney
2 (8-ounce) packages small Italian
    cheese-flavored pizza crusts
    (such as Boboli)
¾ cup (3 ounces) shredded
    reduced-fat Monterey Jack
    cheese

1. Remove roots, outer leaves, and
tops from leeks, leaving 2 inches of
dark leaves; set aside. Cut chiles in

(continued)

half lengthwise; discard stems, seeds, and membranes. Set aside.

2. Prepare grill. Sprinkle adobo seasoning evenly over steaks. Place steaks, leeks, and chile halves on grill rack coated with cooking spray; cover and grill 5 minutes. Turn steaks and vegetables; cover and grill an additional 5 minutes or until steaks are desired degree of doneness. Slice steaks and vegetables into thin strips.

3. Combine salsa and chutney; stir well. Spread evenly over 4 pizza crusts. Top each crust evenly with steak and vegetable strips; sprinkle evenly with cheese. Place pizzas on grill rack coated with cooking spray; cover and grill 3 minutes or until cheese melts. Serve immediately. YIELD: 8 servings (serving size: one-half pizza).

NOTE: If tomato chutney is not available in your area, combine 3 tablespoons fire-roasted garlic salsa and 2 tablespoons sun-dried tomato paste. If fire-roasted garlic salsa is not available, stir 1 teaspoon bottled roasted minced garlic into any basic salsa. Grilling adds a great smoky flavor to these pizzas, but the steak and vegetables may also be broiled. Then bake pizzas at 425° for 5 minutes.

POINTS: 6; **EXCHANGES:** 2 Lean Meat, 1½ Starch, 1 Veg, ½ Fat; **PER SERVING:** CAL 278 (29% from fat); PRO 18.9g; FAT 8.9g (sat 3.4g); CARB 28.7g; FIB 1.1g; CHOL 33.8mg; IRON 3.3mg; SOD 592mg; CALC 247mg

5 INGREDIENTS
Get What You Need

Enjoy your five a day (and then some) with these produce-packed recipes.

You know you should eat at least five servings of fruits and vegetables a day—figuring out where to fit them in is the challenge. So we did it for you, creating recipes for a stir-fry, a crumble, even a pizza that all include at least one serving of fruit or vegetable and, in some cases, as many as five. Getting what you need isn't any easier than this.

SPINACH-AND-CARAMELIZED ONION PIZZA

(pictured on page 27)

Buy creamed spinach, not spinach in butter sauce. To lower fat, use Green Giant boil-in-bag creamed spinach. Other brands are higher in fat.

Cooking spray
1 large onion, thinly sliced and separated into rings
2 tablespoons water
1 tablespoon balsamic vinegar
2 (10-ounce) packages frozen creamed spinach, thawed (such as Green Giant)
1 (10-ounce) package thin Italian cheese-flavored pizza crust (such as Boboli)
¾ cup (3 ounces) crumbled feta cheese with garlic and herbs

1. Preheat oven to 450°.
2. Coat a large nonstick skillet with cooking spray; place over medium-high heat until hot. Add onion; sauté 4 minutes or until crisp-tender. Reduce heat to medium; sauté 10 minutes or until golden brown, adding water, 1 tablespoon at a time, during last 3 minutes. Remove from heat; stir in balsamic vinegar.
3. Spread spinach evenly over pizza crust; top with onion mixture and cheese. Bake at 450° for 10 minutes or until crust is crisp and topping is thoroughly heated. YIELD: 5 servings (serving size: 1 slice).

NOTE: If Green Giant creamed spinach is not available, use the following substitution: Combine 2¼ teaspoons cornstarch and ½ cup fat-free nondairy creamer (such as Cremora) in a 2-cup glass measure; stir until blended. Add 1 tablespoon margarine, ¼ teaspoon butter extract, and ⅛ teaspoon each of onion powder, garlic powder, salt, and sugar; stir well. Microwave at HIGH 1½ minutes or until thick, stirring every 30 seconds. Stir cream sauce into 2 (10-ounce) packages frozen chopped spinach, thawed, drained, and squeezed dry. Spread spinach mixture over cheese-flavored pizza crust as directed.

POINTS: 6; **EXCHANGES:** 2 Starch, 2 Veg, 1½ Fat, ½ Med-fat Meat; **PER SERVING:** CAL 308 (30% from fat); PRO 14g; FAT 10.3g (sat 5g); CARB 40g; FIB 3.5g; CHOL 18mg; IRON 2.4mg; SOD 1002mg; CALC 274mg

PEANUT BUTTER-CHOCOLATE-BANANA SHAKE

2 cups sliced banana
¾ cup 1% low-fat milk
½ cup vanilla low-fat ice cream
½ cup crushed ice
3 tablespoons chocolate-flavored syrup
2 tablespoons reduced-fat creamy peanut butter

1. Arrange banana slices in a single layer on a baking sheet; freeze 45 minutes or until firm.
2. Place frozen bananas and remaining ingredients in a blender; process until smooth. Serve immediately. YIELD: 3 servings (serving size: 1 cup).

POINTS: 5; EXCHANGES: 1½ Starch, 1½ Fruit, ½ L-F Milk; **PER SERVING:** CAL 260 (20% from fat); PRO 7.3g; FAT 5.7g (sat 1.6g); CARB 48g; FIB 3.9g; CHOL 4mg; IRON 0.9mg; SOD 110mg; CALC 117mg

STIR-FRIED SHRIMP AND VEGETABLES

2 (3-ounce) packages Oriental-flavored ramen noodle soup
¼ cup hoisin sauce
1 tablespoon dark sesame oil
2 (16-ounce) packages frozen Peking-style stir-fry vegetables (such as VIP)
1 pound medium shrimp, peeled and deveined

1. Remove seasoning packets from noodles; set aside.
2. Cook noodles according to package directions, omitting seasoning packets. Drain noodles, reserving ¼ cup cooking liquid. Set noodles aside. Combine reserved ¼ cup cooking liquid, seasoning packets, and hoisin sauce; stir well. Set aside.
3. Heat oil in a large nonstick skillet over high heat until hot. Add vegetables; stir-fry 6 minutes or until crisp-tender. Add shrimp; stir-fry 3 minutes. Stir in noodles and hoisin sauce mixture; cook until thoroughly heated. YIELD: 6 servings (serving size: 1⅓ cups).

POINTS: 6; EXCHANGES: 3 Veg, 1½ Very Lean Meat, 1½ Fat, 1 Starch; **PER SERVING:** CAL 282 (28% from fat); PRO 18.1g; FAT 8.8g (sat 3.2g); CARB 29.6g; FIB 4.3g; CHOL 101mg; IRON 2.9mg; SOD 946mg; CALC 74mg

STUFFED SWEET POTATOES

(pictured on page 27)

6 small sweet potatoes (about 2½ pounds)
1 (15-ounce) can pear halves in juice, undrained
¼ cup firmly packed brown sugar
¼ teaspoon salt
¼ cup sweetened dried cranberries (such as Craisins) or raisins
⅓ cup chopped pecans, toasted and divided

1. Preheat oven to 375°.
2. Wrap potatoes in foil; bake at 375° for 50 minutes or until done. Let cool slightly. Cut a slit in top of each potato; carefully scoop out pulp, leaving a ¼-inch-thick shell.
3. Drain pears, reserving ¼ cup juice. Place pear halves and reserved juice in a food processor; process until smooth. Add potato pulp, sugar, and salt; process until blended. Stir in cranberries and 4 tablespoons pecans.
4. Stuff shells with pulp mixture; sprinkle with remaining pecans. Place potatoes on a baking sheet; bake at 375° for 10 minutes or until thoroughly heated. YIELD: 6 servings.

POINTS: 5; EXCHANGES: 1½ Fruit, 3 Starch; **PER SERVING:** CAL 324 (14% from fat); PRO 3.6g; FAT 5g (sat 0.5g); CARB 67.9g; FIB 6.9g; CHOL 0mg; IRON 1.4mg; SOD 131mg; CALC 52mg

APPLE CRUMBLE

⅔ cup quick-cooking oats
⅓ cup firmly packed brown sugar, divided
¼ cup all-purpose flour
3 tablespoons chilled stick margarine, cut into small pieces
3 (12-ounce) packages frozen escalloped apples (such as Stouffer's)

1. Preheat oven to 375°.
2. Combine oats, 4 tablespoons brown sugar, and flour; cut in margarine with a pastry blender or 2 knives until mixture resembles coarse meal.
3. Remove plastic film from apples. Place 3 packages apples in microwave oven; microwave at HIGH 11 minutes or until partially thawed. Spoon apples into an 8-inch square baking dish. Add remaining sugar; stir well. Sprinkle oat mixture over apples. Bake at 375° for 40 minutes or until apple mixture is bubbly and topping is golden. YIELD: 8 servings.

POINTS: 6 EXCHANGES: 2½ Fruit, 1 Starch, 1 Fat; **PER SERVING:** CAL 289 (21% from fat); PRO 2.6g; FAT 6.7g (sat 1.7g); CARB 54g; FIB 4.1g; CHOL 0mg; IRON 1.1mg; SOD 72mg; CALC 14mg

VEGETABLE PASTA SOUP

With only 2 *POINTS* and 120 calories, this soup makes a great lunch for days when you want to splurge at dinner.

3 cups reduced-salt vegetable juice
2 cups water
1 (14½-ounce) can diced tomatoes with basil, garlic, and oregano
1 (1-pound) package frozen pasta, broccoli, corn, and carrots in a garlic seasoned sauce (such as Green Giant Pasta Accents)
1 (16-ounce) package frozen zucchini, cauliflower, and carrot blend
⅓ cup (1⅓ ounces) grated fresh Parmesan cheese
Freshly ground pepper (optional)

1. Combine first 3 ingredients in a Dutch oven; bring to a boil. Stir in frozen vegetables; return to a boil. Reduce heat. Simmer, uncovered, 10 minutes. Ladle soup into bowls; sprinkle with cheese. Serve with pepper, if desired. YIELD: 10 servings (serving size: 1 cup soup and about 1½ teaspoons cheese).

POINTS: 2; **EXCHANGES:** 2 Veg, ½ Starch, ½ Fat; **PER SERVING:** CAL 120 (28% from fat); PRO 4.4g; FAT 3.8g (sat 1.9g); CARB 17.2g; FIB 2.3g; CHOL 6mg; IRON 0.7mg; SOD 559mg; CALC 73mg

FRUITED CHICKEN

6 (6-ounce) skinned chicken breast halves (bone-in)
½ teaspoon salt
¼ teaspoon pepper
1½ cups orange juice
2 (15¼-ounce) cans unsweetened pineapple tidbits, drained
1 (6-ounce) package dried apricots, coarsely chopped (about 1 cup)
½ cup low-sugar orange marmalade

1. Preheat oven to 375°.
2. Place chicken in a 13- x 9-inch baking dish; sprinkle with salt and pepper. Add orange juice. Bake at 375° for 20 minutes, basting occasionally with juice. Add pineapple and apricots; bake an additional 20 minutes or until chicken is done, basting occasionally with juice mixture. Remove chicken and fruit with a slotted spoon, reserving 3 tablespoons orange juice. Set chicken and fruit aside; keep warm.
3. Place marmalade in a saucepan; cook over low heat until marmalade melts. Stir in reserved 3 tablespoons orange juice. Simmer 4 minutes or until slightly syrupy (do not boil).
4. Top chicken breasts evenly with fruit mixture and marmalade mixture. YIELD: 6 servings.

POINTS: 7; **EXCHANGES:** 6 Very Lean Meat, 2 Fruit; **PER SERVING:** CAL 340 (13% from fat); PRO 41g; FAT 4.9g (sat 1.3g); CARB 32.4g; FIB 1.2g; CHOL 109mg; IRON 3mg; SOD 140mg; CALC 46mg

SPAGHETTI SQUASH WITH VEGETABLE RAGOUT

(pictured on page 46)

1 cup water
2 cups frozen black-eyed peas
1 (16-ounce) bag frozen vegetable gumbo mixture (such as McKenzie's)
2 (15-ounce) cans chunky garlic and herb tomato sauce
1½ teaspoons Creole seasoning
¼ teaspoon ground red pepper
1 (2½-pound) spaghetti squash

1. Bring 1 cup water to a boil in a large saucepan; add peas. Cover, reduce heat, and simmer 35 minutes or until tender. Add frozen gumbo mixture and next 3 ingredients; bring to a boil. Reduce heat, and simmer 10 minutes or until thoroughly heated. Set aside; keep warm.
2. Pierce squash several times with a fork, and place on paper towels in a microwave oven. Microwave at HIGH 15 minutes or until tender, turning squash every 3 minutes. Let squash stand 5 minutes; cut in half lengthwise, and discard seeds. Remove spaghetti-like strands with a fork to yield about 6 cups. Spoon vegetable mixture over squash. YIELD: 6 servings (serving size: 1 cup squash and about 1 cup vegetable mixture).

POINTS: 3; **EXCHANGES:** 5 Veg, 1 Starch; **PER SERVING:** CAL 220 (13% from fat); PRO 7.9g; FAT 3.1g (sat 0.2g); CARB 40g; FIB 7g; CHOL 0mg; IRON 2.7mg; SOD 780mg; CALC 178mg

A Cut Above the Rest

A good knife makes slicing, chopping, and paring a pleasure.

Top-notch chefs insist on the best cutlery. "Time in the kitchen should be enjoyable, so why be frustrated by cheap equipment?" says Nicholas Rutyna, executive sous chef of the Grand Hyatt Hotel in New York. Some good brands are Chicago Cutlery, Henckels, Wusthof, and Calphalon (which is new to the cutlery business and currently offered only on-line at www.calphalon.com).

KNOWING KNIVES.

Block sets are nicely priced, but you need only three knives—a chef's knife, a paring knife, and a bread knife.

A chef's knife—or cook's knife, as some call it—is ideal for chopping because of its size and weight. Chef's knives come in a variety of sizes (from 6- to 12-inch blades), but an 8-inch blade is best for most jobs.

A paring knife, which has a 3- to 4-inch blade, peels fruits and vegetables, trims fat from meat, and thinly slices garlic cloves and fresh ginger. For small or delicate jobs, it's the knife to choose.

A bread knife is much more versatile than its name suggests. Because of the sawlike notches on its edge, a good bread knife glides through fresh tomatoes and can cut a large ham into thin slices. But if a bread knife isn't sharp, you'll end up shredding what you want to slice.

In addition to these three knives, every cook should own a sharpening steel. A steel doesn't really sharpen a dull knife—it realigns the blade, postponing (for a long time) the need to sharpen. Unlike knives, a sharpening steel should be replaced after a few years because metal filings collect in its grooves. Any decent steel comes with instructions.

QUALITY QUESTIONS.

Knowing which knives you need is helpful, but remember that not all knives are created equal. The quality of a product is usually reflected in its price, and prices for a single knife can range from $5 to more than $100. Ask yourself the following questions to determine whether a knife is a good value.

WHAT IS IT MADE OF?

Look for knives of high-carbon stainless steel. It holds an edge and resists stains better than carbon, and sharpens more easily than stainless.

HOW IS IT MADE?

A forged knife (made from metal beaten and ground into shape by using high heat) is your best bet—especially for a chef's knife. Stamped knives (cut from thin sheets of metal and sharpened) don't have the same heft as a forged knife, but that's okay for smaller knives like parers.

WHAT TYPE OF EDGE DOES IT HAVE?

Serrated knives stay sharp for a long time and are great for jobs that require a sawing motion like cutting bread. But serrated knives are useless for delicate work like thinly slicing beef. So splurge on good straight-edged chef's and paring knives, and use a steel to realign them.

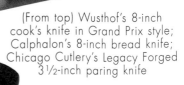

(From top) Wusthof's 8-inch cook's knife in Grand Prix style; Calphalon's 8-inch bread knife; Chicago Cutlery's Legacy Forged 3½-inch paring knife

Going to Pieces

Sometimes a gooey piece of pull-apart bread is all the therapy you need.

Some people find kneading bread therapeutic. But for a busy mother like Sonya Holmes of Marietta, Georgia, getting to bed before midnight is *real* therapy. That's why the idea of lightening her pull-apart bread appealed to us. The recipe calls for frozen bread dough and pantry staples, so it's as easy as homemade bread gets. Serve this gooey treat for breakfast, as a snack, even dessert. Talk about therapeutic.

Light Tricks

- Cut amount of brown sugar in half.
- Decreased amounts of butter and coconut in caramel glaze.
- Omitted dipping dough pieces in butter before arranging them in pan.
- Used evaporated skim milk instead of whole milk.
- Reduced corn syrup and preserves.

CARAMEL UPSIDE-DOWN PULL-APART LOAF

(pictured on page 3)

Frozen bread dough comes with two loaves in each package. Wrap and freeze the remaining loaf for later use.

1 (1-pound) loaf frozen white bread dough
½ cup firmly packed brown sugar
¼ cup evaporated skim milk
2½ tablespoons butter or stick margarine
1 tablespoon light-colored corn syrup
¼ teaspoon ground ginger
¼ cup flaked sweetened coconut
¼ cup pineapple preserves
Butter-flavored cooking spray

1. Thaw bread dough in refrigerator for 12 hours.
2. Combine brown sugar and next 4 ingredients in a saucepan; cook until butter melts, stirring frequently. Bring mixture to a boil over medium-high heat; cover and cook 1 minute. Remove from heat; stir in coconut and preserves. Let cool; cover and chill.
3. Divide dough into 3 equal portions; cut each portion into 16 (1-inch) pieces. Arrange 16 pieces of dough in an 8½- x 4½-inch loaf pan coated with cooking spray. Drizzle with ⅓ cup sugar mixture. Arrange another 16 pieces in pan, and drizzle with ⅓ cup sugar mixture. Add remaining 16 pieces of dough. Set remaining ⅓ cup sugar mixture aside. Cover dough, and let rise in a warm place (85°), free from

drafts, 50 minutes or until doubled in bulk.
4. Preheat oven to 375°.
5. Uncover dough, and bake at 375° for 20 minutes or until brown. Let cool 10 minutes. Place a plate, upside down, on top of pan, and invert bread onto plate. Brush remaining ⅓ cup sugar mixture over top and sides of bread. YIELD: 12 servings (serving size: 4 pull-apart pieces).

POINTS: 4; **EXCHANGES:** 2 Starch, ½ Fat; **PER SERVING:** CAL 179 (22% from fat); PRO 3.5g; FAT 4.3g (sat 2.2g); CARB 32g; FIB 0.1g; CHOL 7mg; IRON 1mg; SOD 217mg; CALC 44mg

VARIATION

APRICOT-CHOCOLATE UPSIDE-DOWN PULL-APART LOAF: Prepare as for Caramel Upside-Down Pull-Apart Loaf, substituting apricot preserves for pineapple preserves. Omit coconut from sugar mixture, and add ¼ cup semisweet chocolate chips. Stir mixture until chocolate chips melt.

POINTS: 4; **EXCHANGES:** 2 Starch, ½ Fat; **PER SERVING:** CAL 187 (24% from fat); PRO 3.6g; FAT 4.9g (sat 2.2g); CARB 33g; FIB 0g; CHOL 7mg; IRON 1mg; SOD 208mg; CALC 45mg

Before		After	
Serving Size	4 pull-apart pieces	Serving Size	4 pull-apart pieces
Calories	384	Calories	179
Fat	19.6g	Fat	4.3g
Percentage of Calories from Fat	46%	Percentage of Calories from Fat	22%
Cholesterol	43mg	Cholesterol	7mg
Sodium	372mg	Sodium	217mg

Over the Top

Simplify supper with these versatile sauces.

Fried chicken fends for itself and grilled steak can stand on its own. But few other dishes are so independent. Take turkey and gravy, macaroni and cheese, ribs with barbecue sauce—these couples were meant to be together. Some sauces may have their soul mates, but others are less committed, pairing with shrimp as well as chicken, or broccoli as well as pasta. Versatile sauces put the culinary world at your fingertips. Simply make the sauce that goes well with whatever you have on hand. Try spooning Cucumber-Yogurt Sauce over grilled salmon; then top off the menu with a baked potato and steamed asparagus. Dinner is served.

MUSHROOM SAUCE

(pictured on page 47)

Use your favorite mushrooms in this beefy sauce. We recommend a mix of button and crimini mushrooms. You can also use portobellos, but they must be chopped because of their size.

1 teaspoon olive oil
4½ cups sliced fresh mushrooms
1 tablespoon minced fresh or 1 teaspoon dried thyme
1½ teaspoons bottled minced garlic
1 tablespoon all-purpose flour
1 (10½-ounce) can beef consommé, undiluted
¼ cup dry red wine
2 tablespoons tomato paste
2 tablespoons chopped fresh parsley

1. Heat olive oil in a large nonstick skillet over medium-high heat. Add mushrooms, and sauté 5 minutes. Reduce heat to medium. Add thyme and garlic, and sauté 1 minute. Add flour, stirring until blended. Gradually add consommé and wine; cook 6 minutes or until mixture is slightly thick, stirring frequently. Add tomato paste, stirring until smooth. Remove from heat, and stir in chopped parsley. YIELD: 6 servings (serving size: ½ cup).

POINTS: 1; **EXCHANGES:** 1 Veg, ½ Fat; **PER SERVING:** CAL 42 (24% from fat); PRO 3.3g; FAT 1.1g (sat 0.2g); CARB 5.8g; FIB 1.1g; CHOL 2mg; IRON 1.2mg; SOD 348mg; CALC 9mg

MAKE IT A MEAL

• Serve Mushroom Sauce with grilled, broiled, or pan-seared filet mignon, sirloin, or flank steak.
• Fill a baked potato with chopped cooked beef, and then top the beef with sauce.
• Spoon sauce over an open-faced steak sandwich or hamburger.
• Top hot cooked egg noodles with sliced cooked steak; spoon sauce over steak and noodles.

TOMATO-HERB MARINARA

(pictured on page 47)

1 teaspoon olive oil
1 cup chopped onion
1 cup chopped carrot
1 teaspoon bottled minced garlic
1 tablespoon minced fresh or 1 teaspoon dried oregano
1½ teaspoons minced fresh or ½ teaspoon dried rosemary
1 (28-ounce) can diced tomatoes with roasted garlic, undrained
¼ cup dry white wine
1 teaspoon sugar
¾ teaspoon salt
½ teaspoon pepper

1. Heat oil in a medium saucepan over medium heat. Add onion, carrot, and garlic; sauté 3 minutes. Add oregano and rosemary; sauté 1 minute. Add tomatoes and remaining ingredients; bring to a boil. Cover, reduce heat, and simmer 30 minutes or until carrot is tender. YIELD: 4 servings (serving size: 1 cup).

POINTS: 1; **EXCHANGES:** 3½ Veg; **PER SERVING:** CAL 89 (13% from fat); PRO 2.2g; FAT 1.3g (sat 0.2g); CARB 17g; FIB 2.5g; CHOL 0mg; IRON 1mg; SOD 1,326mg; CALC 26mg

MAKE IT A MEAL

• Serve Tomato-Herb Marinara over cooked pasta or polenta.
• Top hot cooked spaghetti with baked or pan-seared skinned, boned chicken breasts; spoon sauce over chicken and pasta. Sprinkle with shredded part-skim mozzarella or shredded fresh Parmesan cheese.
• Use as a dip for soft breadsticks.

ZESTY CHEDDAR SAUCE

(pictured on page 47)

2 tablespoons all-purpose flour
½ teaspoon dry mustard
¼ teaspoon salt
¼ teaspoon paprika
Dash of ground red pepper
¾ cup 1% low-fat milk
¾ cup (3 ounces) shredded sharp
    cheddar cheese

1. Combine first 5 ingredients in a saucepan; stir well. Gradually add milk, stirring with a whisk until blended. Place over medium heat; cook 4 minutes or until thick, stirring constantly. Remove from heat; add cheese, stirring until cheese melts. YIELD: 4 servings (serving size: ¼ cup).

POINTS: 3 EXCHANGES: ½ Hi-fat Meat, ½ Sk Milk; **PER SERVING:** CAL 121 (57% from fat); PRO 7.3g; FAT 7.7g (sat 4.8g); CARB 5.6g; FIB 0.1g; CHOL 24mg; IRON 0.4mg; SOD 301mg; CALC 211mg

MAKE IT A MEAL
• Serve Zesty Cheddar Sauce over hot cooked pasta or macaroni.
• Fill a baked potato with chopped cooked broccoli, and top with sauce.
• Spoon sauce over steamed broccoli or cauliflower. Sprinkle with paprika.

FRAGRANT THAI SAUCE

(pictured on page 47)

1 cup one-third-less salt, fat-free
    chicken broth (such as
    Swanson's Natural Goodness)
1 tablespoon brown sugar
3 tablespoons fish sauce
2 tablespoons fresh lime juice
2 teaspoons cornstarch
1 teaspoon vegetable or dark
    sesame oil
2 teaspoons bottled chopped
    ginger or peeled minced fresh
    ginger
1 teaspoon bottled minced garlic
½ teaspoon crushed red pepper
¼ cup minced red bell pepper
¼ cup minced fresh cilantro

1. Combine first 5 ingredients; stir well, and set aside.
2. Heat oil in a saucepan over medium heat. Add ginger, garlic, and red pepper; sauté 1 minute. Add broth mixture. Bring to a boil; cook 1 minute or until slightly thick, stirring constantly. Remove from heat; stir in bell pepper and cilantro. YIELD: 4 servings (serving size: ⅓ cup).

POINTS: 1; EXCHANGES: ½ Starch; **PER SERVING:** CAL 55 (20% from fat); PRO 2.1g; FAT 1.2g (sat 0.2g); CARB 7.6g; FIB 0.4g; CHOL 0mg; IRON 1mg; SOD 574mg; CALC 10mg

MAKE IT A MEAL
• Serve Fragrant Thai Sauce with broiled, baked, or steamed fish such as flounder or snapper.
• Spoon sauce over steamed mussels or shrimp.
• Top cooked Oriental noodles with pan-seared tofu or chicken; spoon sauce over tofu or chicken.

CUCUMBER-YOGURT SAUCE

(pictured on page 47)

To keep the cucumber from watering down the sauce, cut it in half lengthwise and scrape out the seeds before chopping.

1 cup plain low-fat yogurt
⅔ cup peeled seeded chopped
    cucumber
2 tablespoons chopped fresh
    parsley
1 tablespoon chopped fresh dill
¼ teaspoon salt
¼ teaspoon ground cumin
Dash of pepper

1. Combine all ingredients, and stir well. YIELD: 6 servings (serving size: ¼ cup).

POINTS: 1; EXCHANGES: Free; **PER SERVING:** CAL 29 (22% from fat); PRO 2.3g; FAT 0.7g (sat 0.4g); CARB 3.5g; FIB 0.2g; CHOL 2mg; IRON 0.3mg; SOD 128mg; CALC 83mg

MAKE IT A MEAL
• Fill a pita pocket with sliced cooked lamb and Cucumber-Yogurt Sauce.
• Serve sauce with lamb-vegetable kabobs over couscous. Simply skewer leg of lamb cubes and your favorite vegetables. We used mushrooms, red onion wedges, green bell pepper chunks, and cherry tomatoes. Grill or broil kabobs; serve over couscous.
• Spoon sauce over grilled, broiled, or pan-seared salmon fillets or skinned, boned chicken breast halves.

CURRIED APRICOT PURÉE

(pictured on page 47)

½ teaspoon olive oil
¼ cup chopped Vidalia or other
    sweet onion
1 garlic clove, minced
1½ teaspoons curry powder
1 cup chicken broth (such as
    Swanson's)
½ cup chopped dried apricots
    (about 3 ounces)
1½ teaspoons honey
1 teaspoon Dijon mustard

1. Heat oil in a medium nonstick skillet over medium-high heat. Add onion and garlic; sauté 2 minutes. Add curry powder; sauté 30 seconds. Add broth and apricots; cover, reduce heat, and simmer 5 minutes. Remove from heat; let cool slightly.
2. Place apricot mixture, honey, and mustard in a blender or food processor; process until smooth. YIELD: 4 servings (serving size: ¼ cup).

POINTS: 2; **EXCHANGES:** 1 Fruit, ½ Fat;
PER SERVING: CAL 82 (14% from fat);
PRO 2.2g; FAT 1.3g (sat 0.2g); CARB 16.7g;
FIB 1g; CHOL 0mg; IRON 1.4mg;
SOD 247mg; CALC 20mg

MAKE IT A MEAL
• Spoon Curried Apricot Purée onto individual plates; top with grilled, broiled, or pan-seared tuna steak, shrimp, or sea bass, sliced pork tenderloin, sliced leg of lamb, or skinned, boned chicken breast halves. Garnish with fresh herbs; we used thyme. Serve with rice pilaf.
• Use as a basting sauce for grilled chicken or tuna. Serve chicken or tuna with sauce for dipping.

EATING
Clove Encounters

Garlic is famous for warding off cholesterol, high blood pressure, and other ailments. But is this "stinking rose" really that sweet?

The history and folklore of garlic can be found in the ancient cuisines of Asia, Europe, and the Middle East. In America, however, garlic was for a long time avoided like, well, garlic. The flavor—and the odor—kept it out of mainstream dishes, and those who fancied it often hid their passion. Eleanor Roosevelt, a closet garlic lover, cloaked her cloves by dipping them in chocolate.

GOOD NEWS. Over the past 20 years, though, garlic has made a resounding breakthrough. It has gone from being the subject of jokes about bad breath to a staple on our culinary scene. Now garlic is used as a popular flavoring and is regularly found in oils, salsas, and sauces.

Perhaps best of all, our recent love affair with garlic is matched by a number of studies linking the herb to preventive health benefits. Consider this: Its properties have been found to fight high blood pressure, high cholesterol, cardiovascular disease, and certain forms of cancer. There also has been overwhelming evidence that garlic has superior antiviral and antibacterial properties.

To sum it up: Garlic is hot.

WHAT'S INSIDE? Garlic contains healthful substances such as vitamins A and C, sulfur, potassium, phosphorus, and some amino acids. But the most important compound is S-allyl-cysteine, which seems to act like preventive medicine in helping to stave off cancer.

Garlic also reduces the risk of heart disease and strokes through its ability to lower blood pressure and prevent blood clots. It helps decrease production of cholesterol in the liver, which in effect lowers cholesterol levels in the body. Garlic also stimulates white blood cells, improving the immune system and helping ward off viruses, yeasts, and bacteria.

"We are seeing a lot more solid research supporting the health benefits of garlic," says Dina Khader, M.S., R.D., C.D.N. "People used to think of these claims as old wives' tales, but not anymore. There is just too much evidence out there."

The Garlic Information Center at Cornell Medical Center in New York Hospital is dedicated to garlic research. According to Barbara Levine, the center's co-director and associate professor of medicine at Cornell Medical College, as many as 10,000 studies have been conducted internationally in the past decade.

"Research is being done on [garlic's effect on] memory, concentration, and diabetes," she says. Audrey Cross, professor of nutrition

(continued)

at Columbia University's Department of Public Health, adds that Koreans and Italians—who ingest large quantities of garlic in their diets—have one of the lowest rates of heart disease and certain types of cancer.

Then, of course, there is always folklore. Tom Reed, a national speaker on culinary and health benefits of garlic—who eats one to four cloves a day—says the preventive properties of garlic are extensive. "I met a man who had a problem of warts on his hands," says Reed. "He'd had them burned off several times, but they always came back. Four years ago he started eating garlic, and he never had a wart again."

VAMPIRES AND OTHER CRITICS.
While adding garlic to your diet is the traditional way of absorbing its healthful qualities, you can also take supplements in the form of tablets, powders, and oils.

But the jury is still out on garlic supplements: Even though they're odorless and more convenient to consume, supplements supply only specific compounds. On the other hand, fresh garlic gives you the entire package of nutrients. Initial medical research indicates that garlic tablets can act as a regulator for blood pressure and cholesterol levels, but they don't provide the antibacterial protection that raw garlic does.

"People used to think of these claims as old wives' tales, but not anymore. There is just too much evidence out there."

Despite promising research, there are some naysayers. Two recent studies challenge the belief that garlic supplements lower cholesterol. In one study, researchers at the University of Bonn gave commercially available garlic oil to people with cholesterol levels that averaged 291—well above the healthy cutoff point of 200. After 12 weeks their blood cholesterol was unchanged.

In the second study, carried out by Yale University and the Christ Hospital Cardiovascular Research Center in Cincinnati, patients with high cholesterol took either Kwai garlic powder supplements or placebo look-alikes. Neither lowered blood cholesterol.

So when it comes to garlic and health, should we save our breath? Not necessarily. Levine points out that garlic powder does not have the same essential properties of raw garlic and thus cholesterol studies done with the powder will not be as successful. The same, she says, is true for garlic oil.

THE REAL THING.
It's still unclear which garlic is best—raw or processed—but most experts favor the real thing and suggest eating at least one and as many as five cloves a day. "Since garlic is a food and not a medicine, you can't prescribe how much to take a day," says Cross. "It depends on the individual." Either way, this healthful herb still ends up smelling like a rose—well, at least a "stinking" rose.

Finally Fit

ANNETTE LEVIN • **HEIGHT** 5'7" • **BEFORE** 180 LBS. • **AFTER** 125 LBS.

Hint: "It takes time to lose weight and get in good shape. Don't be discouraged. You can do it!"

When Annette Levin's husband joined a health club, she did, too. He found success in the weight room, but Annette found workouts tedious. Her husband's body looked better and better, but her figure didn't seem to change much.

"So I quit working out and turned to food for comfort," says Annette, 29. Four years of steady weight gain led to deep depression. "I felt my life had no worth," she says. "I didn't feel attractive or sexy. The worse I felt, the more I ate." By the time her husband began competing as a bodybuilder, Annette weighed 180 pounds. "I felt so bad, I had to take antidepressant medication."

When the marriage unraveled, "I was divorced, depressed, unemployed, and overweight," she says. "I moved back home with my family and re-evaluated my life. I'd been fat and I'd been thin, but I had never really been fit in mind, body, and spirit."

That changed when Annette began taking long walks that left her feeling stronger physically and emotionally. "I learned that I don't have to exercise in a gym," she says. "I enjoy walking and in-line skating." Now Annette invests at least 30 minutes in both activities three times a week. When she can't work out outdoors, she uses a stair-stepping machine at home.

Annette's job as an airline ticket agent also keeps her active. "If we're not ticketing passengers, we're on the ramp loading luggage. Bags can weigh 70 pounds or more, and that's a good workout."

Changes in her eating habits also made a difference. "I realized I don't have to eat everything on my plate, and I go easy on second helpings." No food is off-limits, but Annette tends to opt for fish, chicken, and vegetables. She snacks on popcorn, fruit, or nonfat yogurt. "I limit portions and eat certain foods less often," she says. "For example, I've decreased red meat to one or two servings per week."

Learning to eat smart and taking her workout outdoors yielded results Annette didn't get in the gym. She lost 55 pounds in a year and has kept it off. Compliments provide more motivation. "It's nice to hear people mention my new figure," she says. "It's nice to be able to wear a bikini."

"I learned that I don't have to exercise in a gym."

Annette no longer takes antidepressants, and she sees a bright, active future. "My next adventure will be a backpacking trip through Europe," she says. "I plan to go to Holland, France, and Spain. I can't wait for the journey to begin."

Mangoes and Cream, page 33

Spaghetti Squash With Vegetable Ragout, page 38

Crab Quesadillas With Poblano Cream, page 34

Clockwise from top: Zesty Cheddar Sauce, page 42; Tomato-Herb Marinara, page 41; Cucumber-Yogurt Sauce, page 42; Curried Apricot Purée, page 43; Fragrant Thai Sauce, page 42; Mushroom Sauce, page 41

Port-Glazed Pears With
Toasted Hazelnuts, page 95

Lemony Spring
Vegetables, page 52

Southwestern Grilled Flank
Steak, page 93, and Marinated
Tomato Salad, page 88

April

Sunday Dinners

At the end of each busy week comes Sunday—wonderful, languorous Sunday. It's the one day most of us can have fun cooking, filling the house with the beguiling aromas of a cake in the oven or a slow-cooked roast—something more exciting than the usual fast weeknight fare. On Sundays, we can enjoy one of life's greatest pleasures: sitting around a table together savoring good food and each other. Sunday dinner is a celebration of family, and special dishes such as these contribute to our well-being.

ROSEMARY-ROASTED CHICKEN WITH MUSHROOM-SHALLOT GRAVY

Roasting vegetables with the chicken imparts a caramelized flavor to the gravy. For easy cleanup, line broiler pan with foil before adding the rack.

    1 tablespoon chopped fresh
        rosemary
    1 teaspoon olive oil
    ½ teaspoon salt
    ¼ teaspoon coarsely ground pepper
    1 (3-pound) chicken
Cooking spray
    2 shallots, halved
    2 unpeeled garlic cloves
    1 (8-ounce) package fresh
        mushrooms
 1½ tablespoons all-purpose flour
    ¾ cup one-third-less salt chicken
        broth
    ⅓ cup 2% reduced-fat milk
    1 tablespoon dry sherry
Rosemary sprigs (optional)

1. Preheat oven to 375°.
2. Combine 1 tablespoon rosemary, oil, salt, and pepper in a small bowl; stir well, and set aside.
3. Remove and discard giblets and neck from chicken. Rinse chicken under cold water, and pat dry. Trim excess fat. Starting at neck cavity, loosen skin from breast and drumsticks by inserting fingers, gently pushing between skin and meat. Rub rosemary mixture under loosened skin over breast and drumsticks. Lift wing tips up and over back, and tuck under chicken.
4. Place chicken, breast side up, on a broiler pan coated with cooking spray. Insert meat thermometer into meaty part of thigh, making sure not to touch bone. Coat shallots and garlic cloves with cooking spray, and arrange around chicken. Bake at 375° for 40 minutes. Coat mushrooms with cooking spray, and arrange around chicken. Bake an additional 30 minutes or until thermometer registers 180°.
5. Remove chicken from broiler pan, reserving pan drippings. Place chicken on a platter; cover loosely with foil. Set aside. Remove vegetables from broiler pan, and slice shallots and mushrooms. Squeeze garlic cloves to extract pulp; place pulp in a medium saucepan. Add flour to pan; gradually add chicken broth and milk, stirring with a whisk until blended. Set aside.
6. Skim fat from reserved drippings. Add skimmed drippings to broth mixture; cook over medium heat 5 minutes or until mixture is thick, stirring constantly with a whisk. Stir in shallots, mushrooms, and sherry; cook until thoroughly heated. Set aside, and keep warm.
7. Remove and discard skin from chicken. Serve chicken with gravy. Garnish with rosemary sprigs, if desired. YIELD: 4 servings (serving size: 3 ounces chicken and 7 tablespoons gravy).

POINTS: 5; **EXCHANGES:** 3 Lean Meat, 2 Veg; **PER SERVING:** CAL 220 (32% from fat); PRO 24.9g; FAT 7.7g (sat 2.1g); CARB 10.6g; FIB 1.1g; CHOL 71mg; IRON 2.1mg; SOD 488mg; CALC 53mg

GOLDEN GARLIC MASHED POTATOES

Use a potato masher if you like a chunky texture. For creamy potatoes, use a handheld mixer. Mash potatoes right in the pan for easy cleanup.

 4½ cups peeled cubed Yukon gold
        or baking potato
    ¾ cup 2% reduced-fat milk
    1 tablespoon butter
    ¾ teaspoon salt
    ⅛ to ¼ teaspoon pepper
    2 garlic cloves, minced

1. Place potato cubes in a medium saucepan, and cover with water; bring to a boil. Reduce heat. Simmer 15 minutes or until potatoes are tender; drain. Mash potato; add milk, butter, salt, pepper, and minced garlic, stirring well. YIELD: 4 servings (serving size: 1 cup).

POINTS: 4; **EXCHANGES:** 2½ Starch, ½ Fat; **PER SERVING:** CAL 214 (17% from fat); PRO 4.7g; FAT 4g (sat 2.4g); CARB 40.8g; FIB 2.7g; CHOL 11mg; IRON 0.7mg; SOD 506mg; CALC 72mg

DIJON POT ROAST AND VEGETABLES

(pictured on page 26)

1 (3-pound) boned chuck roast
3 medium Vidalia or other sweet
   onions, each cut into 6 wedges
1½ pounds carrots, cut into 2-inch
   pieces
2 bay leaves
½ cup beef broth
¼ cup Dijon mustard
3 tablespoons red wine vinegar
1 tablespoon low-salt
   Worcestershire sauce
1½ teaspoons dried thyme
1½ teaspoons dried parsley
¾ teaspoon coarsely ground pepper
½ teaspoon salt
3 garlic cloves, crushed
3½ tablespoons all-purpose flour
3 tablespoons water
1 (12-ounce) package wide egg
   noodles

1. Trim fat from roast.
2. Place roast in a 5-quart electric slow cooker; add onion, carrot, and bay leaves. Combine broth and next 8 ingredients; stir well, and pour over roast. Cover with lid; cook on low-heat setting for 8 hours.
3. Place roast, onion, and carrot on a platter; set aside, and keep warm. Discard bay leaves. Reserve cooking liquid in slow cooker (turn cooker to high-heat setting). Combine flour and 3 tablespoons water in a small bowl; stir with a whisk until blended. Add flour mixture to reserved liquid in slow cooker; cook, uncovered, on high-heat setting 15 minutes or until thick, stirring frequently.
4. Cook noodles according to package directions, omitting salt and fat.

Drain. Spoon gravy over roast and vegetables. Serve with noodles.
YIELD: 9 servings (serving size: 3 ounces roast, 2 onion wedges, one-ninth of carrots, 1 cup noodles, and ⅓ cup gravy).

POINTS: 8; EXCHANGES: 4 Lean Meat, 2 Starch, 1½ Veg; PER SERVING: CAL 411 (21% from fat); PRO 39.1g; FAT 9.7g (sat 3.3g); CARB 39.7g; FIB 3.8g; CHOL 126mg; IRON 6.5mg; SOD 538mg; CALC 54mg

MARINATED BROCCOLI-CORN SALAD

(pictured on page 24)

3½ cups small fresh broccoli florets
¼ cup rice vinegar
1 tablespoon Dijon mustard
1 tablespoon honey
¼ teaspoon salt
¼ teaspoon pepper
1 (16-ounce) package frozen baby
   white corn, thawed
½ cup chopped red bell pepper
½ cup finely chopped red onion

1. Steam broccoli florets, covered, 6 minutes or until crisp-tender. Drain. Rinse under cold water; drain well.
2. Combine vinegar and next 4 ingredients in a medium bowl; stir well. Add broccoli, corn, bell pepper, and onion; stir well. Cover and chill at least 3 hours, stirring occasionally. YIELD: 6 servings (serving size: 1 cup).
NOTE: Substitute frozen shoepeg white corn for baby white corn, if desired.

POINTS: 1; EXCHANGES: 1½ Veg, 1 Starch; PER SERVING: CAL 105 (9% from fat); PRO 4.1g; FAT 1g (sat 0.1g); CARB 23.4g; FIB 3.9g; CHOL 0mg; IRON 1mg; SOD 190mg; CALC 32mg

PARMESAN-ONION ROLLS

Cooking spray
¾ cup finely chopped onion
½ teaspoon dried oregano
½ teaspoon dried basil
1 (16-ounce) box hot roll mix
1 cup warm water (120° to 130°)
2 tablespoons butter, softened
1 large egg white, lightly beaten
1 cup (4 ounces) grated fresh
   Parmesan cheese

1. Coat a nonstick skillet with cooking spray; place over medium-high heat until hot. Add onion, oregano, and basil; sauté until onion is tender. Set aside.
2. Combine contents of roll mix box and enclosed yeast packet in a large bowl; stir well. Add warm water, butter, and egg white, stirring until dough pulls away from sides of bowl. Turn dough out onto a lightly floured surface. Sprinkle with onion mixture; knead until blended. Sprinkle dough with cheese; knead 5 minutes or until dough is smooth and elastic. Place bowl over dough to cover; let rest 10 minutes.
3. Divide dough into 16 equal portions. Shape each portion into a ball. Place 8 balls in each of 2 (8-inch) round cake pans coated with cooking spray. Cover; let rise in a warm place (85°), free from drafts, 25 minutes or until dough doubles in bulk.
4. Preheat oven to 375°.
5. Bake at 375° for 20 minutes or until lightly browned. YIELD: 16 servings (serving size: 1 roll).

POINTS: 4; EXCHANGES: 1½ Starch, 1 Fat; PER SERVING: CAL 156 (29% from fat); PRO 6g; FAT 5g (sat 2.1g); CARB 21.5g; FIB 0.2g; CHOL 10mg; IRON 0.3mg; SOD 249mg; CALC 109mg

LEMONY SPRING VEGETABLES

(pictured on page 48)

2¾ cups diagonally sliced carrot
5½ cups (1-inch) sliced asparagus
    (about 2 pounds)
4¼ cups sugar snap peas, trimmed
  ¼ cup light butter
  3 cups thinly sliced leek (about 3
    medium)
  2 teaspoons grated lemon rind
  2 tablespoons fresh lemon juice
  2 tablespoons chopped fresh
    thyme
  ½ teaspoon salt

1. Arrange carrot in a vegetable steamer in a Dutch oven; cover and steam 4 minutes. Add asparagus, and steam 2 minutes. Add peas; steam 3 minutes. Remove vegetables and steamer from Dutch oven. Set aside. Discard water from Dutch oven.
2. Melt butter in Dutch oven over medium-high heat. Add leek, and sauté 2 minutes. Add vegetables, lemon rind, and remaining ingredients; cook 2 minutes, stirring frequently. YIELD: 10 servings (serving size: 1 cup).

POINTS: 1; **EXCHANGES:** 2½ Veg, ½ Fat;
PER SERVING: CAL 88 (28% from fat);
PRO 3.5g; FAT 2.7g (sat 1.7g); CARB 13.2g;
FIB 3.9g; CHOL 8mg; IRON 1.8mg;
SOD 165mg; CALC 53mg

SICILIAN TUNA WITH FETTUCCINE

(pictured on page 1)

  1 tablespoon olive oil, divided
  4 (4-ounce) tuna steaks (about
    ½ inch thick)
  ½ teaspoon coarsely ground pepper
1½ cups slivered Vidalia or other
    sweet onion
2½ cups chopped plum tomato
    (about 1 pound)
  3 garlic cloves, minced
  ¼ cup sliced green olives
1½ tablespoons capers
  1 tablespoon balsamic vinegar
  1 tablespoon fresh lemon juice
  1 teaspoon dried oregano
  3 cups hot cooked fettuccine,
    cooked without salt or fat

1. Brush 1½ teaspoons olive oil evenly over tuna steaks; sprinkle with pepper. Place a nonstick skillet over medium-high heat until hot. Add tuna steaks. Cook 4 minutes on each side until medium-rare or desired degree of doneness. Remove tuna from skillet; set aside, and keep warm.
2. Add remaining olive oil to skillet. Add onion, and sauté 5 minutes. Add tomato and garlic, and sauté 2 minutes or until tender. Add olives and next 4 ingredients; cook 2 minutes or until thoroughly heated.
3. Place hot fettuccine on individual plates; top with tuna. Spoon tomato mixture over tuna steaks and fettuccine. YIELD: 4 servings (serving size: ¾ cup pasta, 3 ounces tuna, and ½ cup tomato mixture).

POINTS: 8; **EXCHANGES:** 3 Very Lean Meat,
2 Starch, 2 Veg, 1½ Fat; **PER SERVING:** CAL
382 (25% from fat); PRO 33g; FAT 10.7g (sat
2.2g); CARB 38.2g; FIB 3.9g; CHOL 43mg;
IRON 3.7mg; SOD 384mg; CALC 39mg

BOURBON-GLAZED HAM STEAKS

  ¼ cup bourbon
  3 tablespoons brown sugar
  3 tablespoons apple juice
    concentrate, undiluted
  ½ teaspoon stone-ground mustard
Cooking spray
  4 (3-ounce) slices lean boned ham
    (such as Hormel Cure 81)

1. Combine bourbon, brown sugar, apple juice concentrate, and mustard; stir well, and set aside.
2. Coat a large nonstick skillet with cooking spray, and place over medium-high heat until hot. Add ham slices, and cook 2 minutes on each side or until lightly browned. Reduce heat to medium-low, and add bourbon mixture. Cook 7 minutes or until bourbon mixture is slightly thick, stirring mixture and turning ham occasionally. Cut each slice in half, if desired. Place slices on individual plates; top evenly with bourbon mixture. YIELD: 4 servings.

POINTS: 3; **EXCHANGES:** 2 Very Lean Meat,
½ Starch, ½ Fruit; **PER SERVING:** CAL 149
(28% from fat); PRO 15.1g; FAT 4.6g (sat 1.5g);
CARB 12.1g; FIB 0g; CHOL 45mg; IRON 1mg;
SOD 876mg; CALC 9mg

BROWN SUGAR-RUM POUND CAKE WITH STRAWBERRIES

(pictured on page 70)

Rum-flavored sugared strawberries offer a pleasant contrast to this dense, tender cake. Be sure to spoon the syrup over the cake, too.

Cooking spray
⅔ cup butter, softened
1½ cups firmly packed dark brown sugar
1½ cups granulated sugar
1 cup egg substitute
4½ cups sifted cake flour
1½ teaspoons baking soda
¼ teaspoon salt
1 cup low-fat buttermilk
2 tablespoons white rum
1½ teaspoons vanilla extract
4½ cups sliced fresh strawberries
2 tablespoons granulated sugar
1 tablespoon white rum

1. Preheat oven to 325°.
2. Coat a 10-inch tube pan with cooking spray; set aside.
3. Cream butter. Gradually add brown sugar and 1½ cups granulated sugar; beat at medium speed of a mixer until well-blended. Add egg substitute; beat until blended.
4. Combine flour, baking soda, and salt. Add flour mixture to creamed mixture alternately with buttermilk, beginning and ending with flour mixture. Beat in 2 tablespoons rum and vanilla.
5. Pour batter into prepared pan. Bake at 325° for 1 hour and 20 minutes or until a wooden pick inserted in center comes out clean. Let cool in pan 10 minutes on a wire rack; remove from pan. Let cool completely on wire rack.
6. Combine strawberries, 2 tablespoons granulated sugar, and 1 tablespoon rum in a large bowl, and stir well. Let stand 30 minutes, stirring occasionally. Spoon strawberries and liquid over pound cake slices. YIELD: 24 servings (serving size: 1 slice cake and about 2 tablespoons strawberry mixture).

POINTS: 5; EXCHANGES: 3 Starch, ½ Fat; PER SERVING: CAL 237 (21% from fat); PRO 3.1g; FAT 5.5g (sat 3.2g); CARB 43.8g; FIB 0.7g; CHOL 14mg; IRON 1.9mg; SOD 154mg; CALC 36mg

CARROT CAKE WITH CREAM CHEESE FROSTING

Cooking spray
1 tablespoon all-purpose flour
2½ cups all-purpose flour
1½ teaspoons baking soda
1½ teaspoons baking powder
½ teaspoon salt
½ teaspoon ground cinnamon
¼ teaspoon ground allspice
¾ cup sugar
½ cup apple butter
⅓ cup low-fat buttermilk
3 tablespoons butter, melted
2 teaspoons vanilla extract
2 large eggs, lightly beaten
2 cups finely shredded carrot
Cream Cheese Frosting
Carrot strips (optional)

1. Preheat oven to 350°.
2. Coat a 13- x 9-inch baking pan with cooking spray, and dust with 1 tablespoon flour.
3. Combine 2½ cups flour and next 5 ingredients in a large bowl, and make a well in center of mixture. Combine sugar and next 5 ingredients in a bowl; add to dry ingredients. Stir just until moist. Stir in shredded carrot.
4. Pour batter into prepared pan. Bake at 350° for 26 minutes or until a wooden pick inserted in center comes out clean. Let cool completely on wire rack.
5. Spread Cream Cheese Frosting over cake. Garnish with carrot strips, if desired. Store cake tightly covered in refrigerator. YIELD: 16 servings.

POINTS: 6; EXCHANGES: 4 Starch, ½ Fat; PER SERVING: CAL 307 (19% from fat); PRO 4.5g; FAT 6.5g (sat 3.7g); CARB 58.2g; FIB 1g; CHOL 43mg; IRON 1.2mg; SOD 275mg; CALC 46mg

CREAM CHEESE FROSTING:
1 (8-ounce) package Neufchâtel cheese or light cream cheese, chilled
1 teaspoon vanilla extract
¼ teaspoon butter extract
1 (16-ounce) package powdered sugar, sifted

1. Beat first 3 ingredients at low speed of a mixer 1 minute or until smooth. Gradually add sugar, and beat at low speed until smooth (be careful not to overbeat or icing will be runny). YIELD: 2½ cups.

Smart Snacks

When you need energy, think of food as fuel.

Snacking to lose weight may seem illogical, but experts say it makes sense. The problem, says Kristine Clark, Ph.D., R.D., director of sports nutrition at Penn State University, is that most people don't eat the right foods at the right time to have energy for physical activity. More than 70% of people who responded to a national survey said they skip exercise because they are too tired.

Food is the key to breaking this cycle. Clark says, "If you haven't eaten three or four hours before exercise, you'll run out of gas because you have low blood sugar." She suggests having a snack 60 to 90 minutes before exercising. With recipes for these energizing snacks, lack-of-energy excuses evaporate.

CHILI-BEAN DIP

Cannellini beans are white kidney beans. You can substitute Great Northern beans.

1 (19-ounce) can cannellini beans or other white beans, drained
2 tablespoons lime juice
2 teaspoons chili powder
1 teaspoon ground cumin
⅛ teaspoon garlic powder

1. Place all ingredients in a food processor, and process until smooth. Serve dip with assorted raw vegetables. YIELD: 4 servings (serving size: 7 tablespoons).

POINTS: 2; EXCHANGES: 1½ Starch;
PER SERVING: CAL 120 (5% from fat);
PRO 8.4g; FAT 0.7g (sat 0.2g); CARB 21.9g;
FIB 3.9g; CHOL 0mg; IRON 2.5mg;
SOD 273mg; CALC 73mg

ARTICHOKE SPREAD WITH MELBA TOAST

Pack this spread in an insulated lunch box with a freezer block to keep it chilled. Look for Alouette cheese in the specialty cheese case at your market.

½ cup spreadable cheese with garlic and herbs (such as Alouette)
1 (14-ounce) can quartered artichoke hearts, drained and chopped
1 (8-ounce) can sliced water chestnuts, drained and chopped
Dash of pepper
30 melba toast slices

1. Combine first 4 ingredients in a bowl, and stir well. Serve spread with melba toast. YIELD: 6 servings (serving size: ¼ cup spread and 5 melba toast slices).

POINTS: 3; EXCHANGES: 1½ Starch, 1 Veg, ½ Fat; PER SERVING: CAL 164 (26% from fat); PRO 5.7g; FAT 4.8g (sat 3g); CARB 27.1g; FIB 1.8g; CHOL 20mg; IRON 2mg; SOD 281mg; CALC 33mg

MARINATED TOMATOES AND PASTA

Briefly boiling the tomatoes makes the skins split and slip off easily. If the skins don't split, they can be carefully slit with a paring knife and then removed.

8 cups water
1 pint cherry tomatoes
1 cup uncooked gemelli or fusilli (twisted or spiraled pasta)
1 medium cucumber, peeled, halved lengthwise, seeded, and sliced (about 1⅓ cups)
½ cup fat-free Italian dressing
2 tablespoons chopped fresh parsley
¼ teaspoon salt
¼ teaspoon pepper

1. Bring water to a boil in a large saucepan. Add cherry tomatoes, and cook 45 seconds (do not overcook). Remove tomatoes from boiling water with a slotted spoon, and set aside. Add gemelli to boiling water, and cook 12 minutes or until tender. Drain well, and set aside.
2. Remove and discard tomato skins. Combine tomatoes, pasta, cucumber slices, and remaining ingredients in a large bowl; toss gently. Cover and chill at least 4 hours. YIELD: 4 servings (serving size: 1 cup).

POINTS: 3; EXCHANGES: 1½ Starch, 1 Veg;
PER SERVING: CAL 142 (4% from fat);
PRO 3.6g; FAT 0.7g (sat 0.1g); CARB 30.5g;
FIB 1.2g; CHOL 0mg; IRON 0.6mg;
SOD 594mg; CALC 14mg

TRAIL BLAZIN' MIX

1 (18-ounce) box low-fat granola
  with raisins (such as Healthy
  Choice)
½ cup honey
1 (6-ounce) package dried
  chopped tropical fruit medley
  (such as Mariani)
1 cup tropical-flavored gourmet
  jelly beans (such as Jelly Belly)
¼ cup semisweet chocolate
  minichips

1. Preheat oven to 325°.
2. Spread granola in a jelly-roll pan;
drizzle with honey, and toss well.
Spread evenly in pan. Bake at 325°
for 20 minutes, stirring every 7 minutes. Remove from oven, and stir in
dried fruit; return to oven. Turn
oven off, and let mixture stand in
closed oven 30 minutes. Remove
from oven, and let cool completely.
Combine granola mixture, jelly
beans, and minichips in a large bowl;
toss well. YIELD: 27 servings (serving
size: ⅓ cup).

POINTS: 3; **EXCHANGES:** 1 Starch, 1 Fruit;
PER SERVING: CAL 143 (10% from fat);
PRO 1.7g; FAT 1.6g (sat 0.8g); CARB 32.5g;
FIB 1.3g; CHOL 0.1mg; IRON 0.8mg;
SOD 52mg; CALC 7mg

FIG-DATE-BANANA NUT MUFFINS

1 (6.4-ounce) package banana nut
  muffin mix (such as Betty
  Crocker)
⅓ cup low-fat buttermilk
1 large egg, lightly beaten
Cooking spray
¼ cup fig preserves
2 tablespoons chopped dates

1. Preheat oven to 400°.
2. Combine first 3 ingredients in a
bowl; stir just until moist. Spoon 1
tablespoon batter into each of 6 muffin cups coated with cooking spray,
spreading to cover bottom of cups.
Spoon 2 teaspoons preserves and 1
teaspoon dates into center of each
cup; divide remaining batter evenly
among cups to cover fruit. Bake at
400° for 15 minutes. Remove
muffins from pan immediately; place
on a wire rack. YIELD: 6 servings.

POINTS: 4; **EXCHANGES:** 2 Starch, 1 Fat;
PER SERVING: CAL 197 (23% from fat);
PRO 3.6g; FAT 5.1g (sat 1.3g); CARB 33g;
FIB 0.3g; CHOL 35mg; IRON 0.9mg;
SOD 248mg; CALC 22mg

MANGO-BLACK BEAN SALSA

This is a great portable snack to boost
your energy for an after-work workout.

1 (15-ounce) can black beans,
  drained
1 cup peeled diced fresh mango
2 tablespoons chopped fresh
  cilantro
3 tablespoons lime juice
¼ teaspoon salt
Dash of ground red pepper
32 bite-size baked tortilla chips

1. Combine first 6 ingredients in a
bowl; toss well. Cover and chill at
least 1 hour. Serve with tortilla
chips. YIELD: 4 servings (serving size:
½ cup salsa and 8 chips).

POINTS: 2; **EXCHANGES:** 1½ Starch, ½ Fruit;
PER SERVING: CAL 158 (6% from fat);
PRO 7.2g; FAT 1g (sat 0.1g); CARB 32.9g;
FIB 4.1g; CHOL 0mg; IRON 1.7mg;
SOD 402mg; CALC 42mg

POWERHOUSE COOKIES

1 (17.5-ounce) package oatmeal-
  chocolate chip cookie mix
  (such as Betty Crocker)
½ cup finely chopped mixed dried
  fruit
⅓ cup prune baby food
¼ cup roasted salted sunflower
  seeds
¼ cup egg substitute
1 tablespoon water

1. Preheat oven to 375°.
2. Combine all ingredients in a
medium bowl, and stir until well
blended. Drop dough by level
tablespoons 2 inches apart onto
ungreased baking sheets. Bake at
375° for 8 minutes or until edges
are golden brown. Remove from
oven, and let stand 1 minute.
Remove cookies from baking sheets,
and let cool on wire racks.
YIELD: 3 dozen (serving size:
1 cookie).
NOTE: Substitute sweetened
applesauce for prune baby food, if
desired.

POINTS: 3; **EXCHANGES:** 1½ Starch, ½ Fat;
PER SERVING: CAL 149 (25% from fat);
PRO 2.9g; FAT 4.1g (sat 1.6g); CARB 25.4g;
FIB 0.3g; CHOL 0mg; IRON 1.1mg;
SOD 142mg; CALC 4.7mg

WHITE BEAN-PESTO PITA

If you prepare this sandwich the night before you plan to exercise, simply wrap the sandwich in plastic wrap and chill. Lining the pita with a dry lettuce leaf helps protect the bread from moisture.

1 (19-ounce) can cannellini beans or other white beans, undrained
1 tablespoon prepared pesto (such as Pesto Sanremo)
½ cup seeded chopped tomato
2 (7-inch) pita bread rounds, cut in half
4 curly leaf lettuce leaves

1. Drain cannellini beans, reserving 2½ tablespoons bean liquid. Place beans, reserved liquid, and prepared pesto in a food processor. Process until bean mixture is smooth. Combine puréed mixture and tomato in a small bowl, and stir well.
2. Line each pita half with a lettuce leaf; fill each with ½ cup bean mixture. YIELD: 4 servings (serving size: 1 pita half).

POINTS: 4; EXCHANGES: 3 Starch;
PER SERVING: CAL 235 (6% from fat);
PRO 12.5g; FAT 1.5g (sat 0.3g); CARB 44.7g;
FIB 4.3g; CHOL 0mg; IRON 3.4mg;
SOD 389mg; CALC 92mg

Lemon Meringue Pie

Peak perfection is easy to achieve using these step-by-step directions.

LEMON MERINGUE PIE

(pictured on 113)

1 cup all-purpose flour
¼ teaspoon salt
3 tablespoons vegetable shortening
6 tablespoons ice water
Cooking spray
1 large egg yolk
1¼ cups sugar
6 tablespoons cornstarch
1 cup water
⅓ cup fresh lemon juice
2 tablespoons stick margarine
¼ teaspoon grated lemon rind
4 large egg whites (at room temperature)
½ teaspoon cream of tartar
¼ cup sugar

1. Preheat oven to 450°.
2. Combine flour and salt in a bowl; cut in shortening with a pastry blender or 2 knives until mixture resembles coarse meal. Add ice water, 1 tablespoon at a time, tossing with a fork until moist. Press mixture gently into a 4-inch circle on heavy-duty plastic wrap; cover with additional plastic wrap. Roll dough, still covered, into an 11-inch circle. Chill 5 minutes or until plastic wrap can be removed easily.
3. Remove plastic wrap, and fit dough into a 9-inch pie plate coated with cooking spray. Fold edges of dough under, and flute.

Pierce bottom and sides of dough with a fork. Bake at 450° for 10 minutes or until lightly browned. Let cool completely on a wire rack. Reduce oven temperature to 325°.
4. Place egg yolk in a bowl; stir well, and set aside. Combine 1¼ cups sugar and cornstarch in a non-aluminum saucepan; stir well. Stir in 1 cup water and lemon juice; bring to a boil. Cook 1 minute or until thick, stirring constantly with a whisk. Gradually add hot cornstarch mixture to egg yolk, stirring constantly with whisk. Return mixture to pan. Cook over medium heat 2 minutes, stirring constantly. Remove from heat; stir in margarine and lemon rind. Spoon into pastry shell. Cover surface of filling with plastic wrap; set aside.
5. Beat egg whites and cream of tartar with clean, dry beaters at high speed of a mixer until foamy. Gradually add ¼ cup sugar, 1 tablespoon at a time, beating until stiff peaks form. Uncover pie. Spread meringue evenly over hot filling, sealing to edge of crust. Bake at 325° for 25 minutes or until meringue is golden. Let cool completely on a wire rack. Serve at room temperature. Store loosely covered in refrigerator. YIELD: 8 servings.

POINTS: 7; EXCHANGES: 3½ Starch, 1 Fat;
PER SERVING: CAL 304 (23% from fat);
PRO 3.7g; FAT 7.6g (sat 1.0g); CARB 56.1g;
FIB 0.5g; CHOL 27mg; IRON 0.9mg;
SOD 135mg; CALC 9mg

1. Combine flour and salt in a bowl. Cut the shortening into the flour mixture with a pastry blender or two knives. The finished mixture should resemble coarse meal.

2. Add ice water to flour mixture, 1 tablespoon at a time, tossing with a fork until moist.

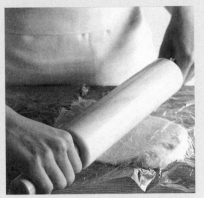

3. Gently press mixture into a 4-inch circle on heavy-duty plastic wrap. Cover with additional plastic wrap. Roll dough, still covered, into an 11-inch circle, and chill.

4. After removing plastic wrap, invert dough into pie plate. Fold under the edges of dough, and flute. Pierce bottom and sides of dough with the tines of a fork.

5. Beat egg whites and cream of tartar in a copper, glass, or metal bowl until foamy. Add 1 tablespoon sugar at a time, beating until stiff peaks form and sugar is dissolved.

6. Dollop meringue onto the hot filling, using a spatula or large spoon.

7. Spread meringue with a spatula or the back of a spoon until it covers the filling and forms a seal around the edges of the crust.

TIPS FROM THE TEST KITCHENS

To make slicing easier, use a knife dipped in hot water. Also, because the meringue weeps when refrigerated, this pie is best eaten the same day it is baked. If you do have leftovers, they should be loosely covered and stored in the refrigerator.

Here's to Your Health

In some cases, moderate drinking can be a toast to your well-being.

Laughter is good medicine. But a glass of wine? A beer? Recent studies show that moderate alcohol intake can improve your health.

"At least 60 studies show that alcohol has a protective effect on the heart," says Eric Rimm, Sc.D., an expert on nutrition and disease at the Harvard School of Public Health. This comes from alcohol's ability to raise HDL cholesterol, which keeps arteries clean. Alcohol also makes the blood less likely to form potentially lethal clots.

According to a study of nearly a half-million people published in 1998, "rates of death from cardiovascular diseases were 30% to 40% lower among men and women reporting at least one drink daily than among nondrinkers."

So we should all be uncorking wine bottles or pouring ourselves cold ones, right? Medical experts are quick to wave a caution flag, despite the many praises for alcohol.

CHEERS AND JEERS.
Alcohol offers risks alongside its benefits. For example, alcohol may increase estrogen levels in the blood. This could be one way that alcohol raises the risk of breast cancer.

One study linked the amount of alcohol consumed with breast cancer. Women who had one drink a day showed a 9% increase in risk (over nondrinkers), but those who had two to five drinks a day were 40% more likely to develop the disease.

Drinking also raises the risk of high blood pressure, stroke, pancreas problems, liver disease, and (paradoxically) heart ailments.

Alcohol might prevent 80,000 deaths from coronary disease a year. But it also contributes to 100,000 deaths from various ailments and accidents, which is why the American Heart Association, the U. S. government, and nearly all doctors neither damn alcohol nor praise it. Instead they urge us to look at our

"Studies show that alcohol has a protective effect on the heart."

individual potential risks and benefits, and decide whether to drink in moderation or not at all.

Those with a family history of alcoholism, liver disease, or pancreatitis, clearly should not drink. The same is true if you have high blood pressure, abnormal heart rhythms, or a peptic ulcer. Also abstain if you're an expectant or nursing mother, or if you're trying to have a baby.

For the rest of us, whether to drink is trickier. Men over 45 and women over 55 are most at risk of heart disease, and stand to benefit most from a drink with dinner. Those under 45, lean, active, and don't smoke won't benefit much. Women with a family history of breast cancer or are at high risk of breast cancer face a tough decision that is best discussed with a physician.

WINE OR BEER?
If you do drink, set limits (see "What's Moderation?"). And it doesn't seem to matter if your choice is wine, beer, or spirits. Reports on the health benefits of red wine got a lot of attention, but if wine confers added benefit, it's likely to be minor. "Much, if not all, of the benefits of alcoholic beverages comes from the ethanol alcohol itself," says Rimm.

As for weight control, some research shows that a calorie from alcohol is more easily metabolized than a calorie from food, and so less likely to wind up as excess baggage.

In terms of calories, however, one drink a day shouldn't ruin your figure. A glass of white table wine has about 70 calories, a bottle of "light" beer about 100, and a mixed drink from 105 for a bourbon and soda to 190 for a tequila sunrise. (A drink made with cream, such as a white Russian, has more.)

What's Moderation?

According to the U.S. government and the American Heart Association, drinking "in moderation" means one to two drinks per day for men and one for women.

Men can have more because they tend to weigh more and because they have more of the enzyme dehydrogenase, which helps metabolize alcohol.

Alcoholic beverages differ in the amount of alcohol they contain, but in general, one "drink" is defined as 12 ounces of beer, 4 to 5 ounces of wine, or a 1 ½-ounce shot of 80-proof spirits. These all contain roughly ½ ounce of pure alcohol.

Be Prepared

A good cook knows the importance of a well-stocked freezer and pantry.

Every good home cook knows the most useful motto is that of the Boy Scouts: Be prepared. Prepared for coming home to an empty fridge, for drop-in dinner guests, and for the family that's hungry even though they ate at Grandma's two hours ago. The only way to do that is to arm yourself with an arsenal of recipes that use only ingredients from your freezer and pantry—dishes that don't call for a single perishable item, so you can stock up. With the ingredients for these recipes on hand, you'll never be caught unprepared.

ORANGE-HOISIN SHRIMP STIR-FRY

(pictured on page 24)

Hoisin or Peking sauce is a spicy, sweet blend of soybeans, chile peppers, garlic, and spices. Find it on the ethnic foods aisle.

⅓ cup hoisin sauce
2 tablespoons frozen orange juice concentrate
1 tablespoon low-salt soy sauce
1 tablespoon bottled minced garlic
⅛ teaspoon crushed red pepper
2 teaspoons dark sesame oil
1 teaspoon ground ginger
1 (16-ounce) package frozen Beijing-style stir-fry vegetables (such as VIP)
1 (8-ounce) can sliced water chestnuts, drained
1 (16-ounce) package frozen cooked and peeled large shrimp, thawed
4 cups hot cooked rice

1. Combine first 5 ingredients in a bowl; stir well. Place wok or a large nonstick skillet over high heat until hot. Add sesame oil, ginger, vegetables, and water chestnuts; stir-fry 3 minutes. Add hoisin sauce mixture and shrimp; stir-fry 2 minutes or until shrimp are warm and vegetables are crisp-tender. Serve over rice.
YIELD: 4 servings (serving size: 1¼ cups stir-fry and 1 cup rice).
NOTE: Frozen Beijing-style stir-fry vegetables include a mixture of carrots, broccoli hearts, snow pea pods, water chestnuts, onions, soybeans, bean sprouts, mushrooms, shoestring bamboo, celery, and red bell pepper.

POINTS: 8; **EXCHANGES:** 2 Very Lean Meat, 3 Veg, 4 Starch; **PER SERVING:** CAL 465 (7% from fat); PRO 31.6g; FAT 3.8g (sat 0.7g); CARB 74.6g; FIB 5.7g; CHOL 221.3mg; IRON 6.2mg; SOD 803mg; CALC 96.3mg

BARBECUED BEANS 'N' RICE

If you prefer mild food, use only one chile.

2 teaspoons olive oil
1 cup frozen chopped onion
1 to 2 drained canned chipotle chiles, minced
1 tablespoon bottled minced garlic
1 (16-ounce) can pinto beans, drained
1 (16-ounce) can kidney beans, drained
1 (15-ounce) can black beans, drained
1 cup hickory barbecue sauce (such as KC Masterpiece)
1 tablespoon Dijon mustard
6 cups hot cooked long-grain rice
Chopped fresh chives (optional)

1. Preheat oven to 350°.
2. Heat oil in a nonstick skillet over medium heat. Add onion, chiles, and garlic; sauté 5 minutes. Remove from heat. Stir in beans, barbecue sauce, and mustard. Spoon mixture into a 1½-quart casserole; cover and bake at 350° for 1 hour. Serve over rice; garnish with chives, if desired.
YIELD: 8 servings (serving size: ½ cup beans and ¾ cup rice).
NOTE: If chipotle chiles aren't available, substitute 1 to 2 drained canned jalapeños and a few drops of mesquite-flavored barbecue smoke seasoning (such as Mesquite Liquid Smoke).

POINTS: 7; **EXCHANGES:** 5 Starch; **PER SERVING:** CAL 372 (5% from fat); PRO 12.2g; FAT 2.1g (sat 0.3g); CARB 76.4g; FIB 5g; CHOL 0mg; IRON 4.6mg; SOD 540mg; CALC 53.3mg

LOUISIANA CRAB JAMBALAYA

This spicy seafood stew has only 135 calories and 2 *POINTS*.

1 tablespoon olive oil
1½ cups frozen chopped onion
1 cup frozen whole-kernel corn
½ cup frozen chopped green bell pepper
1 (14½-ounce) can diced tomatoes with green bell pepper and onion, undrained
1 (10-ounce) package frozen cut okra
2 (6-ounce) cans lump crabmeat, drained
1 (8-ounce) bottle clam juice
1 tablespoon seafood seasoning blend (such as Chef Paul Prudhomme's Seafood Magic)
1 tablespoon bottled minced garlic
1 teaspoon dried fines herbes
¼ teaspoon salt

1. Heat oil in a saucepan over medium-high heat. Add onion, corn, and bell pepper; sauté 5 minutes. Add tomatoes and remaining ingredients; bring to a boil. Reduce heat; simmer, uncovered, 20 minutes, stirring occasionally. Serve over hot cooked rice or with French bread, if desired. YIELD: 6 servings (serving size: 1 cup).

POINTS: 2; **EXCHANGES:** 3½ Veg, ½ Very Lean Meat, ½ Fat; **PER SERVING:** CAL 135 (19% from fat); PRO 9.8g; FAT 2.9g (sat 0.4g); CARB 18.9g; FIB 3.3g; CHOL 37.8mg; IRON 2.1mg; SOD 946mg; CALC 124mg

CURRIED CHICKEN-AND-VEGETABLE COUSCOUS

2 teaspoons olive oil
1 cup frozen chopped onion
2 (16-ounce) cans one-third-less salt chicken broth, divided
1 (16-ounce) package frozen mixed vegetables
1 (15-ounce) can chickpeas (garbanzo beans), drained
1 (10-ounce) can chunk white chicken in water, drained
½ cup golden raisins
¼ cup hot mango chutney
1 tablespoon lemon juice
2½ teaspoons curry powder
2 teaspoons bottled minced garlic
¼ teaspoon ground red pepper
2 tablespoons water
1 (10-ounce) package couscous
¼ cup chopped unsalted, dry-roasted peanuts

1. Heat oil in a nonstick skillet over medium-high heat. Add onion; sauté 3 minutes. Add 1 can broth, vegetables, and next 8 ingredients; bring to a boil. Cover; reduce heat. Simmer 6 minutes or until vegetables are tender.
2. Bring remaining can chicken broth and 2 tablespoons water to a boil in a saucepan. Add couscous; stir well. Remove from heat; cover. Let stand 5 minutes. Fluff with a fork.
3. Spoon couscous into individual bowls; top with vegetable mixture. Sprinkle with peanuts.
YIELD: 8 servings (serving size: about ⅔ cup couscous, ¾ cup vegetable mixture, and 1½ teaspoons peanuts).

POINTS: 8; **EXCHANGES:** 4 Starch, 2 Veg, 1 Lean Meat; **PER SERVING:** CAL 414 (14% from fat); PRO 21.3g; FAT 6.4g (sat 0.6g); CARB 70.3g; FIB 6.1g; CHOL 0mg; IRON 3.1mg; SOD 560mg; CALC 35.5mg

LINGUINE WITH TOMATOES, SPINACH, AND WHITE BEANS

This recipe is surprisingly high in calcium, and provides about 25% of the amount you need in a day.

2 teaspoons olive oil
1 tablespoon bottled minced garlic
2 (14½-ounce) cans diced tomatoes with basil, garlic, and oregano, undrained
1 (15-ounce) can cannellini beans or other white beans, drained
1 (10-ounce) package frozen chopped spinach, thawed, drained, and squeezed dry
6 cups hot cooked linguine (about ¾ pound uncooked pasta)
6 tablespoons grated Romano cheese

1. Heat oil in a large nonstick skillet over medium-high heat. Add garlic; sauté 1 minute. Add tomatoes, beans, and spinach; bring to a boil. Reduce heat, and simmer 15 minutes, stirring occasionally. Spoon sauce over pasta; sprinkle with cheese. YIELD: 6 servings (serving size: 1 cup pasta, 1 cup sauce, and 1 tablespoon cheese).

POINTS: 7; **EXCHANGES:** 3½ Starch, 2½ Veg; **PER SERVING:** CAL 365 (10% from fat); PRO 16.3g; FAT 4.1g (sat 1.3g); CARB 66.8g; FIB 4.9g; CHOL 5.2mg; IRON 6.2mg; SOD 978mg; CALC 239.8mg

May

Our Mothers' Recipes

In honor of Mother's Day, the **Weight Watchers** Magazine staff shares favorite recipes from home.

Most of us learn the most valuable culinary lessons from our mothers. From them we discover that pie is not just dessert, but an offering of love. Here at *Weight Watchers* Magazine, we believe that sharing lightened versions of the dishes we grew up with is a fitting tribute to our mothers. These aren't just the foods of childhood; they're still our favorite recipes. They are a legacy of a mother's love. And that lesson was free.

VEAL MARSALA

"Mom learned this recipe at a gourmet cooking class she took in the seventies. The first time she made it, we all loved it, and it remains one of my favorites."
Alyson Haynes, senior food editor

1 pound veal scaloppine
⅔ cup grated Parmesan cheese, divided
2 tablespoons Italian-seasoned breadcrumbs
¼ teaspoon salt
¼ teaspoon pepper
Cooking spray
1 tablespoon olive oil, divided
1 (8-ounce) package presliced fresh mushrooms
1 cup water
½ cup dry Marsala
1 beef-flavored bouillon cube
¼ teaspoon ground red pepper
3 cups hot cooked vermicelli
Chopped fresh parsley (optional)

1. Place each piece of veal between 2 sheets of heavy-duty plastic wrap; flatten to ¹⁄₁₆-inch thickness, using a meat mallet or rolling pin. Cut large pieces in half; set aside.
2. Combine ⅓ cup Parmesan cheese, breadcrumbs, salt, and pepper in a shallow dish; stir well. Dredge veal in cheese mixture; lightly coat each breaded piece with cooking spray.
3. Coat a nonstick skillet with cooking spray; add 1 teaspoon oil. Place over medium-high heat until hot. Add one-third of veal; cook 1½ minutes on each side or until lightly browned. Remove from skillet, and keep warm. Repeat procedure with remaining oil and veal.
4. Add mushrooms and next 4 ingredients to skillet. Bring to a boil, and cook 6 minutes or until reduced to 1 cup, stirring frequently. Return veal to skillet, turning to coat.
5. Spoon ¾ cup pasta onto each of 4 plates, and divide veal and mushroom mixture evenly over pasta. Sprinkle remaining ⅓ cup Parmesan cheese evenly over each serving; top with chopped parsley, if desired.
YIELD: 4 servings.

POINTS: 8; **EXCHANGES:** 4 Very Lean Meat, 2 Starch, 1 Veg, 1 Fat; **PER SERVING:** CAL 387 (28% from fat); PRO 35g; FAT 12g (sat 4.1g); CARB 33.9g; FIB 2.4g; CHOL 105mg; IRON 3.3mg; SOD 825mg; CALC 213mg

GRAHAM CRACKER CREAM PIE

(pictured on page 111)

"My mother's love lives on through this recipe. The combination of creamy custard and cinnamon-laced crust makes it so wonderful."
Gayle Sadler,
assistant test kitchens director

1 cup plus 1 tablespoon graham cracker crumbs, divided
1 tablespoon sugar
2 teaspoons all-purpose flour
1 teaspoon ground cinnamon
3 tablespoons stick margarine, melted
Cooking spray
⅔ cup sugar
¼ cup cornstarch
¼ teaspoon salt
2 cups 1% low-fat milk
2 large egg yolks, lightly beaten
1 teaspoon stick margarine
1 teaspoon vanilla extract
3 large egg whites (at room temperature)
½ teaspoon cream of tartar
⅓ cup sugar
½ teaspoon vanilla extract

1. Preheat oven to 350°.
2. Combine 1 cup crumbs, sugar, flour, and cinnamon; stir well. Add margarine; toss until moist. Press in bottom and up sides of a 9-inch pie plate coated with cooking spray; lightly coat crust with cooking spray. Bake at 350° for 8 minutes; let cool. Reduce oven temperature to 325°.
3. Combine ⅔ cup sugar, cornstarch, and salt in a saucepan; stir in milk. Bring to a boil over medium heat. Cook 1 minute; stir constantly.

4. Gradually add hot milk mixture to egg yolks, stirring constantly with a whisk. Return mixture to pan. Cook over medium heat 2 minutes or until thick, stirring constantly. Remove from heat; stir in 1 teaspoon margarine and 1 teaspoon vanilla. Pour hot filling into crust.

5. Beat egg whites and cream of tartar with clean, dry beaters at high speed of a mixer until foamy. Gradually add ⅓ cup sugar, 1 tablespoon at a time, beating until stiff peaks form. Add ½ teaspoon vanilla; beat well. Spread over hot filling, sealing to edge of crust. Sprinkle with 1 tablespoon cracker crumbs. Bake at 325° for 25 minutes or until meringue is golden. Let cool. Chill at least 2 hours. YIELD: 8 servings.

POINTS: 6; EXCHANGES: 3 Starch, 1 Fat; PER SERVING: CAL 262 (27% from fat); PRO 5.3g; FAT 7.9g (sat 1.9g); CARB 42.6g; FIB 0.4g; CHOL 57mg; IRON 0.8mg; SOD 257mg; CALC 90mg

MOCHA BROWNIE TORTE

(pictured on page 67)

"Mom has made this family favorite for years. It's an easy way to jazz up brownies for special occasions."
Natalie King, test kitchens staff

⅔ cup hot water
2 tablespoons instant coffee granules
1 (20.5-ounce) box low-fat brownie mix (such as Sweet Rewards)
2 teaspoons vanilla extract
4 large egg whites, lightly beaten
Cooking spray
Coffee Whipped Frosting

1. Preheat oven to 325°.
2. Combine hot water and coffee granules; stir well. Add brownie mix, vanilla, and egg whites; stir until well blended. Pour mixture evenly into 2 (9-inch) cake pans coated with cooking spray. Bake at 325° for 20 minutes. Let cool in pans 5 minutes on a wire rack. Spray wire racks with cooking spray. Loosen brownie layers from sides of pans, using a narrow metal spatula, and turn out onto greased wire racks. Let cool completely.
3. Spread Coffee Whipped Frosting between layers and over top and sides of torte. Serve immediately or store, loosely covered, in refrigerator. YIELD: 12 servings.
NOTE: To loosely cover torte, use a cake dome or place 6 toothpicks in top of torte, spacing evenly to prevent plastic wrap from sticking to whipped topping. Cover with plastic wrap.

POINTS: 5; EXCHANGES: 3 Starch, ½ Fat; PER SERVING: CAL 246 (23% from fat); PRO 4.8g; FAT 6.2g (sat 0.9g); CARB 45.5g; FIB 1.5g; CHOL 0.3mg; IRON 1.7mg; SOD 210mg; CALC 13.8mg

COFFEE WHIPPED FROSTING:
3 cups frozen reduced-calorie whipped topping, thawed
1 tablespoon instant coffee granules

1. Place whipped topping in a bowl; sprinkle with coffee granules. Gently fold coffee into whipped topping (fold only until coffee granules disperse and whipped topping has a speckled look). YIELD: 3 cups.

SUMMER SQUASH CROQUETTES

(pictured on page 66)

"A true Southern cook, my mom always served a meat and three side dishes. Coming up with vegetables that my siblings and I would eat was quite a challenge. This recipe, with its crunchy coating, did the trick."
Kay Fuston, managing editor

1¼ pounds yellow squash, coarsely chopped
½ cup chopped onion
1 cup crushed saltine crackers (about 33 crackers)
¾ teaspoon salt
½ teaspoon sugar
2 large eggs
¼ cup yellow cornmeal
Cooking spray
1 tablespoon vegetable oil, divided
Parsley sprigs (optional)

1. Steam squash and onion, covered, 15 minutes or until vegetables are tender; drain well. Mash squash mixture with a potato masher or fork, and stir in crushed crackers and next 3 ingredients. Cover and chill mixture at least 3 hours.
2. Place ¼ cup yellow cornmeal in a large shallow dish. Divide squash mixture into 12 equal portions. Working quickly, dredge squash mixture, one portion at a time, in cornmeal, shaping into 3-inch patties, and coat each patty with cooking spray.
3. Coat a large nonstick skillet with cooking spray, and add 1 teaspoon vegetable oil. Place skillet over

(continued)

medium-high heat until hot. Add 4 patties, and cook 1½ minutes on each side or until golden. Remove patties from skillet; set aside, and keep warm. Repeat procedure with remaining vegetable oil and patties. Garnish with parsley sprigs, if desired. Serve immediately. YIELD: 6 servings (serving size: 2 croquettes).

POINTS: 3; EXCHANGES: 1 Starch, 1 Veg, 1 Fat; PER SERVING: CAL 161 (35% from fat); PRO 5.2g; FAT 6.3g (sat 1g); CARB 21.4g; FIB 2.6g; CHOL 71mg; IRON 1.7mg; SOD 556mg; CALC 57mg

MRS. PARKER'S CORN-AND-RICE CASSEROLE

(pictured on page 72)

"This casserole was Mom's favorite because it fed an army—and she had seven mouths to feed. The cheesy flavor appeals to me now as much as it did when I was a kid."
Maria Hopkins, copy editor

1 tablespoon margarine
Cooking spray
1 (8-ounce) package presliced fresh mushrooms
½ cup chopped onion
1⅓ cups chicken broth
½ cup uncooked converted rice
1 (10¾-ounce) can reduced-fat reduced-sodium cream of mushroom soup, undiluted
2 (11-ounce) cans vacuum-packed corn with red and green peppers (such as Mexicorn), undrained
½ cup (2 ounces) shredded reduced-fat sharp cheddar cheese
Red bell pepper strips (optional)

1. Preheat oven to 350°.
2. Melt margarine in a saucepan coated with cooking spray over medium-high heat. Add mushrooms and onion; sauté 6 minutes. Add broth; bring to a boil. Add rice; cover, reduce heat, and simmer 20 minutes. Remove from heat; let stand, covered, 5 minutes. Stir in soup and corn. Spoon mixture into an 8-inch square baking dish coated with cooking spray. Bake at 350° for 15 minutes. Top with cheese; bake 5 minutes or until cheese melts. Garnish with red bell pepper strips, if desired. YIELD: 8 servings (serving size: ⅔ cup).

POINTS: 4; EXCHANGES: 2 Starch, ½ Fat; PER SERVING: CAL 176 (21% from fat); PRO 6.7g; FAT 4.1g (sat 1.5g); CARB 29.3g; FIB 1.6g; CHOL 7.9mg; IRON 0.8mg; SOD 780mg; CALC 109mg

HONEY WHEAT BREAD

"My mother baked this bread every week for years and used it for our sandwiches. Back then, I wanted the white gluey kind other kids ate. Now when I make sandwiches for my family, I long for Mom's wheat bread."
Kathleen Phillips, test kitchens director

2 packages dry yeast
⅓ cup honey
1 cup warm water (105° to 115°)
1 cup half-and-half
4 large eggs, lightly beaten
1½ cups whole-wheat flour
1½ teaspoons salt
4¾ cups bread flour
Cooking spray

1. Dissolve yeast and honey in warm water in a mixing bowl; let stand 5 minutes. Add half-and-half and eggs; beat at medium speed of a heavy-duty stand mixer until well blended. Add whole-wheat flour and salt, beating well. Stir in bread flour, ½ cup at a time, to form a soft dough.
2. Turn dough out onto a well-floured surface. Knead until smooth and elastic (about 5 minutes).
3. Place dough in a large bowl coated with cooking spray, turning to coat top. Cover and let rise in a warm place (85°), free from drafts, 45 minutes or until doubled in bulk.
4. Punch dough down; turn dough onto a lightly floured surface, and knead lightly 4 or 5 times. Divide dough into 3 equal portions. Working with one portion at a time (cover remaining dough to keep it from drying out), roll each portion into a 12- x 8-inch rectangle on a lightly floured surface. Roll up each rectangle tightly, starting with a short side. Press firmly to eliminate air pockets; pinch seam and ends to seal. Place each roll of dough, seam side down, in an 8- x 4-inch loaf pan coated with cooking spray.
5. Cover and let rise 30 minutes or until doubled in bulk.
6. Preheat oven to 375°.
7. Bake bread at 375° for 20 minutes or until loaves sound hollow when tapped. Remove bread from pans immediately, and let cool on wire racks. YIELD: 3 loaves, 48 servings (serving size: ½-inch slice).
NOTE: You may use a dough hook and a heavy-duty stand mixer for kneading, if desired.

POINTS: 1; EXCHANGES: 1 Starch; PER SERVING: CAL 72 (16% from fat); PRO 2.6g; FAT 1.3g (sat 0.5g); CARB 12.8g; FIB 0.6g; CHOL 20mg; IRON 0.7mg; SOD 81mg; CALC 11mg

For Better or Worse

MARK BENNETT (WITH AMY) • **HEIGHT** 6'0" • **BEFORE** 242 LBS. • **AFTER** 190 LBS.

Happiest Moment: Not being recognized by old friends

Mark Bennett, a New York graphic designer, is surrounded by food in a city renowned for culinary pleasures. "I was 242 pounds and had no discipline," he recalls. "I'd buy a pizza and a soda and think I was doing fine."

Mark and his wife, Amy, were both overweight when they married. Amy realized that her husband's eating habits were very erratic and unhealthful. "Mine weren't the best, but Mark's food choices were pretty bad," she remembers. Determined not to fulfill the adage that newlyweds always gain weight, Amy joined Weight Watchers.

> *"I started tasting the vegetables and realized they are better without a sauce."*

Mark noticed when Amy started losing weight. But he was only vaguely aware of the program's benefits and certain it wouldn't help him. "My view was that people join groups, exercise, or just stop eating and don't really change," Mark says.

The more Mark encouraged Amy, the more curious he became about making some changes himself. He finally announced that if she gave him a few weeks of the program as a gift, he'd go to the meetings. "I still thought I could do it on my own, but I figured I should give it a try," he explains.

After just one day on the program, he was sold. "The program forced me to be honest with myself," he says. "I gained a control over eating that I wouldn't have otherwise."

Mark kept a food journal, cut out high-fat foods, and reduced the extras. "I started tasting the vegetables and realized they are better without a sauce," he says. In seven months, he lost 42 pounds and was so pleased that he decided to lose another 10.

Mark and Amy stress the importance of partnership. "We encourage each other," Amy says. They feel the difference every day. Last year they helped build a house for Habitat for Humanity, something that wouldn't have been much fun before. "Climbing a ladder was easier without carrying around all the extra weight," says Mark.

"It's all common sense," he says. "There is no silver bullet. I can eat more, or I can eat less, and in the end it's my decision."

Roasted
Asparagus-and-Goat Cheese
Crostini, page 74

Summer Squash
Croquettes, page 63

Mocha Brownie Torte, page 63

Spiced Salmon Fillet With
Fennel Mayonnaise, page 76

Cinnamon-Spiced
Peaches, page 17

Couscous-Stuffed
Portobellos, page 78

Maple-Mustard Pork Roast, page 13,
with Creamed Spiced Rutabaga, page 14

Brown Sugar-Rum Pound Cake
With Strawberries, page 53

Butternut Squash
Crunch, page 73

Springtime
Asparagus Soup,
page 74

Mrs. Parker's Corn-and-Rice
Casserole, page 64

BUTTERNUT SQUASH CRUNCH

(pictured on page 71)

My family ate at the same buffet-style restaurant every Sunday. I'd work my way through the line in anticipation of finding this creamy casserole. Mother begged the chef for the recipe, and it's been a part of our family ever since." Serve this dish as a side or as dessert.

Amy Heise, art director

⅓ cup sugar
¼ cup skim milk
1 teaspoon ground cinnamon
1 teaspoon vanilla extract
¼ teaspoon salt
¼ teaspoon ground nutmeg
1 large egg
1 large egg white
1 (3½-pound) butternut squash
¼ cup water
Cooking spray
1 cup miniature marshmallows
½ cup firmly packed brown sugar
2 tablespoons all-purpose flour
1 tablespoon stick margarine, melted

1. Preheat oven to 350°.
2. Combine first 8 ingredients in a large bowl; stir well, and set aside.
3. Cut squash in half lengthwise, and discard seeds and membrane. Place squash halves, cut sides down, in a shallow baking dish, and add water. Cover with heavy-duty plastic wrap, and vent. Microwave at HIGH 12 minutes or until very tender, rotating dish a half-turn after 5 minutes. Remove squash halves from dish, and discard water. Let squash cool slightly. Scoop out squash pulp, and mash to desired consistency, reserving 4½ cups. Add 4½ cups mashed squash to egg mixture, stirring well. Spoon into a 1½-quart baking dish coated with cooking spray, and top with marshmallows.
4. Combine brown sugar, flour, and margarine in a small bowl; stir well, and sprinkle over marshmallows. Bake at 350° for 25 minutes or until filling is bubbly and marshmallows are lightly browned. YIELD: 7 servings (serving size: about ¾ cup).
NOTE: To make squash easier to cut in half, pierce whole squash with a knife or an ice pick, and microwave at HIGH 2 to 3 minutes. You may substitute 3 (10-ounce) packages frozen butternut squash, thawed, for the fresh, if desired.

POINTS: 4; **EXCHANGES:** 3 Starch;
PER SERVING: CAL 212 (11% from fat);
PRO 3.1g; FAT 2.6g (sat 0.6g); CARB 46.5g;
FIB 1.7g; CHOL 32mg; IRON 1.5mg;
SOD 139mg; CALC 88mg

GOODS

Make a Smile

Nothing beats homemade ice cream on a summer day. Here's the scoop on the best makers.

Today's ice cream makers come in two styles—bucket freezers and cylinder freezers—and are either manual or electric. Both work on the same principle: A paddle blends air into the mixture while freezing it. Differences are convenience, ice cream texture, and price.

BUCKET FREEZERS. A bucket freezer requires salt, ice, and either an electric motor or a strong arm to turn the crank. You can alter the ice cream's consistency by changing the mix of salt and ice. Electric models are noisy and are best for outside use.
WHITE MOUNTAIN ICE CREAM MAKER (4 quarts). A powerful motor and a unique design ensure the smoothest homemade ice cream possible. Available in gourmet shops and catalogs, this model costs more than most (between $150 and $200).
RIVAL ICE CREAM AND YOGURT FREEZER (4 quarts). A good, basic maker, this model has a plastic bucket and a less powerful motor than White Mountain. It costs about $20.

CYLINDER FREEZERS. These rely on a sealed-in coolant and don't need salt or ice. Freeze the cylinder at least 12 hours, add ingredients, and turn it on. The ice cream is ready in 30 minutes—but it won't be as dense as with a bucket-style maker.
MAVERICK ICE CREAM SHOPPE (1 quart). This model makes hard or soft ice cream. Available in department stores, it costs about $50.
KRUPS LA GLACIERE (1½ quarts). Similar to the Maverick, but with a slightly larger capacity. Available in department stores and catalogs, it costs around $60.

Cool Rules

• For speed, chill all ingredients.

• Don't overfill the canister. The mixture will expand as air is incorporated.

• Ice cream is done when it has a soft consistency. For firmer ice cream, freeze it for several hours.

• It's best eaten within a few hours. But it can last several days in an airtight container; place plastic wrap over top before sealing.

Sentinel of Spring

Standing crisp and tall, asparagus is the green god of an early garden.

There's more to asparagus than being hidden under a blanket of hollandaise sauce. For variety, swirl it into a light purée or toss it into a zesty salsa. It can be steamed to retain its color and crunch, roasted to bring forth a sweet nuttiness, or gently simmered to impart an earthy aroma to a soup. If that's not reason enough to explore the wonders of asparagus, consider that it's a healthful source of vitamins A, B, and C.

SPRINGTIME ASPARAGUS SOUP

(pictured on page 71)

2 pounds asparagus spears
2 (14.25-ounce) cans fat-free chicken broth
1 medium baking potato, peeled and sliced
1 tablespoon chopped fresh or 1 teaspoon dried thyme
¼ cup evaporated skim milk or fat-free half-and-half
½ teaspoon salt
Dash of pepper
Lemon slices and thyme sprigs (optional)

1. Snap off tough ends of asparagus spears, and remove scales with a knife or vegetable peeler, if desired. Cut asparagus spears into 1-inch pieces, and set aside.
2. Combine chicken broth, potato, and chopped thyme in a large saucepan; bring mixture to a boil. Cover, reduce heat, and simmer 5 minutes. Add asparagus pieces, and bring to a boil. Cover, reduce heat, and simmer 15 minutes or until vegetables are tender. Remove from heat, and let cool slightly.
3. Drain vegetable mixture through a sieve over a large bowl, reserving 1½ cups cooking liquid. Place vegetable mixture in a food processor, and process until mixture is smooth. Strain puréed vegetable mixture through a sieve into saucepan. Stir in reserved cooking liquid, evaporated skim milk, salt, and pepper. Serve soup warm or chilled. Garnish each serving with lemon slices and thyme sprigs, if desired. **YIELD:** 4 servings (serving size: 1 cup).
NOTE: Vegetable mixture may be puréed in batches in a blender.

POINTS: 1; **EXCHANGES:** 1 Starch, 1 Veg;
PER SERVING: CAL 128 (4% from fat);
PRO 7.3g; FAT 0.5g (sat 0.1g); CARB 23.8g;
FIB 5.2g; CHOL 1mg; IRON 2.1mg;
SOD 322mg; CALC 95mg

ROASTED ASPARAGUS-AND-GOAT CHEESE CROSTINI

(pictured on page 66)

20 thin asparagus spears (about ½ pound)
4 (½-inch-thick) slices French or Italian bread
Garlic-flavored cooking spray
¼ teaspoon kosher or regular salt
¼ cup goat cheese, softened
4 teaspoons chopped fresh chives
1 ounce bottled roasted red bell peppers, cut into strips (about 2 tablespoons)

1. Preheat oven to 400°.
2. Snap off tough ends of spears, and remove scales with a knife or vegetable peeler, if desired. Trim asparagus spears to length of bread slices, and reserve trimmings for another use.
3. Place asparagus in a 9-inch square baking pan; coat asparagus with cooking spray, and sprinkle with salt. Coat one side of bread slices with cooking spray, and set aside. Bake asparagus at 400° for 5 minutes. Turn asparagus spears over, and place bread, coated side up, directly on oven rack next to asparagus. Bake asparagus and bread an additional 10 minutes or until bread is toasted.
4. Combine goat cheese and chives in a small bowl; stir well. Spread goat cheese mixture evenly over bread slices. Top each slice with 5 asparagus spears. Arrange bell pepper strips over asparagus. **YIELD:** 4 servings.

POINTS: 2; **EXCHANGES:** 1 Starch, ½ Fat;
PER SERVING: CAL 103 (25% from fat);
PRO 4.7g; FAT 3g (sat 1.6g); CARB 14.8g;
FIB 1.7g; CHOL 6mg; IRON 1.2mg;
SOD 426mg; CALC 52mg

ASPARAGUS-RASPBERRY SALSA

Serve over chicken, fish, salad greens, or fat-free cream cheese with crackers.

1 pound asparagus spears
1 cup fresh raspberries, halved
¼ cup finely chopped shallot
1 tablespoon raspberry vinegar
1 to 3 teaspoons seeded minced
  jalapeño pepper
¼ teaspoon salt
¼ teaspoon pepper

1. Snap off tough ends of asparagus, and remove scales with a knife or vegetable peeler, if desired. Cut asparagus into ½-inch pieces.
2. Steam asparagus, covered, 3 minutes or until crisp-tender, and drain. Rinse asparagus under cold water, and drain.
3. Combine asparagus, raspberries, and remaining ingredients in a large bowl; toss well. Cover and chill at least 1 hour. YIELD: 4 servings (serving size: ½ cup).

POINTS: 0; **EXCHANGES:** ½ Fruit, ½ Veg; **PER SERVING:** CAL 45 (8% from fat); PRO 2.5g; FAT 0.4g (sat 0.1g); CARB 10g; FIB 4.5g; CHOL 0mg; IRON 1.1mg; SOD 149mg; CALC 30mg

---

Asparagus Tips

You can find this vegetable in markets throughout the year, but it costs less and tastes best from late March through May. Look for firm stalks, tightly closed tips, and ends that aren't dry.

For freshest flavor, refrigerate in a plastic bag and cook within a few days of purchase. To store longer, refrigerate bunches, tips up, in a glass of water, loosely covered.

ASPARAGUS PESTO

A lighter, chunkier version of traditional basil pesto, this condiment complements fish, chicken, pasta, or potatoes.

1 pound asparagus spears
1 cup water
¼ cup grated fresh Parmesan
  cheese
1 tablespoon pine nuts
1 tablespoon extra-virgin olive oil
½ teaspoon salt
¼ teaspoon freshly ground pepper
2 large garlic cloves, peeled and
  quartered

1. Snap off tough ends of asparagus, and remove scales with a knife or vegetable peeler, if desired. Cut asparagus into 1-inch pieces.
2. Bring water to a boil in a saucepan; add asparagus pieces. Cover, reduce heat, and simmer 2 minutes. Drain in a colander over a small bowl, reserving 3 tablespoons cooking liquid. Rinse asparagus under cold water; drain and let cool to room temperature.
3. Place asparagus, cheese, and next 5 ingredients in a food processor, and pulse 10 times or until mixture is finely chopped, scraping sides of processor bowl once. Add reserved cooking liquid; process until blended. YIELD: 6 servings (serving size: ¼ cup).

POINTS: 1; **EXCHANGES:** ½ Veg, 1 Fat; **PER SERVING:** CAL 66 (68% from fat); PRO 3.3g; FAT 5g (sat 1.3g); CARB 3.5g; FIB 1.3g; CHOL 3mg; IRON 0.6mg; SOD 274mg; CALC 70mg

---

ASIAN MARINATED ASPARAGUS

1 pound asparagus spears
2 tablespoons water
¼ cup seasoned rice vinegar
2 tablespoons soy sauce
2 teaspoons bottled chopped fresh
  ginger (such as Christopher
  Ranch)
1 teaspoon dark sesame oil

1. Snap off tough ends of asparagus, and remove scales with a knife or vegetable peeler, if desired. Place asparagus spears and water in a shallow microwave-safe dish. Cover and microwave at HIGH 2 to 4 minutes or until asparagus is crisp-tender; drain. Return asparagus to dish.
2. Combine vinegar and next 3 ingredients in a small bowl; stir with a whisk until mixture is blended. Pour vinegar mixture over asparagus, turning asparagus to coat. Cover and marinate in refrigerator at least 2 hours, turning asparagus occasionally. YIELD: 4 servings.

POINTS: 1; **EXCHANGES:** 1 Veg, ½ Fat; **PER SERVING:** CAL 38 (31% from fat); PRO 2.5g; FAT 1.3g (sat 0.2g); CARB 4.9g; FIB 1.8g; CHOL 0mg; IRON 0.9mg; SOD 518mg; CALC 20mg

The Basics of Blackening

SPICED SALMON FILLET WITH FENNEL MAYONNAISE

(pictured on page 68)

2 teaspoons fennel seeds
1½ teaspoons black peppercorns
¼ teaspoon salt
1 garlic clove, minced
2 tablespoons light mayonnaise
1 tablespoon honey
1 teaspoon lemon juice
4 (4-ounce) skinned salmon fillets
Cooking spray
Fresh fennel fronds (optional)

1. Prepare grill. Place a 10-inch cast-iron skillet on grill rack over hot coals, and let skillet heat at least 10 minutes or until very hot.

2. Combine fennel seeds and peppercorns in a zip-top plastic bag; seal bag. Crush spices, using a meat mallet or rolling pin. Combine crushed spices, salt, and garlic.

3. Combine 1 teaspoon garlic-spice mixture, mayonnaise, honey, and lemon juice; stir well, and set aside.

4. Press remaining garlic-spice mixture onto skinned side of salmon fillets, and coat with cooking spray.

5. Place fillets, spice side down, in preheated skillet, and cook 3 minutes on each side or until fish flakes easily when tested with a fork.

6. Place a fillet, spice side up, on each of 4 plates; serve with mayonnaise mixture. Garnish with fennel fronds, if desired. YIELD: 4 servings (serving size: 1 fillet and about 2 teaspoons mayonnaise mixture).

NOTE: For best blackening results, choose salmon fillets with even thickness and a flat surface area.

POINTS: 5; **EXCHANGES:** 3 Lean Meat, ½ Starch, ½ Fat; **PER SERVING:** CAL 228 (46% from fat); PRO 23.6g; FAT 11.7g (sat 1.65g); CARB 6.2g; FIB 0.4g; CHOL 76mg; IRON 0.9mg; SOD 260mg; CALC 23mg

SWEET ONIONS WITH PISTACHIOS

(pictured on page 22)

2 Vidalia or other sweet onions
¼ cup brown sugar, divided
1 teaspoon ground cinnamon, divided
½ teaspoon freshly ground pepper, divided
¼ teaspoon salt, divided
1 tablespoon balsamic vinegar
1 tablespoon minced pistachios

STEP-BY-STEP

1. Place spices for salmon recipe in a zip-top plastic bag; seal bag, and crush with a meat mallet.

2. Press crushed spice mixture onto skinned side of salmon fillets. For best results and even cooking, choose fillets with even thickness.

3. Place a cast-iron skillet on grill rack over hot coals. The skillet should preheat at least 10 minutes. Add salmon fillets, seasoned side down, and cook until slightly charred.

4. Turn fillets over, and cook until desired degree of doneness.

1. Peel onions; cut a ¼-inch slice from each end so onions sit flat. Cut onions in half crosswise. Place in a large saucepan; add just enough water to cover. Bring to a boil; cover, reduce heat, and simmer 10 minutes or until slightly tender. Drain; let cool completely.

2. Prepare grill. Place a 10-inch cast-iron skillet on grill rack over hot coals; let skillet heat at least 10 minutes or until very hot.

3. Combine 2 tablespoons brown sugar, ½ teaspoon cinnamon, ¼ teaspoon pepper, and ⅛ teaspoon salt in a shallow dish; stir well. Press widest cut side of each onion half in sugar mixture to coat.

4. Place onions, sugar side down, in skillet; cook 6 minutes or until caramelized. Turn onions over; cook an additional 6 minutes. Place onions on a serving plate.

5. Combine vinegar, remaining brown sugar, cinnamon, pepper, and salt. Stir well; drizzle over onions. Sprinkle with pistachios.

YIELD: 4 servings (serving size: ½ onion).

POINTS: 2; EXCHANGES: 1 Veg, 1 Starch; PER SERVING: CAL 97 (14% from fat); PRO 1.5g; FAT 1.5g (sat 0.2g); CARB 20.9g; FIB 1.8g; CHOL 0mg; IRON 0.9mg; SOD 154mg; CALC 38mg

---

Cajun Craze

In blackening, fish, beef, pork, or vegetables are coated with an herb or spice mixture, and then seared in an intensely hot cast-iron skillet. In just minutes, a flavorful crust develops that locks in the food's natural juices.

Blackening produces a lot of smoke, so we recommend cooking outside on a grill. But it can be done inside on a cooktop with a commercial hood vent.

Everyday Vegetarian

Meatless meals don't have to be complicated; just use these simple shortcuts.

Vegetarian cooking is definitely here. It used to be way out there, with hippies who grooved on a plate of sprouts. As veggie cuisine matured, it got a little too chic. If you want meatless meals, you need a simple approach. Luckily, today's excellent convenience products, from fat-free vinaigrettes to wild mushroom couscous mix, give you access to complex flavors that don't have to be created from scratch. We've incorporated them into recipes you can whip up any night of the week.

SPINACH-WALNUT MANICOTTI

(pictured on page 156)

An 8-ounce package of manicotti may contain more than 12 shells; save the extras in case some split when filling.

¾ cup (3 ounces) preshredded part-skim mozzarella cheese, divided
1¼ cups fat-free ricotta cheese
1 cup 2% low-fat cottage cheese
3 ounces block-style fat-free cream cheese (about ⅓ cup), softened
¼ cup chopped walnuts
¼ cup (1 ounce) grated fresh Romano cheese
½ teaspoon dried Italian seasoning
1 (10-ounce) package frozen chopped spinach, thawed, drained, and squeezed dry
1 large egg
1 garlic clove, minced
12 uncooked manicotti
Cooking spray
1 (26-ounce) jar fire-roasted tomato and garlic pasta sauce (such as Classico)

1. Preheat oven to 350°.

2. Combine ½ cup mozzarella cheese, ricotta, and next 8 ingredients in a large bowl; stir well, and set aside.

3. Cook manicotti according to package directions, omitting salt and fat; drain. Rinse under cold water; drain well. Spoon cheese mixture evenly into cooked manicotti, and arrange in a 13- x 9-inch baking dish coated with cooking spray. Pour pasta sauce over stuffed manicotti.

4. Bake, uncovered, at 350° for 25 minutes. Sprinkle with remaining mozzarella; bake 10 minutes or until cheese melts. YIELD: 6 servings.

POINTS: 8; EXCHANGES: 2 Veg, 1½ L-F Milk, 1½ Starch, 1 Lean Meat; PER SERVING: CAL 392 (23% from fat); PRO 29.1g; FAT 10.1g (sat 4g); CARB 47.2g; FIB 4.8g; CHOL 72mg; IRON 3.7mg; SOD 806mg; CALC 433mg

CURRIED CHICKPEAS IN COCONUT-CILANTRO BROTH

Regular coconut milk (rather than light) adds a rich flavor to this dish.

1 teaspoon butter or stick margarine
1 cup chopped onion
1 garlic clove, minced
1 (14.5-ounce) can diced tomatoes, undrained
⅔ cup canned coconut milk
1 tablespoon seeded minced jalapeño pepper
1 to 2 teaspoons curry powder
1 (19-ounce) can chickpeas (garbanzo beans), drained
⅓ cup chopped fresh cilantro
5 cups hot cooked basmati rice

1. Heat butter in a large skillet over medium-high heat. Add onion and garlic; sauté 3 minutes or until tender. Stir in tomatoes and next 3 ingredients; reduce heat, and simmer 5 minutes. Add chickpeas; partially cover, and simmer 15 minutes. Remove from heat; stir in cilantro. Serve over rice. YIELD: 5 servings (serving size: ¾ cup chickpea mixture and 1 cup rice).

POINTS: 8; **EXCHANGES:** 4 Starch, 2 Veg, 1 Fat; **PER SERVING:** CAL 423 (20% from fat); PRO 12.3g; FAT 9.5g (sat 6.5g); CARB 73.3g; FIB 4.3g; CHOL 2mg; IRON 5.8mg; SOD 442mg; CALC 81mg

COUSCOUS-STUFFED PORTOBELLOS

(pictured on page 68)

1 (6-ounce) package fat-free couscous with wild mushrooms (such as Marrakesh Express)
1½ cups water
¾ cup finely chopped red bell pepper
1 cup chopped arugula
¾ cup (3 ounces) preshredded fresh Parmesan cheese, divided
½ cup (2 ounces) crumbled feta cheese
1 tablespoon balsamic vinegar
1 teaspoon olive oil
¼ teaspoon pepper
4 large portobello mushroom caps (about 1 pound)

1. Preheat oven to 350°.
2. Combine seasoning packet from couscous and water in a saucepan; bring to a boil. Gradually stir in couscous and bell pepper. Remove from heat; cover and let stand 7 minutes. Fluff with a fork; stir in arugula, ½ cup Parmesan cheese, and feta cheese. Set aside.
3. Combine vinegar, oil, and pepper; brush over mushroom caps. Top each cap with 1 cup couscous mixture, pressing firmly to pack. Place stuffed caps in a shallow roasting pan; add water to pan to depth of ¼ inch. Bake at 350° for 20 minutes. Sprinkle with remaining Parmesan cheese; bake 10 minutes or until cheese melts. YIELD: 4 servings.

POINTS: 7; **EXCHANGES:** 2 Starch, 1½ Veg, 1 Med-fat Meat, ½ Fat; **PER SERVING:** CAL 310 (30% from fat); PRO 18.4g; FAT 10.3g (sat 5.9g); CARB 36.7g; FIB 2.7g; CHOL 27mg; IRON 2.6mg; SOD 739mg; CALC 339mg

BROCCOLI-TOFU STIR-FRY WITH CASHEWS

3 tablespoons soy sauce
2 tablespoons seasoned rice vinegar
1½ teaspoons bottled minced garlic
2 teaspoons fresh or bottled chopped ginger
1 (1-pound) package firm tofu, drained and cut into ½-inch cubes
1 tablespoon dark sesame oil, divided
5 cups fresh broccoli florets
½ cup chopped green onions
2 tablespoons seeded minced jalapeño pepper
⅓ cup cashews
5 cups hot cooked somen (wheat noodles) or angel hair pasta

1. Combine first 4 ingredients in a shallow dish, and stir well. Add tofu cubes, stirring gently to coat. Let stand 15 minutes. Remove tofu from dish, reserving marinade.
2. Heat 2 teaspoons oil in a wok or nonstick skillet over high heat. Add tofu; cook 2 minutes or until browned. Remove tofu; set aside, and keep warm.
3. Add remaining 1 teaspoon oil, broccoli, green onions, and jalapeño pepper to pan; sauté 2 minutes. Stir in reserved marinade, tofu, and cashews; serve over noodles.
YIELD: 5 servings (serving size: about 1½ cups stir-fry and 1 cup noodles).

POINTS: 7; **EXCHANGES:** 2½ Starch, 2 Veg, 2 Fat, 1 Very Lean Meat; **PER SERVING:** CAL 358 (29% from fat); PRO 17.5g; FAT 11.4g (sat 1.8g); CARB 49g; FIB 5.8g; CHOL 0mg; IRON 8.1mg; SOD 567mg; CALC 145mg

GRILLED VEGETABLE SANDWICH

1 (1-pound) eggplant, cut crosswise into ½-inch slices
2 yellow squash, sliced
½ small red onion, sliced
1 red bell pepper, quartered
⅔ cup fat-free balsamic vinaigrette (such as Gerard's), divided
Cooking spray
2 tablespoons light mayonnaise
1 tablespoon minced fresh basil
1 (8-ounce) loaf French bread, cut in half lengthwise
4 (¾-ounce) slices provolone cheese, each cut in half

1. Place first 4 ingredients in a large dish; brush half of vinaigrette over vegetables. Let stand 10 minutes. Set remaining vinaigrette aside.
2. Prepare grill. Place bell pepper on grill rack coated with cooking spray; cover and grill 3 minutes. Add onion; cover and grill 2 minutes. Add eggplant and squash; cover and grill 6 minutes, turning vegetables and basting occasionally with remaining vinaigrette.
3. Combine mayonnaise and basil, and spread over top half of bread. Arrange half of cheese slices on bottom half of bread; top with vegetables, remaining cheese slices, and top half of bread.
4. Place sandwich on grill rack coated with cooking spray; grill 2 minutes or until cheese melts and bread is toasted. YIELD: 4 servings.

POINTS: 6; **EXCHANGES:** 2½ Veg, 2 Starch, 1½ Fat, ½ Med-fat Meat; **PER SERVING:** CAL 318 (29% from fat); PRO 12.8g; FAT 10.3g (sat 4.4g); CARB 44.5g; FIB 6.4g; CHOL 18mg; IRON 2.5mg; SOD 773mg; CALC 230mg

PESTO-BEAN PIZZA WITH FRESH TOMATOES

½ cup drained canned cannellini beans or other white beans
⅓ cup fresh basil leaves
2 tablespoons water
2 garlic cloves, minced
1 (10-ounce) package thin Italian cheese-flavored pizza crust (such as Boboli)
½ cup (2 ounces) grated Romano cheese, divided
1 large tomato, cut into thin wedges
1 small yellow bell pepper, cut into rings
½ cup (2 ounces) crumbled feta cheese with garlic and herbs
½ teaspoon freshly ground pepper

1. Preheat oven to 425°.
2. Place first 4 ingredients in a food processor; process until smooth. Spread over pizza crust; sprinkle with 3 tablespoons Romano cheese. Top with tomato, bell pepper, remaining Romano cheese, feta cheese, and pepper.
3. Place pizza on oven rack or baking sheet; bake at 425° for 8 minutes or until cheese melts. YIELD: 6 servings.

POINTS: 5; **EXCHANGES:** 1½ Starch, 1 Veg, 1 Med-fat Meat; **PER SERVING:** CAL 225 (29% from fat); PRO 11.9g; FAT 7.3g (sat 3.9g); CARB 27.6g; FIB 2.1g; CHOL 22mg; IRON 2mg; SOD 511mg; CALC 215mg

EATING

Follow the Leader

There are two rules for getting children to eat healthfully: Start early and lead the way.

Beth Ludwin, a registered nurse in Philadelphia, is reaping the rewards of teaching her children to make healthful food choices.

When the two oldest were toddlers, she began monitoring the food that came into the house. "They grew up with the idea of eating good food." explains Ludwin. "Now as teens, they want to look good and they know that eating right is part of that. It has become second nature for them to make healthful choices."

WEIGHTY MATTERS. Ludwin's children are the fortunate exceptions. The number of overweight children in the United States doubled between 1965 and 1995, according to the U.S. Center for Disease Control and Prevention at Tulane University. A third of kids ages 6 to 11 are overweight, and the number of overweight children ages 4 to 5 rose from 5.8% in 1974 to 10% in 1994.

"Being overweight affects more children than any other disease," says Naomi Neufeld, a pediatric endocrinologist at the University of California at Los Angeles. Overweight children have a greater chance of

(continued)

being overweight adults, she says. That increases the risk of health problems like diabetes, heart disease, high blood pressure, stroke, and cancer.

EXAMINING WHY. Helping kids develop good eating habits when they're young enhances their potential for greater lifelong health. But the effort is a challenge for both parents and kids.

Suzanne Polo, M.S., R.D., an adjunct assistant professor of nutrition at Marymount Manhattan College in New York City, says today's hectic family life is part of the problem. "Families don't eat together as often as they used to," she says. "Parents with busy schedules often rely too much on fast food or leave children with sitters or in situations where they are able to snack more."

To further complicate matters, public schools allow brand-name fast food, such as Taco Bell and Pizza Hut, to be sold in their cafeterias. Vending machines stocked with sodas and empty-calorie snacks are within easy reach. It's little wonder that the CDC at Tulane estimates that only 1% of American children meet the requirements laid out in the U.S. Department of Agriculture's Food Guide Pyramid.

MAKE POSITIVE CHANGES. The first step for parents is to be better educated about nutrition and set good examples. "Parents have a great influence over how their children will approach food," says Polo. "It's important that children see them eating healthfully, too." She adds that parents should speak with their child's pediatrician and a certified nutrition counselor for advice.

Once parents know what their child should be eating regularly and in what amounts, they can begin steering their children in the right direction. Here are some ways.

MARKET VALUE. "Introduce your child to fresh produce at the market. Suggest he or she pick out carrots, oranges, or apples for the family. This fosters an interest in selecting healthful food," says Polo. It will also help engage children in simple food preparation, which increases the desire to eat what they helped make. "It can be as simple as helping make a fruit cup," she says.

> *"If the right snack foods . . . are readily available, you can instill healthful snacking habits."*

SNACK ATTACKS. Children can snack healthfully. The trick is to encourage wholesome alternatives to cookies, potato chips, and other fatty finger foods. "If the right snack foods, like fruit, cheese, raisins, or baby carrots, are readily available, you can instill healthful snacking habits, which is important if you're not always there to watch what they eat," says Laurie Jones, R.D., health promotions manager for Medifit Corporation at PSE&G in Newark, New Jersey.

TABLE TALK. Several studies link adults with eating disorders to homes where mealtime was stressful. "The table is not the place to bring up negatives like a bad report card,"

says Polo. "It also doesn't matter if children finish everything at a meal. Like adults, they'll have times when they are not hungry." Adds Ellyn Satter, author of *How to Get Your Kid to Eat . . . But Not Too Much* (Bull Publishing, 1987), "Parents are responsible for what the child is offered, and the child is responsible for how much he or she eats."

LOOKS ARE EVERYTHING. "Kids eat a lot with their eyes. If it looks good, they'll eat it," says Tracey McBride, mother of three and author of *Frugal Luxuries: Simple Pleasures to Enhance Your Life and Comfort Your Soul* (Bantam Books, 1997). For example, her kids insist on drinking milk and juice from funky-looking glasses she picked up at a flea market. "Sometimes just cutting foods in interesting shapes is all it takes to make food more appealing to the eye," says McBride.

REPEAT PERFORMANCE. One study showed young children are more likely to eat something they've seen often—even if they've never tried it. "A casserole won't appeal to a child because they can't identify the foods in it," says Jones. "But if you present a child with a plate that has three distinct foods on it—such as chicken, potatoes, and carrots—they will be more responsive."

These tactics will probably succeed in the long run, but expect to reinforce them every day, says Ludwin. Her teenagers are nutrition-savvy, but her 10-year-old is still learning. "Perhaps he's bucking the system because he's the youngest," she says. No surprise there—kids will be kids.

June

Fresh from the Sea

The variety of ocean fare offers a dish for every taste.

The French call seafood "les fruits de mer," fruits of the sea. Poetry and veracity in one phrase. Americans, on the other hand, call it "brain food." Scientists say seafood contains acids that are essential to brain function. Seafood is a low-calorie source of protein that's low in saturated fat and high in the fatty acids that contribute to heart health. Best of all, it tastes great. Because seafood cooks quickly, it's a natural for busy evenings—you can get a healthful, delicious meal on the table in less than 30 minutes. That's simply delicious in any language.

CURRY-CRUSTED OYSTER SALAD

(pictured on page 92)

Remoulade Dressing
  6 tablespoons yellow cornmeal
  1 tablespoon curry powder
  1 teaspoon dried oregano
  ½ teaspoon salt
  ¼ teaspoon ground red pepper
  ⅓ cup all-purpose flour
  2 large egg whites
  2 (8-ounce) containers standard oysters, drained
Cooking spray
  12 cups mixed baby salad greens
  ½ cup thinly sliced red onion, separated into rings
  2 tomatoes, cut into 24 wedges

1. Prepare Remoulade Dressing; cover and chill.
2. Preheat oven to 475°.
3. Combine cornmeal and next 4 ingredients in a shallow dish; stir well. Place flour in a shallow dish. Place egg whites in a bowl; stir well with a whisk. Dredge oysters, one at a time, in flour. Dip each oyster in egg whites; dredge in cornmeal mixture. Place breaded oysters on a baking sheet coated with cooking spray. Lightly coat oysters with cooking spray. Bake at 475° for 5 minutes. Turn oysters over; bake an additional 4 minutes or until golden.
4. Combine salad greens and onion; toss. Spoon 3 cups salad into each of 4 bowls; top each with 6 tomato wedges. Divide oysters evenly over salads. Drizzle 2½ tablespoons Remoulade Dressing over each salad. Serve immediately. YIELD: 4 servings.
NOTE: These oysters are so crunchy and tasty you'll want to serve them solo, too. One serving of oysters by themselves provides 3 *POINTS*.

POINTS: 4; **EXCHANGES:** 3 Veg, 1 Starch, 1 Lean Meat, ½ Fat; **PER SERVING:** CAL 234 (23% from fat); PRO 14.3g; FAT 6g (sat 0.7g); CARB 32.1g; FIB 6.1g; CHOL 50mg; IRON 9.3mg; SOD 727mg; CALC 152mg

REMOULADE DRESSING:
  ¼ cup plain fat-free yogurt
  2 tablespoons minced fresh onion
  2½ tablespoons capers
  2½ tablespoons light mayonnaise
  1 tablespoon lemon juice
  1 teaspoon Worcestershire sauce

1. Combine all ingredients in a bowl; stir well. YIELD: ⅔ cup.

VEGETABLE-STEAMED ORANGE ROUGHY

  1 tablespoon olive oil
  1 cup green bell pepper strips
  1 cup red bell pepper strips
  1 cup chopped onion
  3 garlic cloves, minced
  1 large yellow squash, cut in half lengthwise and sliced (about 2 cups)
  ⅓ cup water
  2 tablespoons fresh lemon juice
  1 tablespoon fresh thyme, divided
  ¾ teaspoon salt, divided
  ¼ teaspoon hot sauce
  4 (6-ounce) orange roughy fillets
  ¼ teaspoon pepper

1. Heat olive oil in a 2-inch-deep, straight-sided skillet or Dutch oven over medium-high heat. Add bell pepper strips, onion, and garlic; sauté 2 minutes. Add squash; sauté 2 minutes. Reduce heat to medium, and add water, lemon juice, 2 teaspoons thyme, ½ teaspoon salt, and hot sauce. Arrange fish fillets in a single layer over vegetable mixture, and sprinkle fillets with remaining 1 teaspoon thyme, ¼ teaspoon salt, and pepper. Cover, reduce heat, and simmer 12 minutes or until fish flakes easily when tested with a fork.
YIELD: 4 servings (serving size: 1 fillet and 1 cup vegetables).

POINTS: 3; **EXCHANGES:** 2 Very Lean Meat, 2 Veg, 1 Fat; **PER SERVING:** CAL 161 (26% from fat); PRO 18.7g; FAT 4.7g (sat 0.6g); CARB 11.9g; FIB 3.1g; CHOL 23mg; IRON 2.2mg; SOD 518mg; CALC 40mg

PASTA WITH WHITE CLAM SAUCE

2 (10-ounce) cans baby clams
2 tablespoons olive oil
6 garlic cloves, sliced
1 (8-ounce) bottle clam juice
1 teaspoon dried basil
½ to ¾ teaspoon crushed red pepper
¼ cup fresh lemon juice
6 cups hot cooked linguine
(about 12 ounces uncooked)
½ cup chopped fresh parsley
1 teaspoon grated lemon rind
¼ teaspoon salt
¼ teaspoon pepper
¼ cup (1 ounce) preshredded fresh
Parmesan cheese

1. Drain clams, reserving juice. Set clams and juice aside.
2. Heat olive oil in a saucepan over medium heat. Add garlic; sauté 2 minutes or until golden (do not allow to burn or garlic will be bitter). Add reserved clam juice, bottled juice, basil, and red pepper; bring to a boil. Reduce heat; simmer, uncovered, 3 minutes. Add clams and lemon juice; cook 3 minutes or until clams are thoroughly heated.
3. Combine pasta and clam sauce in a large bowl. Add chopped parsley, lemon rind, salt, and pepper; toss well. Spoon 1 cup pasta into each of 6 individual shallow bowls, dividing clam sauce evenly. Sprinkle 2 teaspoons Parmesan cheese over each serving. YIELD: 6 servings.

POINTS: 7; **EXCHANGES:** 3 Starch, 1 Very Lean Meat, 1 Fat; **PER SERVING:** CAL 323 (20% from fat); PRO 16.5g; FAT 7g (sat 1.6g); CARB 47.1g; FIB 1.6g; CHOL 34mg; IRON 6.4mg; SOD 786mg; CALC 126mg

SALMON WITH MOROCCAN TOMATO RELISH

(pictured on page 136)

½ teaspoon salt, divided
4 (6-ounce) skinned salmon fillets
2 teaspoons olive oil, divided
1¾ cups chopped red onion
1 tablespoon peeled minced fresh
ginger
4½ cups coarsely chopped tomato
1 teaspoon grated orange rind
2 tablespoons fresh orange juice
1 teaspoon grated lemon rind
1 tablespoon fresh lemon juice
1 tablespoon capers
¼ teaspoon ground cinnamon
¼ cup chopped fresh mint
3 tablespoons chopped fresh
cilantro
Mint sprigs (optional)

1. Sprinkle ¼ teaspoon salt evenly over salmon. Heat 1 teaspoon oil in a large nonstick skillet over medium-high heat until hot. Add salmon; cook 3 minutes on each side or until lightly browned. Remove from skillet; set aside, and keep warm.
2. Add remaining oil to skillet; place over medium-high heat until hot. Add onion and ginger; sauté 2 minutes. Add remaining ¼ teaspoon salt, tomato, and next 6 ingredients; cook 5 minutes, stirring occasionally.
3. Return salmon to skillet, nestling fillets in tomato mixture; cook 3 minutes until salmon is medium-rare or desired degree of doneness. Remove from heat; place salmon on individual plates. Stir chopped mint and cilantro into tomato mixture; spoon mixture around each fillet. Garnish with mint sprigs, if desired.

YIELD: 4 servings (serving size: 1 fillet and ¾ cup tomato relish).

POINTS: 7; **EXCHANGES:** 4½ Lean Meat, 3 Veg; **PER SERVING:** CAL 334 (35% from fat); PRO 39.3g; FAT 13.1g (sat 2.3g); CARB 14.9g; FIB 3.1g; CHOL 66mg; IRON 2.4mg; SOD 559mg; CALC 28mg

TUNA WITH CORIANDER MAYONNAISE

(pictured on page 90)

2 tablespoons light mayonnaise
4 teaspoons skim milk
1 tablespoon plain fat-free yogurt
⅛ teaspoon ground coriander
⅛ teaspoon freshly ground pepper
¼ cup coriander seeds
½ teaspoon salt
¼ teaspoon freshly ground pepper
4 (6-ounce) tuna steaks (about ¾
inch thick)
Cooking spray

1. Combine first 5 ingredients. Chill. Place seeds in a heavy-duty, zip-top plastic bag; seal. Crush seeds with a rolling pin. Sprinkle salt and ¼ teaspoon pepper over tuna; press crushed coriander into both sides of steaks.
2. Coat a large nonstick skillet with cooking spray; place over medium-high heat until hot. Add tuna; cook 4 minutes on each side until medium-rare or desired degree of doneness. Serve tuna with mayonnaise mixture. YIELD: 4 servings (serving size: 1 tuna steak and about 1 tablespoon mayonnaise mixture).

POINTS: 6; **EXCHANGES:** 6 Very Lean Meat, 1½ Fat; **PER SERVING:** CAL 286 (36% from fat); PRO 40.8g; FAT 11.4g (sat 2.2g); CARB 3.9g; FIB 1.5g; CHOL 67mg; IRON 2.6mg; SOD 422mg; CALC 50mg

BALSAMIC-GLAZED SCALLOPS

2 cups water
1 tablespoon balsamic vinegar
¼ teaspoon salt
1 cup uncooked long-grain rice
1 tablespoon olive oil
1½ pounds sea scallops
¼ cup balsamic vinegar
1 tablespoon honey
1 teaspoon dried marjoram
Chives with blossoms (optional)

1. Combine first 3 ingredients in a medium saucepan; bring to a boil. Add rice; cover, reduce heat, and simmer 20 minutes or until rice is tender and liquid is absorbed. Remove from heat; set aside (do not uncover rice).
2. Heat oil in a large nonstick skillet over medium-high heat until hot. Add scallops; sauté 5 minutes. Remove scallops from skillet; set aside.
3. Add vinegar, honey, and marjoram to skillet; bring to a boil. Reduce heat to medium; cook 3 minutes. Return scallops to skillet; cook 2 minutes or until thoroughly heated. Serve scallops and sauce over rice. Garnish with chives, if desired. YIELD: 4 servings (serving size: one-fourth of scallop mixture and ¾ cup rice).

POINTS: 8; **EXCHANGES:** 3 Starch, 3 Very Lean Meat, ½ Fat; **PER SERVING:** CAL 365 (12% from fat); PRO 31.9g; FAT 5g (sat 0.7g); CARB 45.7g; FIB 0.6g; CHOL 56mg; IRON 2.8mg; SOD 423mg; CALC 57mg

CATFISH BAKED WITH TOMATO-KALAMATA TOPPING

2¼ cups seeded chopped plum tomato
½ cup pitted chopped kalamata olives
⅓ cup chopped fresh cilantro
4 (6-ounce) farm-raised catfish fillets

1. Preheat oven to 375°.
2. Combine first 3 ingredients in a bowl; stir well.
3. Place catfish fillets in a 13- x 9-inch baking dish; top with tomato mixture. Bake fillets at 375° for 25 minutes or until fish flakes easily when tested with a fork. YIELD: 4 servings (serving size: 1 fillet and about ¾ cup tomato topping).

POINTS: 5; **EXCHANGES:** 4 Very Lean Meat, 1½ Fat, 1 Veg; **PER SERVING:** CAL 232 (36% from fat); PRO 31.2g; FAT 9.3g (sat 2g); CARB 5.3g; FIB 1.6g; CHOL 97mg; IRON 2.7mg; SOD 268mg; CALC 89mg

SHRIMP WITH CILANTRO AND LIME

1¾ pounds large shrimp, peeled and deveined
2 tablespoons fresh lime juice
½ teaspoon ground cumin
¼ teaspoon ground ginger
2 garlic cloves, minced
1 tablespoon olive oil
¼ cup chopped fresh cilantro
1 teaspoon grated lime rind
½ teaspoon salt
¼ teaspoon pepper

1. Combine first 5 ingredients in a large bowl; toss well. Heat oil in a large nonstick skillet over medium-high heat. Add shrimp mixture, and sauté 4 minutes or until shrimp is done. Remove from heat; stir in cilantro and remaining ingredients. YIELD: 4 servings (serving size: about 1½ cups).

POINTS: 5; **EXCHANGES:** 5 Very Lean Meat, 1 Fat; **PER SERVING:** CAL 217 (27% from fat); PRO 34.8g; FAT 6.4g (sat 1g); CARB 3.2g; FIB 0.2g; CHOL 259mg; IRON 4.5mg; SOD 546mg; CALC 98mg

CORFU-STYLE COD

1 tablespoon olive oil
2 cups chopped leek
2 garlic cloves, minced
1½ teaspoons paprika
¼ teaspoon ground red pepper
1 cup dry red wine
1 tablespoon tomato paste
1 teaspoon salt
4 (6-ounce) cod fillets

1. Heat oil in a large nonstick skillet over medium-high heat until hot. Add leek and garlic; sauté 3 minutes. Add paprika and red pepper; sauté 1 minute. Add wine and tomato paste; reduce heat, and simmer 4 minutes.
2. Sprinkle salt evenly over both sides of fillets. Add to skillet, nestling fillets in leek mixture. Cover, reduce heat, and simmer 15 minutes or until fish flakes easily when tested with a fork. YIELD: 4 servings (serving size: 1 fillet and ⅓ cup sauce).

POINTS: 4; **EXCHANGES:** 4 Very Lean Meat, 1½ Veg, ½ Fat; **PER SERVING:** CAL 204 (21% from fat); PRO 31.3g; FAT 4.8g (sat 0.7g); CARB 7.8g; FIB 0.9g; CHOL 73mg; IRON 1.9mg; SOD 689mg; CALC 59mg

ORANGE-TERIYAKI FISH KABOBS

(pictured on page 91)

3 tablespoons low-salt soy sauce
1 tablespoon rice vinegar
1 tablespoon honey
1 teaspoon peeled minced fresh
  ginger
1½ pounds skinned swordfish,
  grouper, or other firm fish
  fillets, cut into 1-inch pieces
1 (8-ounce) package fresh
  mushrooms
1 medium-size green bell pepper,
  cut into 1½-inch pieces
1 medium-size red bell pepper,
  cut into 1½-inch pieces
Cooking spray
6 tablespoons orange juice

1. Combine first 4 ingredients in a
shallow dish; stir well. Add fish, stirring to coat. Cover; marinate in
refrigerator 15 minutes. Remove fish
from dish, reserving marinade. Thread
fish, mushrooms, and bell pepper
alternately onto 8 (10-inch) skewers.
Place kabobs on a broiler pan coated
with cooking spray; broil 6 minutes.
Turn kabobs over; broil 6 minutes or
until vegetables are tender and fish
flakes easily when tested with a fork.
2. Combine marinade and orange
juice in a saucepan; bring to a boil.
Reduce heat; simmer 5 minutes or
until reduced to ½ cup. Drizzle over
kabobs.
YIELD: 4 servings (serving size: 2
kabobs and 2 tablespoons sauce).

POINTS: 6; **EXCHANGES:** 5 Very Lean Meat,
1½ Fat, 1 Veg, ½ Fruit;**PER SERVING:** CAL 284
(26% from fat); PRO 37.6g; FAT 8.3g (sat 1.7g);
CARB 12.9g; FIB 1.8g; CHOL 87mg;
IRON 3mg; SOD 432mg; CALC 67mg

5 INGREDIENTS

Island Hop

Travel to a world of warm breezes and sparkling turquoise seas
with these slightly exotic island desserts.

These desserts pack a tropical punch—every bite is as satisfying as
the feel of sun on your face. But be warned, one luscious taste and
you may never go back—to the same old desserts, that is.

MANGO CRISP

4 cups peeled cubed ripe mango
  (about 5 mangoes)
5 tablespoons brown sugar, divided
¼ cup butter or stick margarine,
  melted and divided
2 (1.62-ounce) packets instant
  cinnamon and spice oatmeal
  (such as Quaker)
4 cups vanilla fat-free ice cream

1. Preheat oven to 375°.
2. Combine mango cubes, 3 tablespoons brown sugar, and 1 tablespoon melted butter in a large bowl;
stir well. Spoon mango mixture into
an 8-inch square baking dish.
3. Combine remaining brown sugar,
remaining melted butter, and oatmeal in a bowl; toss with a fork
until well blended. Sprinkle over
mango mixture. Bake at 375° for 35
minutes or until bubbly. Serve warm
with ice cream. YIELD: 8 servings
(serving size: one-eighth of crisp and
½ cup ice cream).

POINTS: 6; **EXCHANGES:** 2½ Starch, 1 Fruit,
½ Fat; **PER SERVING:** CAL 288 (20% from fat);
PRO 5.4g; FAT 6.4g (sat 1.2g); CARB 55.2g;
FIB 1.9g; CHOL 2.6mg; IRON 1.2mg;
SOD 196mg; CALC 142mg

COCONUT-LIME BRUSHED POUND CAKE WITH FROZEN YOGURT

⅓ cup cream of coconut (such as
  Coco Lopez)
1 tablespoon grated lime rind
2½ tablespoons fresh lime juice
1 teaspoon rum flavoring
1 (13.6-ounce) fat-free golden
  loaf cake (such as Entenmann's)
2 cups strawberry fat-free frozen
  yogurt or pineapple sherbet

1. Preheat oven to 350°.
2. Combine first 4 ingredients in a
small bowl; stir well, and set aside.
3. Cut cake into 8 (1-inch-thick)
slices; place on a large baking sheet.
Brush cream of coconut mixture
evenly over tops of cake slices. Bake
at 350° for 10 minutes. Let cool.
Place cake slices on individual plates;
top with frozen yogurt. YIELD: 8 servings (serving size: 1 slice cake and ¼
cup frozen yogurt).

POINTS: 5; **EXCHANGES:** 2½ Starch, ½ Fat;
PER SERVING: CAL 227 (14% from fat);
PRO 4.4g; FAT 3.5g (sat 3.1g); CARB 41.7g;
FIB 0.7g; CHOL 0mg; IRON 0.2mg;
SOD 200mg; CALC 78mg

TROPICAL SORBET SANDWICHES

½ (18-ounce) package refrigerated
    sugar cookie dough
1 tablespoon unsweetened cocoa
⅓ cup flaked sweetened coconut
2 cups mango or other flavor
    sorbet, slightly softened

1. Combine cookie dough and
cocoa in a bowl; knead until well
blended. Cover and chill 15
minutes.
2. Preheat oven to 350°.
3. Turn dough out onto a lightly
floured surface; roll dough to
⅛-inch thickness. Cut 6 cookies
with a 3-inch-round cookie cutter;
place cookies on a baking sheet.
Reroll dough, and cut 6 more cookies; place on baking sheet. Sprinkle
coconut evenly over cookies; lightly
press coconut into dough. Bake at
350° for 10 minutes; let cool on pan
10 minutes. Remove cookies from
pan; cool completely on wire racks.
4. Spread ⅓ cup sorbet onto each of
6 cookies, and top with remaining
cookies, pressing gently. Wrap sandwiches; freeze at least 30 minutes.
YIELD: 6 servings (serving size: 1
sandwich).
NOTE: If you prefer plain sugar
cookies, simply omit the cocoa, and
proceed with the recipe.

POINTS: 6; **EXCHANGES:** 3 Starch, 1 Fat;
PER SERVING: CAL 280 (29% from fat);
PRO 1.8g; FAT 9g (sat 3.8g); CARB 49.1g;
FIB 0.6g; CHOL 5mg; IRON 0.3mg;
SOD 198mg; CALC 2mg

CREAMY COCONUT RICE PUDDING

Try sprinkling toasted flaked sweetened
coconut on each serving. It adds a
kick of flavor and a little crunch.

1 (14-ounce) can light coconut
    milk
¾ cup water
¼ teaspoon salt
¾ cup uncooked long-grain rice
½ cup sugar
¼ teaspoon coconut extract

1. Combine coconut milk, water,
and salt in a medium saucepan;
bring to a boil. Stir in rice. Cover,
reduce heat, and simmer 25 minutes
or until rice is tender and liquid is
absorbed, stirring gently after 10
minutes. Remove from heat; stir in
sugar and extract. Let stand, covered,
5 minutes. Stir gently before serving.
YIELD: 5 servings (serving size:
½ cup).

POINTS: 5; **EXCHANGES:** 3 Starch;
PER SERVING: CAL 229 (17% from fat); PRO 2g;
FAT 4.4g (sat 2.9g); CARB 45g; FIB 0.4g;
CHOL 0mg; IRON 1.7mg; SOD 150mg;
CALC 8mg

SPICED RUM FLAN

1¼ cups sugar, divided
5 large eggs
2½ cups 1% low-fat milk
¼ cup spiced rum or dark rum
1 teaspoon vanilla extract

1. Preheat oven to 325°.
2. Place ¾ cup sugar in a small
heavy skillet over medium heat;
cook 3 minutes or until sugar
dissolves (do not stir). Cook an

additional 3 minutes or until golden,
stirring constantly. Immediately pour
into a 9-inch round cake pan, tipping quickly until caramelized sugar
coats bottom of cake pan.
3. Place eggs in a medium bowl;
stir with a whisk until well blended.
Set aside. Combine remaining sugar,
milk, rum, and vanilla in a large
heavy saucepan; stir well. Place over
medium heat; cook 5 minutes or
just until mixture comes to a simmer. Gradually add hot milk mixture to eggs, stirring constantly with
a whisk.
4. Pour milk mixture into prepared
pan; place cake pan in a large shallow baking pan. Add hot water to
baking pan to a depth of 1 inch.
Bake at 325° for 55 minutes or until
a knife inserted near center comes
out clean. Remove cake pan from
water; let cool completely on a
wire rack. Cover and chill at least
3 hours.
5. Loosen edge of flan with a knife
or rubber spatula. Place a serving
plate, upside down, on top of pan;
invert flan onto serving plate.
Drizzle any remaining caramelized
syrup over flan. YIELD: 8 servings.
NOTE: When caramelizing sugar, do
not use a nonstick skillet. After sugar
dissolves, watch it carefully because
it caramelizes quickly. If it gets too
brown it will be bitter.

POINTS: 4; **EXCHANGES:** 2½ Starch;
PER SERVING: CAL 203 (18% from fat);
PRO 6.6g; FAT 4g (sat 1.5g); CARB 35.3g;
FIB 0g; CHOL 141mg; IRON 0.5mg;
SOD 79mg; CALC 110mg

PASSION FRUIT SORBET

(pictured on page 4)

2 cups water
¾ cup sugar
1½ cups passion fruit nectar
3 tablespoons fresh lemon
  juice

1. Combine water and sugar in a small saucepan; bring to a boil, and cook 5 minutes. Pour into an 8-inch square baking dish; freeze 20 minutes. Stir in nectar and lemon juice, and freeze 30 minutes. Stir well with a fork; freeze 1½ hours or until solid (do not stir). Let stand at room temperature until slightly softened. Break frozen mixture into chunks. Place frozen chunks in a food processor; pulse 5 times or until smooth. Serve immediately. YIELD: 3 servings (serving size: 1 cup).

POINTS: 5; EXCHANGES: 4 Fruit;
PER SERVING: CAL 248 (0% from fat);
PRO 0.1g; FAT 0g (sat 0g); CARB 63.9g;
FIB 1g; CHOL 0mg; IRON 0.4mg; SOD 9.6mg;
CALC 10.6mg

ISLAND FRUIT TART

(pictured on page 90)

1 (12-ounce) peeled and cored
  fresh pineapple
1 (9-inch) refrigerated piecrust
  (such as Pillsbury)
2 bananas (about ½ pound),
  sliced
2 teaspoons cinnamon-sugar,
  divided
1½ to 2 teaspoons water
1 (12-ounce) jar guava jelly

1. Preheat oven to 425°.
2. Cut pineapple crosswise into ¼-inch-thick slices; cut each slice in half. Set aside.
3. Roll piecrust to a 13-inch circle on a lightly floured surface. Place piecrust on baking sheet lined with parchment paper. Arrange banana slices over crust, leaving a 2-inch border (banana slices may overlap). Sprinkle 1 teaspoon cinnamon-sugar over banana slices. Arrange pineapple slices over banana. Fold 2-inch border of dough over fruit, pressing firmly (dough will cover only outside edge of fruit). Brush border of dough with water; sprinkle with remaining cinnamon-sugar.
4. Bake at 425° for 30 minutes or until crust is golden. Let cool slightly. Carefully slide tart onto a serving platter, using a spatula. Cut tart into 8 wedges.
5. Place jelly in a small saucepan, and cook over medium heat 10 minutes or until jelly melts, stirring occasionally. Remove from heat; let cool 10 minutes. Drizzle jelly evenly over each serving. YIELD: 8 servings (serving size: 1 slice tart and 2 tablespoons jelly).

POINTS: 6; EXCHANGES: 2½ Starch, 1 Fruit,
1 Fat; PER SERVING: CAL 299 (22% from fat);
PRO 1g; FAT 7.3g (sat 3.1g); CARB 55.7g;
FIB 1.2g; CHOL 5mg; IRON 0.3mg;
SOD 101mg; CALC 5mg

BANANA-RAISIN BREAD PUDDING

1 cup skim milk
½ cup sugar
3 large eggs
12 (1-ounce) slices cinnamon-
  raisin bread, cut into ¾-inch
  cubes
3 bananas (about ¾ pound), cut
  into ¼-inch-thick slices
Cooking spray
1 tablespoon sugar

1. Preheat oven to 350°.
2. Combine milk, ½ cup sugar, and eggs in a large bowl; stir mixture well with a whisk. Add bread and banana; toss gently to moisten. Cover and let stand 10 minutes.
3. Spoon mixture into a shallow 1½-quart baking dish coated with cooking spray. Sprinkle 1 tablespoon sugar evenly over bread mixture. Bake at 350° for 25 minutes or until golden and set. YIELD: 8 servings (serving size: about ¾ cup).

POINTS: 4; EXCHANGES: 2½ Starch, ½ Fruit;
PER SERVING: CAL 234 (15% from fat);
PRO 6.8g; FAT 3.8g (sat 1.1g); CARB 44.8g;
FIB 2.6g; CHOL 80mg; IRON 1.5mg;
SOD 192mg; CALC 75mg

If You Can't Stand the Heat

. . . get out of the kitchen, and head outside. These recipes give new meaning to the term "dining out."

Hot weather is no reason to stop making supper. It's easy to prepare delicious meals—even meals worthy of guests—and still keep your cool. Eat in the backyard, on the deck, or by the pool. Grilling lets you talk with friends and family as they play or swim. Round out the menu with our no-cook marinated salads and quick throw-together appetizer and dessert.

FENNEL-AND-ORANGE SALAD

This traditional Italian salad is crunchy and slightly sweet. It works well with all three entrées in this story.

    4 cups chopped fennel bulb
        (about 2 [1-pound] bulbs)
    ½ cup fresh orange juice
    3 large navel oranges, peeled and
        coarsely chopped
    2 tablespoons chopped fresh mint
    2 tablespoons sherry vinegar
    1 tablespoon extra-virgin olive oil
    ½ teaspoon salt
    ½ teaspoon freshly ground pepper

1. Combine all ingredients in a large bowl; toss well. Cover and chill 3 hours. YIELD: 6 servings (serving size: 1 cup).

POINTS: 1; **EXCHANGES:** 1 Veg, ½ Fruit, ½ Fat; **PER SERVING:** CAL 81 (29% from fat); PRO 2.5g; FAT 2.6g (sat 0.3g); CARB 13.7g; FIB 3.5g; CHOL 0mg; IRON 1.8mg; SOD 202mg; CALC 93mg

MARINATED TOMATO SALAD

(pictured on page 48)

Marinating the tomatoes makes them especially juicy. The success of this dish depends on vine-ripe summer tomatoes.

    5 medium tomatoes (about
        2 pounds), cut into ¾-inch-
        thick wedges
    12 large kalamata olives, pitted and
        chopped
    1 tablespoon capers
    2 teaspoons minced fresh oregano
    ¼ teaspoon salt
    ¼ teaspoon pepper
    2 tablespoons red wine vinegar
    2 teaspoons extra-virgin olive oil

1. Combine first 6 ingredients in a large bowl. Drizzle vinegar and olive oil over salad; toss gently to coat. Cover and marinate at room temperature 1 hour. Toss gently before serving. YIELD: 7 servings (serving size: 1 cup).

POINTS: 1; **EXCHANGES:** 2 Veg, ½ Fat; **PER SERVING:** CAL 63 (43% from fat); PRO 1.7g; FAT 3g (sat 0.5g); CARB 9.3g; FIB 2.3g; CHOL 0mg; IRON 1.3mg; SOD 299mg; CALC 25mg

LEMON-GARLIC GRILLED CHICKEN

For more flavor, rub herb mixture under chicken skin and chill until ready to cook.

    3 (6-ounce) chicken breast halves
        (bone-in)
    3 (5-ounce) chicken thighs
    4 garlic cloves, peeled
    1 cup fresh parsley sprigs
    1 teaspoon grated lemon rind
    3 tablespoons fresh lemon juice
    ½ teaspoon salt
    ¼ teaspoon pepper
    Garlic-flavored cooking spray

1. Rinse chicken under cold water, and pat dry. Loosen skin from chicken by inserting fingers under skin and gently pushing fingers between skin and meat.
2. Drop garlic through food chute with food processor on; process until minced. Add parsley and next 4 ingredients; process until finely minced. Rub parsley mixture over chicken under loosened skin. Coat chicken with cooking spray.
3. Prepare grill. Place chicken on grill rack; cover and grill 30 minutes or until chicken is done, turning occasionally. Remove skin before serving. YIELD: 6 servings.

POINTS: 4; **EXCHANGES:** 2 Very Lean Meat, 2 Lean Meat; **PER SERVING:** CAL 188 (35% from fat); PRO 27.1g; FAT 7.4g (sat 2g); CARB 2.1g; FIB 0.5g; CHOL 85mg; IRON 1.8mg; SOD 286mg; CALC 31mg

(continued on page 93)

Model Behavior

TAMI COLBY • **HEIGHT** 5'3" • **BEFORE** 160 LBS. • **AFTER** 116 LBS.

Proudest moment: "Winning Athlete of the Month at my gym. They said they gave it to me because I'm so motivated and excited about working out."

Most of us look at old photos of ourselves and wish we still looked that good. But Tami Colby wouldn't turn back the clock. "I feel younger now than I did when I was 18."

Tami, 36, turns heads at the music company where she works. An aspiring model, Tami says, "I'm having fun doing things I passed up as a teenager because I didn't want people to see how I looked. Now I feel like I'm free."

Tami flirted with weight-loss programs, including a five-day fast that put her in the hospital when she was 13. "It was a puzzle I couldn't figure out," she says. "I'd eat a salad with dressing, bacon bits, and extra stuff on it, and not understand why I didn't lose weight."

Tami, a petite 5'3", has weighed as much as 160 pounds. Although that was obviously too much for her, she began to accept being overweight as her fate. "I remember my grandmother telling me when I was a teenager that I'd never be thin," she says. "Those kinds of comments made me feel hopeless. So I concentrated on my hair and makeup, trying to make everything else perfect. But I found myself saying, 'This isn't fair. Why can't I be thin?' "

The big change in Tami's life was triggered when she received a new driver's license in the mail. The photograph stunned her. "I'd never weighed that much before. Reality hit me in the face, and I said, 'That's not me because I'm not going to let it be me.' "

Tami and two friends joined a Weight Watchers At Work program. "I saw this as a chance to change my life," she says. It took eight months to reach her goal weight, but Tami relished the challenge. "It made me feel proud and strong that I had willpower," she says. "I kept track of everything I ate."

One day, Tami went to the gym near her office for a lunch-hour workout. "I wanted to try everything that first day. They had to send me back to work so I wouldn't overdo it," she recalls. "I've been

"I eat a single, mouthwatering chocolate every afternoon at work. But just one."

going ever since, five days a week for nearly three years, and I can't believe how my body has changed."

Tami says that physical activity gives her the freedom to eat more of what she likes. "I don't deprive myself," she says. "In fact, I eat a single, mouthwatering chocolate every afternoon at work. But just one." Indeed, life is sweet for Tami, who recently got her first modeling contract. The 18-year-old Tami never would have done that.

Tuna With Coriander
Mayonnaise, page 83

Dijon Chicken-Mushroom
Stroganoff, page 95

Island Fruit Tart, page 87

Orange-Teriyaki Fish Kabobs,
page 85

Cherry Tomato Salsa, page 105

Turkey Burgers With Sweet Red Onion Relish, right

Curry-Crusted Oyster Salad, page 82

TURKEY BURGERS WITH SWEET RED ONION RELISH

(pictured at left)

    1 tablespoon extra-virgin olive oil
2½ cups finely chopped red onion
      (about 2 medium)
    3 tablespoons balsamic vinegar,
      divided
    1 teaspoon chopped fresh thyme
1½ pounds ground turkey breast
    ¼ cup chili sauce
    2 tablespoons grape jelly
    ½ teaspoon salt
    ¼ teaspoon pepper
Cooking spray
    6 curly leaf lettuce leaves
    6 (1½-ounce) sesame hamburger
      buns, split

1. Heat oil in a nonstick skillet over medium-high heat. Add onion; sauté 10 minutes or until lightly browned, stirring occasionally. Add 2 tablespoons vinegar and thyme; sauté 30 seconds or just until liquid evaporates. Remove from heat; keep warm.
2. Combine remaining 1 tablespoon vinegar, turkey, and next 4 ingredients in a bowl; stir until blended. Divide mixture into 6 equal portions, shaping into ½-inch-thick patties.
3. Prepare grill. Place patties on grill rack coated with cooking spray; grill 5 minutes on each side or until done.
4. Place 1 lettuce leaf on bottom half of each bun; top each with a patty, 3 tablespoons onion relish, and top half of bun. YIELD: 6 servings.

POINTS: 6; **EXCHANGES:** 3½ Very Lean Meat, 2 Starch, ½ Veg; **PER SERVING:** CAL 304 (19% from fat); PRO 31g; FAT 6.4g (sat 1.9g); CARB 32.8g; FIB 1.9g; CHOL 60mg; IRON 1.8mg; SOD 791mg; CALC 53mg

SOUTHWESTERN GRILLED FLANK STEAK

(pictured pn page 48)

A homemade spice mix takes just a minute or two to assemble and gives flank steak a real flavor boost.

    1 (1½-pound) lean flank steak
      (about ¾ inch thick)
    2 tablespoons Hungarian sweet
      paprika
    1 tablespoon chili powder
    2 teaspoons ground cumin
    1 teaspoon ground cinnamon
    ½ teaspoon salt
Cooking spray

1. Trim excess fat from steak. Combine paprika and next 4 ingredients; rub over both sides of steak. Place steak in a dish; cover and marinate in refrigerator at least 4 hours.
2. Prepare grill. Place steak on grill rack coated with cooking spray; cover and grill 4 minutes on each side or until desired degree of doneness. Remove steak from grill; let stand 5 minutes before slicing. Cut steak diagonally across the grain into thin slices. YIELD: 6 servings (serving size: 3 ounces).

POINTS: 7; **EXCHANGES:** 4 Lean Meat, 1 Fat; **PER SERVING:** CAL 271 (55% from fat); PRO 27.5g; FAT 16.5g (sat 6.9g); CARB 2.6g; FIB 1.1g; CHOL 74mg; IRON 4mg; SOD 298mg; CALC 25mg

BAKED GINGER PEACHES AND YOGURT

A simple cookie topping accents the sweet flavor of summer peaches.

    3 large fresh peaches, peeled,
      halved, and pitted
Butter-flavored cooking spray
    ½ teaspoon vanilla extract
    14 gingersnaps, crushed
    2 tablespoons brown sugar
    3 cups vanilla low-fat frozen
      yogurt

1. Preheat oven to 375°.
2. Place peach halves, cut sides up, in an 11- x 7-inch baking dish coated with cooking spray; sprinkle vanilla evenly over peach halves.
3. Combine crushed gingersnap cookies and brown sugar in a small bowl; stir well. Fill the center of each peach half with crushed cookie mixture. Bake at 375° for 25 minutes or until thoroughly heated. Serve peaches warm with frozen yogurt. YIELD: 6 servings (serving size: 1 peach half and ½ cup yogurt).
NOTE: If fresh peaches are unavailable, substitute 2 (15-ounce) cans peach halves in light syrup, drained.

POINTS: 5; **EXCHANGES:** 2 Starch, ½ Fruit, ½ Fat; **PER SERVING:** CAL 221 (21% from fat); PRO 4.6g; FAT 5.1g (sat 2.2g); CARB 40.5g; FIB 1.3g; CHOL 17mg; IRON 1.1mg; SOD 61mg; CALC 138mg

CROSTINI WITH ROASTED PEPPER SPREAD

½ cup drained bottled roasted red
    bell peppers (about 4 ounces)
2 tablespoons chopped walnuts
2 tablespoons fresh parsley leaves
¼ teaspoon salt
¼ teaspoon freshly ground pepper
18 (½-inch-thick) slices thin
    French bread baguette, toasted

1. Press bell peppers gently between
paper towels until barely moist, and
set aside.
2. Place walnuts and parsley in a
food processor; pulse until coarsely
ground, scraping sides of processor
bowl once. Add bell peppers; process
until smooth. Spoon into a bowl; stir
in salt and pepper. Cover and chill at
least 4 hours.
3. Spread about 1 teaspoon bell
pepper mixture over each bread
slice. Serve immediately.
YIELD: 6 servings (serving size:
 3 crostini).

POINTS: 1; **EXCHANGES:** ½ Starch, ½ Fat;
PER SERVING: CAL 74 (29% from fat);
PRO 2.6g; FAT 2.4g (sat 0.3g); CARB 10.9g;
FIB 1g; CHOL 0mg; IRON 0.8mg;
SOD 470mg; CALC 26mg

HOW TO
Power Poaching

We coined the term "power poaching" for this technique
because it allows you to retain the food's water-soluble vitamins.
We concentrate the cooking liquid by reducing it and then using
it as the base for the accompanying sauce.

STEP-BY-STEP

1. Keep the poaching liquid
below the boiling point, or barely
trembling, while cooking. If the
liquid boils, the food toughens
and cooks too quickly.

2. The food needs to be in a single layer and surrounded by the
poaching liquid, not submerged.
Once covered with a tight-fitting
lid, the pan allows enough steam
to form to self-baste the food and
keep it moist.

3. Check food a minute or two
before the timer says it's ready.
Vegetables and fruits are done
when a fork easily pierces the surface. Chicken should appear
opaque and feel resilient to the
touch. Fish should flake easily
when tested with a fork.

4. After removing the food, reduce
the poaching liquid by vigorously
cooking over high heat until the
liquid is thick and syrupy. Syrup
should hold ribbons on bottom of
skillet when scraped with a spoon.

PORT-GLAZED PEARS WITH TOASTED HAZELNUTS

(pictured on page 48)

2 large Anjou pears (about
   1 pound)
1 cup port or other sweet red wine
1 cup cranberry juice cocktail
½ cup water
⅓ cup fresh mint leaves
3 tablespoons honey
1⅓ cups vanilla low-fat ice cream
2 tablespoons chopped blanched
   hazelnuts, toasted

1. Peel and core pears; cut each pear in half lengthwise. Cut a ¼-inch slice from rounded side of each pear half so pears sit flat. Combine wine and next 4 ingredients in a skillet; bring mixture to a boil. Cover, reduce heat, and simmer 5 minutes. Arrange pears, cut sides down, in skillet; cover and simmer 8 minutes (do not boil). Turn pear halves over; cover and simmer an additional 8 minutes or until tender. Remove pears from skillet with a slotted spoon; place pears in a shallow dish.
2. Bring poaching liquid to a boil; cook, uncovered, 10 minutes or until reduced to ½ cup. Pour poaching liquid through a sieve over pears in dish; discard mint leaves. Turn pears over to coat; cover and chill.
3. Arrange 1 pear half, cut side up, on each of 4 plates; top each with ⅓ cup ice cream. Drizzle 2 tablespoons poaching liquid over each serving, and sprinkle with 1½ teaspoons hazelnuts. YIELD: 4 servings.

POINTS: 4; **EXCHANGES:** 2 Starch, 1½ Fruit; **PER SERVING:** CAL 232 (16% from fat); PRO 2.9g; FAT 4g (sat 0.9g); CARB 49.7g; FIB 3.3g; CHOL 3.3mg; IRON 0.6mg; SOD 36mg; CALC 91mg

DIJON CHICKEN-MUSHROOM STROGANOFF

(pictured on page 90)

1 cup fat-free chicken broth
1 cup water
½ cup chopped onion
2 tablespoons Dijon mustard
1 teaspoon dried thyme
¼ teaspoon salt
Dash of white pepper
1 garlic clove, minced
1 (8-ounce) package fresh
   mushrooms
4 (4-ounce) skinned, boned
   chicken breast halves
½ cup low-fat sour cream
2 cups hot cooked egg noodles
   (about 4 ounces uncooked)
Thyme sprigs (optional)

1. Combine first 9 ingredients in a skillet. Bring to a boil. Cover, reduce heat, and simmer 5 minutes (poaching liquid will appear curdled). Arrange chicken in a single layer in skillet; cover and simmer 15 minutes (do not boil). Remove from skillet with a slotted spoon; keep warm.
2. Bring poaching liquid to a boil. Cook, uncovered, 8 minutes or until reduced to ½ cup. Remove from heat; let cool slightly. Stir in sour cream. Return chicken and juices to skillet, turning chicken to coat.
3. Serve chicken and sauce over noodles. Garnish with thyme sprigs. YIELD: 4 servings (serving size: ½ cup cooked noodles, 1 chicken breast half, and about ⅓ cup sauce).

POINTS: 6; **EXCHANGES:** 4 Very Lean Meat, 1½ Starch, 1 Veg, ½ Fat; **PER SERVING:** CAL 307 (21% from fat); PRO 33g; FAT 7g (sat 2.9g), CARB 26.3g; FIB 2.8g; CHOL 103mg; IRON 3.3mg; SOD 583mg; CALC 67mg

EATING

Tapping the Source

Is bottled water safer than what comes out of the faucet?

The United States has one of the best drinking water supplies in the world, experts say, but concerns about tap water are leading more consumers to drink bottled water.

NEWS ON TAP. Drinking water is monitored by each state based on Environmental Protection Agency guidelines, which regulate more than 80 contaminants.

But problems still occur. In 1993, a parasite contaminated the water in Milwaukee, killing dozens and causing illness in 400,000 others. The city changed the way it treats its drinking water, and the EPA is now requiring all cities to upgrade efforts to eliminate dangerous microorganisms in drinking water.

BOTTLE-FED. Bottled water is regulated by the Food and Drug Administration (FDA). A study of 103 brands of bottled water sold in the U.S. found most waters were high quality. But in one sample, a third of the tested brands did not meet bacterial guidelines.

Choosing tap or bottled water is a personal decision. Some people are so accustomed to local tap water that it tastes like home to them. Others crave the strong flavor of some bottled waters with high mineral contents.

July/August

Summer Crush

Taste the fruits of the season and fall in love.

Summer, how do we love thee? Let us count the ways: long days, family vacation, and abundant produce. We've taken the juicy fruits of summer and transformed them into a variety of heavenly indulgences. To make your enjoyment complete, there's even a nonfruit offering for the die-hard chocoholic. So go ahead, let yourself fall in love.

LEMON CHEESECAKE WITH BLACKBERRY SAUCE

(pictured on page 115)

18 graham crackers (2½-inch squares)
¼ cup sugar
1 tablespoon chilled butter
1 teaspoon ground cinnamon
1 large egg white
Cooking spray
1 (16-ounce) carton 2% low-fat cottage cheese
1 (8-ounce) block ⅓-less-fat cream cheese (Neufchâtel), softened
1 cup sugar
¼ cup cornstarch
¼ teaspoon salt
3 large egg yolks
1½ teaspoons grated lemon rind
¼ cup fresh lemon juice
2 teaspoons vanilla extract
3 large egg whites (at room temperature)
3 tablespoons sugar
Blackberry Sauce
Edible flowers (optional)

1. Preheat oven to 325°.
2. Place graham crackers in a food processor; process 10 seconds. Add ¼ cup sugar, butter, and cinnamon; process 20 seconds or until mixture resembles coarse meal. Add 1 egg white; pulse 15 times or just until moist (do not overprocess). Press crumb mixture into bottom of a 9-inch springform pan coated with cooking spray. Bake at 325° for 20 minutes. Let cool completely on a wire rack. Reduce oven temperature to 300°.
3. Place cottage cheese in a food processor; process 2 minutes or until smooth. Add cream cheese; process 40 seconds, scraping sides of processor bowl once. Add 1 cup sugar, cornstarch, salt, and egg yolks; process until mixture is smooth. Add lemon rind, lemon juice, and vanilla; process an additional 10 seconds (mixture will be thin).
4. Beat egg whites with clean, dry beaters at high speed of a mixer until soft peaks form. Gradually add 3 tablespoons sugar, 1 tablespoon at a time, beating until stiff peaks form. Add egg white mixture to cheese mixture in food processor; pulse 6 times or just until blended.
5. Pour cheese mixture into prepared pan. Cover loosely, and bake at 300° for 50 minutes. Turn off oven; uncover cheesecake, and let stand in closed oven 1 hour. Remove cheesecake from oven, and let cool completely on a wire rack. Cover and chill 12 hours. Serve cheesecake with Blackberry Sauce. Garnish with edible flowers, if desired. YIELD: 12 servings (serving size: 1 slice cheesecake and 3 tablespoons sauce).

POINTS: 7; EXCHANGES: 3½ Starch, 1 Fat; PER SERVING: CAL 330 (24% from fat); PRO 10g; FAT 8.7g (sat 4.4g); CARB 52.7g; FIB 2.4g; CHOL 75mg; IRON 1mg; SOD 370mg; CALC 65mg

BLACKBERRY SAUCE:

2 tablespoons cornstarch
2 tablespoons crème de cassis (black currant-flavored liqueur)
1 pound fresh blackberries (about 4 cups)
½ cup sugar
½ cup water
1 tablespoon fresh lemon juice

1. Combine cornstarch and liqueur in a small bowl; stir well, and set aside.
2. Combine blackberries, sugar, water, and lemon juice in a large heavy saucepan. Bring mixture to a boil over medium heat, stirring occasionally. Reduce heat, and simmer, uncovered, 5 minutes, stirring occasionally. Add cornstarch mixture; cook 2 minutes or until thick, stirring constantly. Pour sauce into a bowl, and let cool. Cover surface of sauce with plastic wrap, and chill. YIELD: 2⅔ cups (serving size: 3 tablespoons).

RASPBERRY COBBLER

1 cup firmly packed dark brown
    sugar
½ cup water
4 teaspoons cornstarch
2 teaspoons vanilla extract
½ teaspoon ground cinnamon
¼ teaspoon ground nutmeg
6 cups fresh raspberries
Cooking spray
1 cup all-purpose flour
¼ cup sugar
1 teaspoon baking powder
¼ teaspoon baking soda
¼ teaspoon salt
5 tablespoons chilled unsalted
    butter, cut into small pieces
½ cup low-fat buttermilk

1. Preheat oven to 400°.
2. Combine first 6 ingredients in a
large bowl. Add raspberries, and toss
gently to coat. Spoon raspberry
mixture into a shallow 2-quart baking dish coated with cooking spray.
3. Combine 1 cup flour, sugar, baking powder, baking soda, and salt in
a bowl; cut in butter with a pastry
blender or 2 knives until mixture
resembles coarse meal. Add low-fat
buttermilk, tossing with a fork just
until mixture forms a soft dough.
Spoon dough into 8 mounds on top
of raspberry mixture. Bake at 400°
for 30 minutes or until topping is
lightly browned and filling is bubbly.
Serve warm or at room temperature.
YIELD: 8 servings.

POINTS: 4; **EXCHANGES:** 2½ Starch, 1 Fat, ½
Fruit; **PER SERVING:** CAL 248 (29% from fat);
PRO 2.9g; FAT 8.1g (sat 4.5g); CARB 42.7g;
FIB 6.1g; CHOL 19mg; IRON 1.5mg;
SOD 189mg; CALC 87mg

RUSTIC RED PLUM TART

1¼ cups all-purpose flour
1 tablespoon sugar
¼ teaspoon salt
4 tablespoons chilled unsalted
    butter
¼ cup ice water
½ teaspoon cider vinegar
¼ cup chopped walnuts
¼ cup all-purpose flour
1 teaspoon ground cinnamon,
    divided
1½ pounds ripe red plums (about
    9), each cut into 12 wedges
⅓ cup sugar
¼ teaspoon ground nutmeg
1½ tablespoons water, divided
¼ cup apricot preserves

1. Preheat oven to 400°.
2. Place first 3 ingredients in a food
processor; pulse 2 times or until
blended. Add butter; pulse 4 times or
until mixture resembles coarse meal.
Combine ice water and vinegar.
With processor on, add mixture
through food chute, processing just
until blended (do not form a ball).
Press mixture gently into a 4-inch
circle on heavy-duty plastic wrap;
cover with additional plastic wrap.
Roll dough, still covered, into a
14-inch circle. Chill dough 15 minutes or until plastic wrap can be
removed easily.
3. Remove plastic wrap. Fit dough
into a 12- or 13-inch round pizza
pan, allowing edges of dough to
extend over edges of pan. Set aside.
4. Place walnuts, ¼ cup flour, and ½
teaspoon cinnamon in a food
processor; process 20 seconds or
until walnuts are finely ground (do
not overprocess to a paste). Set aside.

5. Sprinkle walnut mixture evenly
over pastry, leaving a 1- to 2-inch
border. Working from the outside
edge of pan to the center, arrange
plum wedges in a spiral pattern,
overlapping wedges slightly.
6. Combine ⅓ cup sugar, remaining ½ teaspoon cinnamon, and nutmeg; stir well. Reserve 1 tablespoon
sugar mixture; set aside. Sprinkle
remaining sugar mixture evenly over
plum wedges. Fold edges of pastry
over plums (pastry will cover only
outside edges of fruit). Brush edge
of pastry with 1½ teaspoons water,
and sprinkle with reserved 1 tablespoon sugar mixture.
7. Bake at 400° for 45 minutes or
until pastry is lightly browned. Let
cool in pan on a wire rack.
8. Combine remaining 1 tablespoon
water and apricot preserves in a
small saucepan; bring to a boil over
medium heat. Reduce heat, and
simmer 1 minute, stirring constantly.
Gently brush apricot mixture over
plums. Let cool completely.
YIELD: 10 servings.

POINTS: 4; **EXCHANGES:** 2 Starch, 1 Fat, ½
Fruit; **PER SERVING:** CAL 207 (30% from fat);
PRO 3.1g; FAT 6.8g (sat 3.1g); CARB 35.2g;
FIB 2.2g; CHOL 12mg; IRON 1.1mg;
SOD 63mg; CALC 13mg

VERY BERRY SUMMER FRUIT COMPOTE

(pictured on page 135)

1 vanilla bean
1½ cups water
1 cup sugar
1 (3-inch) cinnamon stick
2 cups fresh raspberries
2 cups fresh blackberries
2 cups fresh blueberries
Pineapple-mint sprigs or spearmint
    sprigs (optional)

1. Split vanilla bean lengthwise, and scrape seeds from bean into a large saucepan. Add vanilla bean to pan. Add water, sugar, and cinnamon stick; stir well. Bring to a boil; reduce heat, and simmer 5 minutes, stirring occasionally. Add berries; cook 1 minute, stirring gently. Remove from heat; let stand 10 minutes.

2. Drain berry mixture, reserving sugar syrup. Place berries, vanilla bean, and cinnamon stick in a medium bowl; set aside. Return sugar syrup to pan; bring to a boil. Cook 10 minutes or until slightly thick. Pour syrup over berry mixture; cover and chill 2 hours. Discard vanilla bean and cinnamon stick just before serving. Garnish with mint sprigs, if desired. YIELD: 4 servings (serving size: 1 cup).

POINTS: 4; **EXCHANGES:** 3½ Starch, 1½ Fruit; **PER SERVING:** CAL 290 (2% from fat); PRO 1.4g; FAT 0.8g (sat 0g); CARB 73.8g; FIB 8.8g; CHOL 0mg; IRON 0.8mg; SOD 5mg; CALC 35mg

TICKLE-ME-PINK STRAWBERRY CREAM ROLL

(pictured on page 115)

Cooking spray
1 tablespoon all-purpose flour
4 large egg yolks
3 tablespoons sugar
1 teaspoon vanilla extract
1½ teaspoons grated lemon rind
¼ cup all-purpose flour
¼ teaspoon salt
6 large egg whites (at room
    temperature)
2 tablespoons sugar
2 cups sliced fresh strawberries
2 tablespoons sugar
1 teaspoon lemon juice
1 teaspoon vanilla extract
1 (8-ounce) container frozen
    fat-free whipped topping,
    thawed
2 tablespoons powdered sugar
Fresh strawberries (optional)

1. Preheat oven to 375°.
2. Coat a 15- x 10-inch jelly-roll pan with cooking spray; line bottom with wax paper. Coat wax paper with cooking spray; sprinkle with 1 tablespoon flour. Set aside.
3. Beat yolks at high speed of a mixer 4 minutes. Gradually add 3 tablespoons sugar, beating well. Add vanilla and lemon rind; beat until blended. Combine ¼ cup flour and salt; add to yolk mixture, stirring gently to combine.
4. Beat egg whites with clean, dry beaters at high speed of a mixer until foamy. Gradually add 2 tablespoons sugar, 1 tablespoon at a time, beating until stiff peaks form. Gently fold egg white mixture into yolk mixture.

5. Spoon batter into prepared pan. Bake at 375° for 15 minutes or until cake springs back when touched lightly in center. Loosen cake from sides of pan, and turn out onto a slightly damp dishtowel; carefully peel off wax paper. Let cool 1 minute. Starting at narrow end, roll up cake and towel together. Place cake, seam side down, on a wire rack, and let cool completely.
6. Combine strawberries and next 3 ingredients; toss gently. Let stand 30 minutes, stirring once. Drain strawberries through a sieve, reserving juice. Mash strawberries with a fork. Fold whipped topping into berries.
7. Unroll cake carefully, and remove towel. Drizzle reserved strawberry juice over cake; spread strawberry mixture over cake, leaving a ½-inch border around outside edges. Reroll cake; place, seam side down, on a platter. Cover and chill 2 hours. Sift powdered sugar over cake. Garnish with strawberries, if desired.
YIELD: 4 servings.

POINTS: 7; **EXCHANGES:** 3½ Starch, 1 Fat; **PER SERVING:** CAL 332 (15% from fat); PRO 9.2g; FAT 5.6g (sat 1.7g); CARB 55.8g; FIB 1.7g; CHOL 218mg; IRON 1.2mg; SOD 268mg; CALC 38mg

BLUEBERRY PIE WITH AMARETTI STREUSEL

(pictured on page 158)

1 cup all-purpose flour
1 tablespoon powdered sugar
2 tablespoons chilled vegetable shortening, cut into small pieces
¼ teaspoon salt
2 tablespoons chilled unsalted butter, cut into small pieces
3 tablespoons ice water
½ teaspoon cider vinegar
Cooking spray
12 amaretti cookies (about 3 ounces)
½ cup sugar
⅓ cup all-purpose flour
1 teaspoon ground cinnamon
5 teaspoons chilled unsalted butter, cut into small pieces
2 large egg whites (at room temperature)
⅛ teaspoon salt
2 tablespoons sugar
4 cups fresh blueberries (about 1¼ pounds)
1 tablespoon fresh lime juice

1. Preheat oven to 400°.
2. Place first 4 ingredients in a food processor, and pulse 2 times or until blended. Add 2 tablespoons chilled butter; pulse 4 times or until mixture resembles coarse meal. Combine ice water and vinegar. With processor on, add vinegar mixture through food chute, processing just until combined (do not form a ball). Press mixture gently into a 4-inch circle on heavy-duty plastic wrap, and cover with additional plastic wrap. Roll dough, still covered, into an 11-inch circle. Chill dough 15 minutes or until plastic wrap can be removed easily.
3. Remove plastic wrap; fit dough into a 9-inch pie plate coated with cooking spray. Fold edges under, and flute. Pierce bottom and sides of dough with a fork; bake at 400° for 15 minutes. Let cool on a wire rack. Reduce oven temperature to 350°.
4. Place cookies in a heavy-duty zip-top plastic bag; coarsely crush with a mallet or rolling pin, and set aside. Combine ½ cup sugar, ⅓ cup flour, and cinnamon in a small bowl. Cut in 5 teaspoons butter with a pastry blender or 2 knives until mixture resembles coarse meal. Stir in cookie crumbs. Sprinkle ¼ cup crumb mixture over bottom of prepared piecrust. Set remaining crumb mixture aside.
5. Beat egg whites and ⅛ teaspoon salt with clean, dry beaters at high speed of a mixer until foamy. Add 2 tablespoons sugar, 1 tablespoon at a time, beating until stiff peaks form. Gently fold blueberries and lime juice into egg white mixture. Spoon blueberry mixture into prepared crust, spreading evenly (crust will be very full). Sprinkle remaining crumb mixture evenly over blueberry mixture. Bake at 350° for 45 minutes. Shield edges of piecrust with foil after 30 minutes to prevent over-browning, if necessary. Let cool completely on a wire rack.
YIELD: 10 servings.

POINTS: 6; **EXCHANGES:** 2½ Starch, 1 Fat, ½ Fruit; **PER SERVING:** CAL 289 (29% from fat); PRO 4g; FAT 9.4g (sat 3.3g); CARB 49g; FIB 2.4g; CHOL 14mg; IRON 2.1mg; SOD 134mg; CALC 11mg

MANGO MOUSSE WITH RASPBERRY SAUCE

(pictured on page 25)

4 cups peeled cubed mango (about 4 large)
2 tablespoons fresh lime juice
1 envelope unflavored gelatin
⅓ cup water
3 large egg whites
½ cup sugar
Raspberry Sauce
¾ cup frozen reduced-calorie whipped topping, thawed
Fresh raspberries (optional)

1. Place mango and lime juice in a food processor; process until smooth, scraping sides of processor bowl occasionally. Set aside.
2. Sprinkle gelatin over ⅓ cup water in a 1-cup heatproof glass measure; let stand 10 minutes. Fill a 1-quart saucepan half-full with water; place over medium heat until very hot. Place glass measure in saucepan; stir until gelatin dissolves. Stir gelatin mixture into mango mixture; set aside.
3. Combine egg whites and sugar in the top of a double boiler, and place over gently simmering water. Stir egg white mixture with a rubber spatula, scraping sides and bottom of pan frequently; cook 9 minutes or until mixture is 140°, stirring constantly. Remove from heat. Beat egg white mixture at high speed of a mixer until stiff peaks form (do not over-beat). Gently fold half of egg white mixture into mango mixture. Fold mango mixture into remaining egg white mixture. Divide mixture evenly among 6 (8-ounce) dessert glasses. Cover and chill 3 hours or until set.

4. Spoon about 3 tablespoons Raspberry Sauce over each serving; top each with 2 tablespoons whipped topping. Garnish with fresh raspberries, if desired. YIELD: 6 servings.

POINTS: 4; EXCHANGES: 2 Starch, 2 Fruit; PER SERVING: CAL 235 (3% from fat); PRO 4g; FAT 0.8g (sat 0.1g); CARB 57.7g; FIB 4.7g; CHOL 0mg; IRON 0.6mg; SOD 32mg; CALC 33mg

RASPBERRY SAUCE:

4 cups fresh raspberries
6 tablespoons sugar
2 tablespoons fresh lime juice

1. Place raspberries in a blender or food processor; process until smooth. Press raspberry purée through a fine sieve into a medium bowl, and discard seeds. Add sugar and lime juice to raspberry purée; stir well. Cover and chill. YIELD: 1⅓ cups.

PEACH ICE CREAM

2 cups peeled, coarsely chopped peaches (about 2 large)
¼ cup sugar
¼ teaspoon almond extract
1⅓ cups 1% low-fat milk, divided
¼ cup nonfat dry milk
2 large egg yolks
1 (14-ounce) can fat-free sweetened condensed skim milk
1 tablespoon lemon juice
1 tablespoon vanilla extract
Mint sprigs (optional)

1. Combine peaches and sugar in a 1-quart saucepan; partially mash peaches with a fork or potato masher. Place over medium heat, and cook 20 minutes or until thick

and bubbly, stirring frequently. Pour into a bowl, and stir in almond extract. Cover surface of peach mixture with plastic wrap; let cool to room temperature. Chill.

2. Combine ⅔ cup 1% low-fat milk, dry milk, and yolks in a saucepan. Heat over medium-low heat to 180° or until tiny bubbles form around edge of pan, stirring frequently (do not boil). Remove from heat; add remaining ⅔ cup milk, sweetened condensed skim milk, lemon juice, and vanilla, stirring with a whisk until well blended. Cover and chill.

3. Combine milk mixture and peach mixture; stir well. Pour into the freezer can of an ice cream freezer. Freeze according to manufacturer's instructions. Spoon into a freezer-safe container; cover and freeze 2 hours or until firm. Garnish with mint sprigs, if desired. YIELD: 8 servings (serving size: ½ cup).

POINTS: 5; EXCHANGES: 2 Starch, 1 Sk Milk; PER SERVING: CAL 231 (7% from fat); PRO 7.5g; FAT 1.8g (sat 0.7g); CARB 44.9g; FIB 0.7g; CHOL 63mg; IRON 0.2mg; SOD 93mg; CALC 232mg

FUDGY PIE WITH ICE CREAM

(pictured on cover)

Dutch process cocoa adds a richer, darker flavor than regular cocoa, and it's less acidic.

Cooking spray
2 tablespoons dry breadcrumbs
3 tablespoons unsalted butter
1 (1-ounce) square unsweetened chocolate
½ cup Dutch process cocoa
1⅓ cups sugar
¼ cup all-purpose flour
¼ cup finely chopped walnuts
¼ cup warm water
2 teaspoons vanilla extract
¼ teaspoon salt
2 large egg yolks, lightly beaten
3 large egg whites (at room temperature)
2 tablespoons sugar
½ cup fat-free hot fudge topping (such as Hershey's)
½ cup vanilla low-fat ice cream or frozen yogurt
Fresh strawberries (optional)

1. Preheat oven to 350°.
2. Coat a 9-inch pie plate with cooking spray; dust with breadcrumbs. Turn pie plate upside down to remove excess breadcrumbs; discard. Set prepared pie plate aside.
3. Melt butter and chocolate over low heat in a medium heavy saucepan, stirring with a whisk until smooth. Stir in cocoa, and cook over medium heat 1 minute, stirring constantly. Stir in 1⅓ cups sugar (mixture will be very thick), and cook 1 minute, stirring constantly. Remove

(continued)

from heat; add flour and next 5 ingredients, stirring until mixture is well blended. Set aside.

4. Beat egg whites with clean, dry beaters at high speed of a mixer until foamy. Gradually add 2 tablespoons sugar, 1 tablespoon at a time, beating until stiff peaks form. Gently stir one-third of egg white mixture into chocolate mixture; gently fold in remaining egg white mixture. Pour into prepared pie plate, spreading evenly.

5. Bake at 350° for 30 minutes. Turn off oven; let pie stand in closed oven 5 minutes. Remove from oven; let cool completely on a wire rack.

6. Cut pie into 8 slices. Top each slice with 1 tablespoon hot fudge topping and 1 tablespoon ice cream. Garnish with strawberries, if desired. Serve immediately. **YIELD:** 8 servings.

POINTS: 7; EXCHANGES: 3½ Starch, 1½ Fat; PER SERVING: CAL 339 (28% from fat); PRO 6.4g; FAT 10.6g (sat 5g); CARB 56g; FIB 1.1g; CHOL 68mg; IRON 1.8mg; SOD 185mg; CALC 50mg

HOW TO
Take Up Smoking

This cooking method can be addictive, but it's a good habit to pick up. Get started with these recipes and the step-by-step photographs below.

JERK SMOKED CHICKEN

(pictured on page 112)

  2 medium limes
  1 medium-size orange
  ⅔ cup sliced green onions
  ¼ cup habanero pepper sauce
1½ tablespoons dried thyme
1½ teaspoons ground allspice
  1 teaspoon freshly ground pepper
  ½ teaspoon salt
  ¼ teaspoon ground cloves
  3 garlic cloves, peeled
  2 (3-pound) chickens
  4 (3-inch) chunks hickory wood

1. Squeeze juice from orange and limes; set citrus rinds aside. Combine citrus juice, onions, and next 7 ingredients in a blender or food processor; process until well blended.

2. Remove and discard giblets and neck from chickens. Rinse chickens under cold water; pat dry. Trim excess fat from chickens. Starting at neck cavities, loosen skin from breasts and drumsticks by gently pushing fingers between skin and meat. Place citrus rinds in body cavities. Tie legs together with string, and lift wings up and over backs; tuck under chickens.

3. Place chickens in a large zip-top plastic bag. Pour juice mixture under loosened skin of chickens. Seal bag, and marinate in refrigerator at least 2 hours, turning bag occasionally.

STEP-BY-STEP

1. Fill charcoal pan with 8 to 10 pounds of briquettes. Carefully light charcoal. Allow to burn 20 minutes or until coals are covered with gray ash. Place soaked wood chunks on top of coals, using long tongs.

2. Place water pan in smoker. Carefully fill pan with hot water or other liquid as specified in recipe to within 1 inch below the rim of the water pan. Work quickly so smoke and heat do not escape.

3. Coat grill racks with cooking spray for easy cleanup; place racks in the smoker. Arrange food on racks. Cover with smoker lid, and cook food according to recipe directions.

4. Use the access door to add liquid or charcoal. A long heavy-duty metal funnel or watering can with a long spout works best for refilling water pan and long tongs can be used for adding charcoal.

Lessons in Lighting Up

• Place the smoker on a heat-proof surface away from flammable material. A large piece of heavy-duty foil can be placed under the smoker for a drip pan and ash guard.

• A full water pan should last about 4 hours. If you hear sizzling coming from the smoker, it needs more liquid. Check the coals periodically through the access door, and add as needed.

• Three or four wood chunks should be plenty to lend a smoky flavor to meats. Wood chips burn fast and are recommended only for smoking foods such as fish that cook quickly. A lot of smoke is produced the first hour of cooking, but then dies down. It is not necessary to add additional wood.

• Do not use instant-lighting charcoal that is pretreated with lighter fluid.

• Don't be tempted to lift the smoker lid to check the meat before the minimum recommended cooking time. Each time the smoker is opened, heat and moisture escape and 15 minutes must be added to the cooking time. Most smokers have built-in thermometers that indicate an ideal cooking range. If the smoker is not hot enough, open the side access door to allow more air to reach the fire.

---

4. Soak hickory chunks in water 30 minutes to 1 hour. Drain well.

5. Prepare charcoal fire in meat smoker; let burn 15 to 20 minutes or until center coals are covered with gray ash. Place soaked hickory chunks on top of coals. Remove chickens from bag, reserving marinade. Place water pan in smoker; add reserved marinade and hot water to pan to within 1 inch of rim.

6. Place chickens, breast side up, on rack in smoker, allowing enough room between chickens for air to circulate. Insert meat thermometer into thickest portion of thigh, making sure not to touch bone. Cover with lid; cook 3 hours or until thermometer registers 185°. Refill water pan and add charcoal to fire as needed.

7. Remove chickens from smoker; let stand 10 minutes. Remove and discard skin before serving.

YIELD: 8 servings (serving size: 3 ounces chicken).

NOTE: If habanero pepper sauce isn't available, substitute any red hot sauce.

POINTS: 4; EXCHANGES: 2 Lean Meat, 1 Very Lean Meat; **PER SERVING:** CAL 158 (31% from fat); PRO 23g; FAT 5.5g (sat 1.5g); CARB 3.1g; FIB 0.5g; CHOL 68mg; IRON 2.1mg; SOD 258mg; CALC 38mg

---

SPICY PORK ROAST

1 tablespoon cumin seeds
1 tablespoon coriander seeds
1½ teaspoons black peppercorns
1½ teaspoons mustard seeds
1 tablespoon dark brown sugar
2¼ teaspoons chili powder
1½ teaspoons paprika
½ teaspoon salt
¼ teaspoon ground red pepper
¼ teaspoon ground cinnamon
1 (3-pound) lean, boned pork loin roast
4 (3-inch) chunks mesquite wood
6 (12-ounce) cans beer or 9 cups hot water

1. Place a small skillet over medium heat until hot. Add first 4 ingredients; sauté 2 minutes or until fragrant. Remove from heat; let cool completely. Place spice mixture in a spice grinder, mini food processor, or blender; process until ground.

2. Combine freshly ground spices, brown sugar, and next 5 ingredients; set aside. Trim fat from roast; rub spice mixture evenly over roast. Place roast in a large heavy-duty zip-top plastic bag; seal bag, and

marinate in refrigerator 8 hours, turning bag occasionally.

3. Soak mesquite chunks in water 30 minutes to 1 hour. Drain well.

4. Prepare charcoal fire in meat smoker; let burn 15 to 20 minutes or until center coals are covered with gray ash. Place soaked mesquite wood chunks on top of coals. Place water pan in smoker; add beer or hot water to pan to within 1 inch of rim.

5. Place roast on rack in smoker; insert meat thermometer into thickest portion of roast. Cover with smoker lid; cook 4 hours or until thermometer registers 160° (slightly pink). Refill water pan with water and add charcoal to fire as needed.

6. Remove roast from smoker; let stand 10 minutes before slicing. Serve with hamburger buns or barbecue bread and barbecue sauce.

YIELD: 12 servings (serving size: 3 ounces pork).

POINTS: 5; EXCHANGES: 2 Med-fat Meat, 1 Lean Meat; **PER SERVING:** CAL 211 (51% from fat); PRO 22.9g; FAT 11.9g (sat 4.1g); CARB 1.4g; FIB 0.3g; CHOL 77mg; IRON 1.3mg; SOD 162mg; CALC 14mg

Music to Your Mouth

Salsas, with their bright, bold colors and flavors, give sparkle and soul to a simple meal, much like the music with which they share a name.

Salsas combine ingredients in lively accord—usually with some acid, a little (or a lot of) heat, and very little fat to create a melody of flavor. These salsas span a variety of uses. They all pair harmoniously with the recipes from "Grilling Discovery" on page 106, and we offer some serving suggestions. But you can also use them to top any grilled meat or chicken, add sizzle to a salad, or give punch to leftovers. Once you see how much flavor you can get with just five ingredients, you may find your cooking moves to a whole new beat.

GRILLED-VEGETABLE SALSA

This smoky salsa suits Herb-Marinated Shrimp, page 108.

  1 pound red bell peppers
  1 pound yellow bell peppers
  1 pound green bell peppers
Cooking spray
  2 portobello mushroom caps
    (about 8 ounces)
  1 medium-size red onion, cut
    into ½-inch-thick slices
  1 tablespoon chopped fresh thyme
  1 tablespoon balsamic vinegar
  ½ teaspoon salt
  ¼ teaspoon pepper

1. Cut each bell pepper in half; discard stems, seeds, and membranes.
2. Prepare grill. Place bell pepper halves, skin side down, on grill rack coated with cooking spray. Add mushroom caps and onion slices to rack; cover and grill 20 minutes or until vegetables are tender, turning mushroom caps and onions after 10 minutes (do not turn bell pepper halves). Remove vegetables from grill rack. Set mushroom caps and onions aside. Place bell pepper halves in a large zip-top plastic bag immediately; seal bag, and let stand 15 minutes.
3. Peel bell pepper halves, and coarsely chop. Coarsely chop mushroom caps and onion slices. Combine chopped vegetables, thyme, and remaining ingredients in a bowl; stir well. Serve warm or at room temperature. YIELD: 6 servings (serving size: ½ cup).

NOTE: The flavor and color of this salsa are best when all three colors of bell pepper are used, but you may use only one color pepper, if desired.

POINTS: 1; **EXCHANGES:** 2 Veg; **PER SERVING:** CAL 57 (13% from fat); PRO 2.3g; FAT 0.8g (sat 0.1g); CARB 12g; FIB 3.3g; CHOL 0mg; IRON 2.5mg; SOD 202mg; CALC 22mg

PICCALILLI-FLAVORED SALSA

Serve this sweet and sour relish with Carolina-Style Barbecued Pork Sandwiches, page 106.

  3 cups coarsely chopped green
    bell pepper (about 1¼ pounds)
  1 cup chopped onion
2½ tablespoons sugar
  2 tablespoons cider vinegar
  1 tablespoon water
  ½ teaspoon salt
  ¼ teaspoon pepper
  ⅛ teaspoon ground cloves

1. Place a large nonstick skillet over medium heat until hot. Add all ingredients; sauté 10 minutes or until most of liquid evaporates. Serve warm or at room temperature.
YIELD: 5 servings (serving size: ½ cup).

POINTS: 1; **EXCHANGES:** 1 Veg, ½ Starch; **PER SERVING:** CAL 54 (7% from fat); PRO 1g; FAT 0.4g (sat 0.1g); CARB 13g; FIB 1.7g; CHOL 0mg; IRON 1.1mg; SOD 238mg; CALC 11mg

PLUM SALSA

Ruby-hued plums and onion add spark to Moroccan Chicken Thighs, page 107.

1¼ pounds ripe plums (about 7),
    quartered and pitted
  1 small red onion (about 4
    ounces), quartered
  1 cup fresh cilantro sprigs
  ¾ cup fresh mint leaves
  1 tablespoon white wine vinegar
  ½ teaspoon salt
  ¼ teaspoon pepper
  ⅛ teaspoon ground red pepper

1. Place plums and onion in a food processor; pulse 10 times, scraping sides of processor bowl occasionally. Add cilantro and remaining ingredients; pulse 5 times or until mixture is chopped (do not overprocess or salsa will be mushy). Serve at room temperature. YIELD: 6 servings (serving size: ½ cup).

POINTS: 1; EXCHANGES: 1½ Fruit, 1 Veg;
PER SERVING: CAL 113 (10% from fat);
PRO 2.1g; FAT 1.2g (sat 0.1g); CARB 26.3g;
FIB 4.5g; CHOL 0mg; IRON 0.8mg;
SOD 395mg; CALC 31mg

WHITE BEAN-AND-ARUGULA SALSA

Serve with Rosemary-Mustard Lamb Chops, page 108

1 (15-ounce) can cannellini beans or other white beans, rinsed and drained
4 cups chopped arugula
2⅓ cups diced tomato (about 1 pound)
1 tablespoon extra-virgin olive oil
½ teaspoon crushed red pepper
2½ teaspoons white wine vinegar
¼ teaspoon salt

1. Combine all ingredients in a bowl, and stir well. Let stand 15 minutes, stirring occasionally. Serve at room temperature. YIELD: 5 servings (serving size: 1 cup).

POINTS: 2; EXCHANGES: 1 Starch, 1 Veg;
PER SERVING: CAL 113 (27% from fat);
PRO 6.1g; FAT 3.4g (sat 0.5g); CARB 16.6g;
FIB 2.9g; CHOL 0mg; IRON 1.5mg;
SOD 277mg; CALC 90mg

CHERRY TOMATO SALSA

(pictured on page 92)

Spice up Chili-Crusted Flank Steak Fajitas, page 107, with this piquant salsa.

20 cherry tomatoes (about 10 ounces), quartered
½ cup chopped fresh cilantro
½ cup diced red onion
2 tablespoons seeded minced jalapeño pepper
1 tablespoon fresh lime juice
½ teaspoon salt

1. Combine all ingredients in a bowl; stir well. Let stand at least 15 minutes, stirring occasionally. Serve at room temperature. YIELD: 3 servings (serving size: ¾ cup).

POINTS: 0; EXCHANGES: 1½ Veg;
PER SERVING: CAL 34 (11% from fat);
PRO 1.3g; FAT 0.4g (sat 0.1g); CARB 7.8g;
FIB 1.7g; CHOL 0mg; IRON 0.7mg;
SOD 402mg; CALC 15mg

CURRIED NECTARINE SALSA

This savory-sweet combination complements Citrus-Teriyaki Tuna, page 108.

1 teaspoon curry powder
2 cups diced nectarine (about ¾ pound)
½ cup diced red bell pepper
¼ cup diced red onion
¼ teaspoon salt

1. Place curry in a large skillet; cook over high heat 30 seconds or until fragrant, stirring occasionally.

Remove skillet from heat; add nectarine and remaining ingredients, stirring until well blended. Serve warm or at room temperature. YIELD: 5 servings (serving size: ½ cup).

POINTS: 0; EXCHANGE: ½ Fruit;
PER SERVING: CAL 37 (10% from fat);
PRO 0.7g; FAT 0.4g (sat 0g); CARB 8.7g;
FIB 1.8g; CHOL 0mg; IRON 0.5mg;
SOD 118mg; CALC 7mg

ROSEMARY-ONION SALSA

This pairs well with Rosemary-Mustard Lamb Chops, page 108.

2 teaspoons olive oil
5 cups slivered red onion (about 1¼ pounds)
1 tablespoon sugar
2 tablespoons red wine vinegar
1½ teaspoons minced fresh or ¾ teaspoon dried rosemary, crushed
¼ teaspoon salt
¼ teaspoon pepper

1. Heat oil in a large nonstick skillet over medium-high heat. Add onion, and sauté 7 minutes or until lightly browned. Add sugar and remaining ingredients; reduce heat to medium, and sauté an additional 5 minutes. Serve warm or at room temperature. YIELD: 4 servings (serving size: ½ cup).

POINTS: 2; EXCHANGES: 4 Veg, ½ Fat;
PER SERVING: CAL 115 (20% from fat);
PRO 2.5g; FAT 2.6g (sat 0.4g); CARB 21.9g;
FIB 4g; CHOL 0mg; IRON 0.6mg;
SOD 153mg; CALC 46mg

PAN-ROASTED CORN SALSA

(pictured on page 113)

The basil and lemon in this salsa pair well with Herb-Marinated Shrimp, page 108.

1 (10-ounce) package frozen baby lima beans
1¾ cups fresh corn kernels (about 3 ears)
Cooking spray
2 cups chopped tomato
1 cup thinly sliced fresh basil leaves
1 teaspoon grated lemon rind
1 tablespoon fresh lemon juice
½ teaspoon salt
¼ teaspoon pepper

1. Bring 1 cup water to a boil in a large saucepan; add baby lima beans, and return to a boil. Cover, reduce heat, and simmer 12 minutes. Add corn; cover and simmer an additional 2 minutes. Drain well.
2. Coat a large nonstick skillet with cooking spray, and place over high heat until hot. Add bean mixture, and sauté 4 minutes or until lightly browned. Remove skillet from heat; stir in tomato and remaining ingredients. Serve warm or at room temperature. YIELD: 8 servings (serving size: ½ cup).

POINTS: 1; **EXCHANGES**: 1 Starch, ½ Veg; **PER SERVING**: CAL 83 (7% from fat); PRO 4.2g; FAT 0.6g (sat 0.1g); CARB 17g; FIB 2.3g; CHOL 0mg; IRON 1.4mg; SOD 208mg; CALC 19mg

Grilling Discovery

It's easy, delicious, and good for you, and the options are tantalizing.

Grilling is an easy cooking method, and it's also one of the most healthful. It requires little, if any, added fat, and when you grill meat or poultry, a lot of the inherent fat is cooked off. And grilling is a very versatile cooking method, so you're not limited to burgers and chicken. Even the novice cook can prepare these diverse dishes with ease.

These recipes are special in their own right, but spectacular when paired with the salsas in "Music to Your Mouth," page 104. Look for recommendations of our favorite combinations. You can't go wrong with flavors as bold and as bright as the summer sun, and recipes as easy as a summer breeze.

CAROLINA-STYLE BARBECUED PORK SANDWICHES

For a taste of the South, serve this sandwich with Piccalilli-Flavored Salsa, page 104.

1 (1-pound) pork tenderloin
¼ cup dark brown sugar, divided
¼ cup cider vinegar
2 tablespoons ketchup
½ teaspoon salt, divided
¼ teaspoon ground red pepper, divided
1 teaspoon paprika
1 teaspoon ground cumin
½ teaspoon dry mustard
¼ teaspoon garlic powder
Cooking spray
4 (2-ounce) sesame seed sandwich rolls, split
12 dill pickle slices

1. Trim fat from pork, and set pork aside.
2. Combine 2 teaspoons brown sugar, vinegar, ketchup, ¼ teaspoon salt, and ⅛ teaspoon ground red pepper; stir well. Set sauce aside.
3. Combine remaining brown sugar, remaining salt, remaining red pepper, paprika, and next 3 ingredients; stir well. Rub mixture over pork.
4. Prepare grill. Place pork on grill rack coated with cooking spray; cover and grill 22 minutes or until thermometer registers 160° (slightly pink), turning pork occasionally.
5. Remove pork from grill; let stand 5 minutes. Cut pork into ¼-inch-thick slices. Spoon 1 tablespoon barbecue sauce onto bottom half of each roll; top with sliced pork and remaining sauce. Top each sandwich with 3 pickle slices and top half of roll. YIELD: 4 servings.
NOTE: To prepare indoors, place a grill pan over medium heat until hot; coat with cooking spray. Add pork, and cook 24 minutes or until thermometer registers 160° (slightly pink), turning occasionally.

POINTS: 7; **EXCHANGES**: 3½ Very Lean Meat, 2½ Starch; **PER SERVING**: CAL 330 (20% from fat); PRO 32g; FAT 7.4g (sat 2g); CARB 35g; FIB 1g; CHOL 84mg; IRON 4mg; SOD 1005mg; CALC 84mg

CHILI-CRUSTED FLANK STEAK FAJITAS

(pictured on page 2)

Cherry Tomato Salsa, page 105, is a refreshing companion with this dish.

1 (½-pound) lean flank steak
1 medium-size red bell pepper, quartered and seeded
1 medium-size green bell pepper, quartered and seeded
1 medium-size yellow bell pepper, quartered and seeded
4 plum tomatoes, cut in half
2 tablespoons lime juice, divided
2 tablespoons Worcestershire sauce, divided
¾ teaspoon salt, divided
3 garlic cloves, minced and divided
1½ teaspoons chili powder
1 medium-size red onion, cut into ¼-inch-thick slices
Cooking spray
8 (6½-inch) flour tortillas
4 tablespoons fat-free sour cream

1. Trim fat from steak, and set aside.
2. Combine bell pepper pieces, tomato halves, 1 tablespoon lime juice, 1 tablespoon Worcestershire sauce, ¼ teaspoon salt, and half of minced garlic in a bowl. Toss gently.
3. Combine remaining lime juice, remaining Worcestershire sauce, ¼ teaspoon salt, remaining garlic, and flank steak in a zip-top plastic bag; seal bag, and marinate in refrigerator at least 30 minutes. Remove steak from bag, reserving marinade. Rub chili powder over steak. Remove bell pepper pieces and tomato halves from bowl, reserving marinade.
4. Prepare grill. Place steak, bell pepper pieces, tomato halves, and onion slices on grill rack coated with cooking spray. Grill tomato halves 3 minutes on each side. Grill steak 5 minutes on each side or until desired degree of doneness, basting occasionally with reserved marinade. Grill bell pepper pieces and onion slices 6 minutes on each side or until tender, basting occasionally with reserved marinade.
5. Remove steak and vegetables from grill. Let steak stand 5 minutes; cut steak diagonally across grain into thin slices. Cut bell pepper pieces into ¼-inch-thick strips; cut onion slices in half. Sprinkle remaining ¼ teaspoon salt evenly over vegetables.
6. Heat flour tortillas according to package directions. Place 2 tortillas on each of 4 plates. Divide steak, bell pepper, and onion evenly among tortillas. Top each fajita with ½ tomato and 1½ teaspoons fat-free sour cream; roll up tortillas. Serve warm.
YIELD: 4 servings (serving size: 2 fajitas).

NOTE: To prepare indoors, cut each bell pepper in half lengthwise; discard seeds and membranes. Place halves, skin sides up, on a broiler pan lined with foil. Flatten peppers with hand. Place onion slices on broiler pan, and broil 5 minutes. Turn onions over; add tomatoes, and broil 5 minutes or until onions, peppers, and tomatoes are lightly browned.

While vegetables cook, place a grill pan over medium-high heat until hot; coat with cooking spray. Add steak; cook 3 minutes on each side or until desired degree of doneness.

POINTS: 5; **EXCHANGES:** 1 Veg, 2½ Starch, 1½ Lean Meat; **PER SERVING:** CAL 303 (22% from fat); PRO 18.2g; FAT 8.1g (sat 3.4g); CARB 46.6g; FIB 11g; CHOL 28mg; IRON 4mg; SOD 661mg; CALC 139mg

MOROCCAN CHICKEN THIGHS

The sweet spices in this dish work well with fruity Plum Salsa, page 104.

4 (4-ounce) skinned, boned chicken thighs
1½ teaspoons ground cumin
2 teaspoons grated lemon rind
½ teaspoon ground ginger
½ teaspoon salt
¼ teaspoon ground cinnamon
2 garlic cloves, minced
2 teaspoons olive oil
Cooking spray

1. Trim fat from chicken thighs, and set aside.
2. Combine cumin and next 5 ingredients in a large bowl. Brush olive oil evenly over chicken. Add chicken to bowl, and toss well to coat chicken with spice mixture. Let stand 10 minutes.
3. Prepare grill. Place chicken on grill rack coated with cooking spray. Cover; grill 6 minutes on each side or until done. Serve with pita bread, if desired. YIELD: 4 servings.

NOTE: To prepare indoors, place a grill pan over medium-high heat until hot; coat with cooking spray. Add chicken; cook 7 minutes on each side or until done.

POINTS: 4; **EXCHANGES:** 3 Lean Meat; **PER SERVING:** CAL 161 (39% from fat); PRO 22.5g; FAT 6.9g (sat 1.5g); CARB 1.3g; FIB 0.2g; CHOL 94mg; IRON 1.8mg; SOD 392mg; CALC 25mg

ROSEMARY-MUSTARD LAMB CHOPS

Serve with Rosemary-Onion Salsa, page 105, or White Bean-and-Arugula Salsa, page 105.

2 tablespoons Dijon mustard
2 tablespoons chopped fresh rosemary
¼ teaspoon salt
¼ teaspoon pepper
2 garlic cloves, minced
8 (4-ounce) lean lamb loin chops (about 1¼ inches thick)
Cooking spray

1. Combine first 5 ingredients in a small bowl; stir well. Rub mixture evenly over both sides of lamb chops. Place chops on a baking sheet or platter; cover and marinate in refrigerator at least 30 minutes.
2. Prepare grill. Place lamb loin chops on grill rack coated with cooking spray; grill 8 minutes on each side or until lamb is desired degree of doneness. YIELD: 4 servings (serving size: 2 lamb chops).

NOTE: To prepare indoors, place a grill pan over high heat until hot; coat with cooking spray. Add lamb, and cook 8 minutes on each side or until desired degree of doneness.

POINTS: 5; **EXCHANGES:** 3½ Lean Meat; **PER SERVING:** CAL 203 (39% from fat); PRO 27.3g; FAT 8.5g (sat 2.9g); CARB 2.1g; FIB 0.8g; CHOL 86mg; IRON 3mg; SOD 459mg; CALC 40mg

CITRUS-TERIYAKI TUNA

The flavors of Curried Nectarine Salsa, page 105, enhance this recipe.

1 cup orange juice
¼ cup peeled minced fresh ginger
¼ cup chopped green onions
¼ cup low-salt teriyaki sauce
3 tablespoons fresh lemon juice
2 garlic cloves, minced
3 drops hot sauce
4 (6-ounce) tuna steaks (about ¾ inch thick)
Cooking spray
Sliced green onions (optional)

1. Combine first 7 ingredients in a shallow dish. Add tuna, turning to coat. Cover. Marinate in refrigerator 30 minutes, turning tuna occasionally. Remove from dish; reserve marinade.
2. Strain marinade through a sieve into a saucepan, discarding solids. Bring marinade to a boil over high heat; cook 6 minutes or until slightly thick. Set sauce aside; keep warm.
3. Prepare grill. Place tuna steaks on grill rack coated with cooking spray, and grill 4 minutes on each side until tuna is medium-rare or until desired degree of doneness. Serve tuna with prepared sauce, and sprinkle with sliced green onions, if desired. YIELD: 4 servings.
NOTE: To prepare indoors, place a grill pan over medium-high heat until hot; coat with cooking spray. Add tuna, and cook 3 minutes on each side until tuna is medium-rare or until desired degree of doneness.

POINTS: 6; **EXCHANGES:** 5½ Very Lean Meat, 1½ Fat, ½ Fruit; **PER SERVING:** CAL 285 (26% from fat); PRO 39.5g; FAT 8.1g (sat 2.1g); CARB 11.7g; FIB 0.4g; CHOL 63mg; IRON 1.9mg; SOD 323mg; CALC 15mg

HERB-MARINATED SHRIMP

(pictured on page 114)

Serve with Grilled-Vegetable Salsa, page 104, or Pan-Roasted Corn Salsa, page 106.

⅓ cup fresh basil leaves
¼ cup fresh mint leaves
2 tablespoons fresh oregano leaves
½ teaspoon salt
¼ teaspoon pepper
3 garlic cloves, halved
2½ teaspoons extra-virgin olive oil
1½ pounds large shrimp, peeled
Cooking spray

1. Combine first 6 ingredients in a food processor, and pulse until mixture is coarsely chopped. Add olive oil, and process until well blended.
2. Combine herb mixture and shrimp in a large bowl, and toss to coat. Cover and marinate shrimp in refrigerator 30 minutes.
3. Thread shrimp onto 12 (6-inch) skewers.
4. Prepare grill. Place skewers on grill rack coated with cooking spray; grill 3 minutes on each side or until done. YIELD: 4 servings (serving size: about 4 ounces).

NOTE: To prepare indoors, place a large grill pan over medium-high heat until hot; coat grill pan with cooking spray. Place 6 skewers on grill pan, and cook 3 minutes on each side or until done. Repeat procedure with remaining skewers.

POINTS: 3; **EXCHANGES:** 4 Very Lean Meat; **PER SERVING:** CAL 153 (26% from fat); PRO 25g; FAT 4.4g (sat 0.8g); CARB 2.5g; FIB 0.4g; CHOL 228mg; IRON 4.8mg; SOD 556mg; CALC 94m

Dressed for Success

DEALIA YANCEY • **HEIGHT** 5'5" • **BEFORE** 205 LBS. • **AFTER** 130 LBS.

Happiest Moment: "I went to the mall and bought a gorgeous power suit and heels, and then walked into a job interview. It felt great."

Forgive Dealia Yancey if you are startled by her gleeful screams from behind the curtain of a dressing room. For this working mom, shopping is now cause for celebration.

"My size and appearance were embarrassing, so I refused to shop," Dealia says. "I went to the large size department and saw things a grandmother would wear. Now," she says, "my husband and daughter are embarrassed to shop with me, because I scream when I try on something great that fits."

What began as a struggle with her weight during childhood and adolescence became an epic battle for Dealia in 1994. "I was back in college full time, raising a child, and my husband was in Korea," she says. "Due to stress, I ate more, and a burger and fries were the easiest foods to get."

In 1997, a friend urged Dealia to try the new Weight Watchers 1•2•3 Success® Plan. Dealia had been a Weight Watchers member since 1973, but hadn't maintained her weight losses. "I set unrealistic goals," she says. "I deprived myself to lose weight quickly." But when she saw advertisements featuring a svelte Sarah Ferguson, Duchess of York, she decided it was time to do it right.

Dealia's social engagements require her to eat out often. "Now, if I'm going to a potluck, I volunteer to bring a veggie or fruit tray, or

I bring a *Weight Watchers* Magazine recipe." Before going out to dinner or grocery shopping, she has a healthful snack to take the edge off her hunger.

Dealia makes time for exercise. "It's amazing what 20 minutes a day can do," she says about her treadmill. "My energy is really up."

"My success came not just from following a plan, but from changing the way I think about food and how I deal with stress," she adds. "I accepted that I live in a world where food is a constant temptation." And Dealia learned to focus on the positive. "I can't be perfect all the time, but I can follow the program and concentrate on my goal." Dealia's focus shifted from a number on the scale to her personal well-being.

> *"If I'm going to a potluck, I volunteer to bring a veggie tray."*

Dealia's new confidence allowed her to make a career move she wouldn't have made 75 pounds ago. "For the first time, I feel truly successful and confident," she says. These days, Dealia loves an opportunity to get dressed up. "I used to think I would never look different. Now I have such pride that I don't ever want to go back to the way it was."

Light
Guacamole,
page 32

Black-Eyed Pea-and-Chutney
Chili, page 19

Graham Cracker
Cream Pie, page 62

Jerk Smoked Chicken,
page 102

112

Pan-Roasted Corn Salsa,
page 106

Lemon Meringue Pie,
page 56

Herb-Marinated Shrimp,
page 108

Mediterranean Vegetable
Pasta, page 14

Tickle-Me-Pink Strawberry
Cream Roll, page 99

Lemon Cheesecake With
Blackberry Sauce, page 97

115

Encore, Encore

CLAUDIA AIKMAN • **HEIGHT** 5'7" • **BEFORE** 216 LBS. • **AFTER** 147 LBS.

Happiest moment: *"On my honeymoon, I wore a two-piece bathing suit. And, to toot my own horn, I didn't look half-bad."*

When Claudia Aikman first wrote to us, we were glad to hear from her. But by the time we got in touch, she was eight months pregnant. "After the baby is born, let us know how you're doing," we said. A few months later, Claudia wrote back. "Yippie! I did it again," she said. "I'm back to my goal weight of 150 pounds." Making your goal twice—now *that*, we thought, is a real success story.

Claudia grew up with poor eating habits and little exercise in a small town in Newfoundland. She began to change her habits when she heard coworkers singing the praises of *Weight Watchers*. "I figured it wouldn't hurt to go to meetings. I was doubtful I could change myself; the idea of the group sold me," she says.

Claudia started eating more healthful foods and incorporating exercise into her day. "Steve (her fiancé) cooked low-fat dinners for me every night while I went to the gym after work," she says. "If I'd had to face making dinner for us after working out, I wouldn't have gone as often. His offering to cook made all the difference."

Claudia went on to drop 5 dress sizes and 69 pounds, and she was exercising regularly. "I felt like a new person," Claudia recalls. A newlywed, Claudia was loving life.

But just as she was settling into her skinnier self, Claudia became pregnant. She was happy—and nervous. "Exercise had become a part of my life, and I feared that all the effort would go to waste."

But Claudia reasoned that if these new habits were so good for her, they'd be good for her baby, too. Her doctor recommended that she should continue exercising during pregnancy.

After Sara was born, it took six months for Claudia to return to her pre-pregnancy weight. "I walked around the neighborhood pushing Sara in a stroller," she says. "It was amazing how the pounds came off." Just as before, Claudia's husband supported her, cooking and doing anything he could.

Now back at work, Claudia wants to spend evenings with Sara. So she works out at the gym during her lunch hour several times a

"If I'd had to face making dinner for us after working out, I wouldn't have gone as often."

week. And on weeknights and weekends, she still takes her daughter for strolls.

Claudia admits that motherhood was intimidating at first, but it gives her even more incentive to stay healthy. "We got rid of the deep-fryer a long time ago," she says. "We intend to eat right and stay fit for our child."

116

September

Party Over Easy

Brunch lets you entertain without a care.

Brunch is informal, relaxed. It can be as simple as serving warm scones with cream cheese spread and vanilla-scented fruit or assembling an egg-and-tortilla casserole before you go to bed, and then putting it in the oven when you get up. Of course, if you're expecting a crowd, you could whip up all of these recipes for an amazing buffet.

CORNMEAL-PECAN PANCAKES

(pictured on page 134)

1 cup all-purpose flour
½ cup yellow cornmeal
¼ cup finely chopped pecans, toasted
1 tablespoon sugar
1 tablespoon baking powder
½ teaspoon baking soda
½ teaspoon salt
2 cups low-fat buttermilk
1 tablespoon vegetable oil
1 large egg, lightly beaten
¾ cup maple syrup

1. Combine first 7 ingredients in a bowl; stir well. Combine buttermilk, oil, and egg; stir well. Add to flour mixture, stirring until smooth.
2. Spoon about ¼ cup batter for each pancake onto a hot nonstick griddle or nonstick skillet. Turn pancakes when tops are covered with bubbles and edges look cooked. Serve hot with maple syrup. YIELD: 8 servings (serving size: 2 pancakes and 1½ tablespoons syrup).

POINTS: 5; EXCHANGES: 3 Starch, ½ Fat; PER SERVING: CAL 247 (23% from fat); PRO 5.5g; FAT 6.2g (sat 0.7g); CARB 43.1g; FIB 1.1g; CHOL 27mg; IRON 1.7mg; SOD 387mg; CALC 168mg

SOUTHWESTERN EGG CASSEROLE

12 (6-inch) corn tortillas
8 large eggs
4 large egg whites
2½ cups skim milk
1 cup 1% low-fat cottage cheese
¾ teaspoon salt
¾ teaspoon freshly ground pepper
1½ cups (6 ounces) crumbled feta cheese
1 cup thinly sliced green onions
Cooking spray
1½ cups salsa
¼ cup diagonally sliced green onion tops (optional)

1. Cut tortillas in half; slice tortilla halves crosswise into 1-inch strips. Set aside.
2. Combine eggs and egg whites in a large bowl; stir well with a whisk. Add skim milk, cottage cheese, salt, and pepper; stir well. Add tortilla strips, feta cheese, and 1 cup green onions; stir well. Pour into a 13- x 9-inch baking dish coated with cooking spray. Cover with foil, and chill 8 hours.
3. Preheat oven to 325°.
4. Bake, covered, at 325° for 1 hour. Uncover and bake an additional 20 minutes or just until set (casserole will continue to firm as it cools). Let cool 5 minutes, and cut into 12 squares. Spoon 2 tablespoons salsa over each serving, and top each with 1 teaspoon sliced green onion tops, if desired. YIELD: 12 servings.

POINTS: 4; EXCHANGES: 1 L-F Milk, ½ Starch, 1 Med-fat Meat; PER SERVING: CAL 194 (35% from fat); PRO 13.3g; FAT 7.5g (sat 3.4g); CARB 18.8g; FIB 1.8g; CHOL 156mg; IRON 1.2mg; SOD 517mg; CALC 220mg

CHERRY TOMATO SALAD

3 pounds cherry tomatoes (about 4 pints), divided
2 tablespoons water
1 tablespoon white wine vinegar
2 teaspoons extra-virgin olive oil
½ teaspoon salt
¼ teaspoon freshly ground pepper
1 garlic clove, peeled
¼ cup chopped fresh mint
Freshly ground pepper (optional)

1. Place ½ pound tomatoes (about ¾ pint), water, and next 5 ingredients in a blender; process until smooth.
2. Cut remaining tomatoes in half; place in a large bowl. Add puréed tomato mixture and mint; toss gently to coat. Sprinkle with ground pepper, if desired. YIELD: 8 servings (serving size: 1 cup).

POINTS: 1; EXCHANGES: 1 Veg, ½ Fat; PER SERVING: CAL 47 (33% from fat); PRO 1.5g; FAT 1.7g (sat 0.2g); CARB 8.1g; FIB 1.9g; CHOL 0mg; IRON 0.8mg; SOD 162mg; CALC 10mg

TOASTED OAT SCONES

(pictured on page 155)

1¼ cups regular oats
1½ cups all-purpose flour
½ cup sugar
2 teaspoons baking powder
¼ teaspoon baking soda
½ teaspoon salt
½ teaspoon ground nutmeg
4 tablespoons chilled stick
    margarine, cut into small pieces
½ cup chopped dates
¾ cup low-fat buttermilk
1 teaspoon vanilla extract
Cooking spray
1 tablespoon stick margarine, melted

1. Preheat oven to 450°.
2. Spread oats on a baking sheet; bake at 450° for 3 minutes or until lightly toasted, stirring once. Let cool completely.
3. Combine 1 cup toasted oats, flour, and next 5 ingredients; cut in 4 tablespoons margarine with a pastry blender or 2 knives until mixture resembles coarse meal. Add dates; toss well. Add buttermilk and vanilla, stirring just until moist.
4. Turn dough out onto a floured surface; with floured hands, knead lightly 4 times. Pat dough into a 9-inch circle on a baking sheet coated with cooking spray. Brush melted margarine over dough; sprinkle with remaining oats. Cut dough into 12 wedges, separating wedges slightly. Bake at 450° for 12 minutes or until golden. Serve warm. YIELD: 12 servings.

POINTS: 4; **EXCHANGES:** 2 Starch, ½ Fat;
PER SERVING: CAL 189 (27% from fat);
PRO 3.6g; FAT 5.7g (sat 1.1g); CARB 31.4g;
FIB 1.8g; CHOL 0mg; IRON 1.2mg;
SOD 232mg; CALC 59mg

POTATO, CORN, AND RED PEPPER HASH

Be sure to use the shelled, green kernel of the pumpkinseed, not the whole seed. If pumpkinseed kernels are not available, substitute roasted sunflower seed kernels or toasted pine nuts.

1 pound Yukon gold or red
    potatoes
1½ teaspoons olive oil, divided
1 cup chopped onion
1 cup fresh corn kernels or frozen
    whole-kernel corn
1 cup drained chopped bottled
    roasted red bell peppers (about
    7 ounces)
1 teaspoon ground cumin
Dash of ground red pepper
2 tablespoons chopped, unsalted
    pumpkinseed kernels, toasted
3 tablespoons chopped fresh
    parsley
½ teaspoon salt
¼ teaspoon black pepper

1. Place potatoes in a large Dutch oven, and cover with water; bring to a boil. Reduce heat, and simmer 30 minutes or until tender; drain. Let cool; peel potatoes, and cut into ½-inch cubes.
2. Heat ½ teaspoon olive oil in a large nonstick skillet over medium-high heat. Add onion; sauté 5 minutes. Add corn; sauté 3 minutes. Stir in roasted peppers, cumin, and ground red pepper. Spoon mixture into a bowl; set aside.
3. Heat ½ teaspoon olive oil in skillet over medium-high heat. Add half of potato cubes, and cook 5 minutes or until lightly browned, stirring once (frequent stirring prevents browning). Add potatoes to corn

mixture, and set aside. Repeat procedure with remaining ½ teaspoon olive oil and potatoes.
4. Return potato-corn mixture to skillet; cook over medium-high heat 1 minute or until warm. Remove from heat; stir in pumpkinseed kernels, parsley, salt, and black pepper.
YIELD: 8 servings (serving size: ½ cup).

POINTS: 2; **EXCHANGES:** 1 Starch;
PER SERVING: CAL 89 (22% from fat);
PRO 2.8g; FAT 2.2g (sat 0.4g); CARB 16.3g;
FIB 2g; CHOL 0mg; IRON 1.6mg;
SOD 517mg; CALC 28mg

STRAWBERRY-ALMOND CREAM CHEESE

Serve this creamy spread with Toasted Oat Scones, bagels, or biscuits.

3 tablespoons pure almond paste
    (such as Betty Crocker)
1 (8-ounce) tub light cream
    cheese
2 tablespoons powdered sugar
½ cup chopped fresh strawberries

1. Place almond paste in a food processor; process until paste is very finely ground. Add cream cheese and sugar; process just until blended (do not overprocess or mixture will be thin). Add strawberries; process just until blended. Cover and chill at least 1 hour. YIELD: 1⅓ cups (serving size: 1 tablespoon).

POINTS: 1; **EXCHANGES:** ½ Fat;
PER SERVING: CAL 37 (58% from fat);
PRO 1.4g; FAT 2.4g (sat 1.1g); CARB 2.6g;
FIB 0.2g; CHOL 6mg; IRON 0.1mg;
SOD 61mg; CALC 20mg

SMOKY MOLASSES-GLAZED TURKEY

1 (2-pound) skinned, boned smoked turkey breast (such as Sara Lee)
1 cup molasses
½ cup brewed coffee
2 tablespoons tomato paste
2 tablespoons cider vinegar
¼ teaspoon salt
¼ teaspoon freshly ground pepper
1 drained canned chipotle chile in adobo sauce
1 garlic clove, peeled

1. Preheat oven to 325°.
2. Place turkey in a shallow baking pan; add ½ cup water. Cover with foil. Bake at 325° for 45 minutes.
3. Place molasses and next 7 ingredients in a blender, and process until smooth. Strain mixture through a sieve into a medium saucepan; discard solids. Bring mixture to a boil over medium-high heat. Reduce heat to medium, and simmer 25 minutes or until mixture is reduced to 1 cup, stirring occasionally.
4. Drain turkey, and return to baking pan. Brush ¼ cup molasses glaze over turkey. Bake, uncovered, an additional 20 minutes, basting turkey occasionally with pan drippings. Thinly slice turkey, and serve with remaining molasses glaze. YIELD: 8 servings (serving size: 3 ounces turkey and 1½ tablespoons glaze).

POINTS: 5; EXCHANGES: 4 Very Lean Meat, 2 Starch; PER SERVING: CAL 268 (3% from fat); PRO 34.3g; FAT 1g (sat 0.3g); CARB 29.6g; FIB 0.3g; CHOL 94.1mg; IRON 3.9mg; SOD 175mg; CALC 101mg

PLUM COBBLER

1¾ cups sugar, divided
2 tablespoons all-purpose flour
8 cups sliced ripe plums (about 3 pounds)
Cooking spray
2 cups all-purpose flour
2 teaspoons baking powder
½ teaspoon baking soda
½ teaspoon salt
¾ cup low-fat buttermilk
¼ cup vegetable oil
1 teaspoon vanilla extract
1 large egg, lightly beaten
1 large egg white, lightly beaten
1½ teaspoons sugar

1. Preheat oven to 350°.
2. Combine 1 cup sugar and 2 tablespoons flour in a large bowl; stir well. Add plums, and toss well to coat. Spoon plum mixture into a 13- x 9-inch baking dish coated with cooking spray.
3. Combine 2 cups flour, baking powder, baking soda, and salt in a bowl; make a well in center of mixture. Combine ¾ cup sugar, buttermilk, and next 4 ingredients in a bowl; stir well. Add to flour mixture, stirring just until moist. Spoon batter over plum mixture, spreading gently to edges of dish. Sprinkle 1½ teaspoons sugar over batter.
4. Bake at 350° for 35 minutes or until golden. Cool on a wire rack. Serve cobbler warm or at room temperature. YIELD: 12 servings.

POINTS: 6; EXCHANGES: 3 Starch, 1 Fruit, ½ Fat; PER SERVING: CAL 307 (18% from fat); PRO 4.4; FAT 6.1g (sat 1g); CARB 60.7g; FIB 2.9g; CHOL 18mg; IRON 1.2mg; SOD 203mg; CALC 58mg

WHITE SANGRIA FIZZ

1 medium navel orange, sliced
1 lemon, sliced
1 lime, sliced
⅓ cup fresh orange juice
¼ cup sugar
1 (750-milliliter) bottle dry white wine
1½ cups seltzer, chilled

1. Combine first 5 ingredients in a pitcher; stir until sugar is nearly dissolved. Stir in wine. Chill 8 hours.
2. Add seltzer just before serving. Pour into glasses; divide fruit evenly. YIELD: 7 servings (serving size: 1 cup).

POINTS: 2; EXCHANGES: 1 Fat, ½ Starch, ½ Fruit; PER SERVING: CAL 121 (0% from fat); PRO 0.6g; FAT 0.1g (sat 0g); CARB 13.8g; FIB 1.1g; CHOL 0mg; IRON 0.6mg; SOD 20mg; CALC 25mg

END-OF-SUMMER FRUIT IN VANILLA SYRUP

1 cup fresh blueberries
1 cup fresh raspberries
1 cup peeled sliced peaches
½ cup water
¼ cup sugar
1 vanilla bean, split lengthwise

1. Combine fruit in a bowl.
2. Combine water and sugar in a saucepan. Scrape seeds from vanilla bean; add seeds and bean to sugar mixture. Bring to a boil. Pour boiling syrup over fruit; let cool. Cover; chill 8 hours. Discard bean. YIELD: 6 servings (serving size: ½ cup).

POINTS: 1; EXCHANGES: 1 Fruit; PER SERVING: CAL 68 (3% from fat); PRO 0.5g; FAT 0.2g (sat 0g); CARB 17.3g; FIB 2.6g; CHOL 0mg; IRON 0.2mg; SOD 2mg; CALC 7mg

Second Time Around

Don't throw out stale bread; give it new life in these scrumptious dishes.

Bread gone hard is not bread gone bad. Frugal pioneers planned for bread left at the end of the week. Yankee settlers soaked it with egg, sugar, and milk and made bread pudding; fishermen ladled seafood stew over crusty ends to soak up the broth. Try these satisfying dishes and you may find yourself hiding bread, in hopes it'll go stale before someone eats it.

PANZANELLA WITH TUNA

¼ cup extra-virgin olive oil
3 tablespoons red wine vinegar
½ teaspoon salt
¼ teaspoon pepper
12 cups (¾-inch) cubed stale French bread (about 12 ounces)
5 cups coarsely chopped tomato (about 2 pounds)
1¼ cups thinly sliced red onion, separated into rings
1 cup chopped fresh basil
⅓ cup chopped fresh mint
3 (6-ounce) cans albacore tuna in water, drained and flaked
Freshly ground pepper (optional)

1. Combine first 4 ingredients in a small bowl; stir well with a whisk.
2. Combine bread and next 4 ingredients in a large bowl; toss gently. Add vinaigrette and tuna; toss gently. Cover and let stand at least 10 minutes. Sprinkle each serving with freshly ground pepper, if desired.
YIELD: 8 servings (serving size: 2 cups).

POINTS: 6; **EXCHANGES:** 2 Very Lean Meat, 1½ Starch, 1½ Veg, 1½ Fat; **PER SERVING:** CAL 290 (31% from fat); PRO 19.5g; FAT 9.9g (sat 1.6g); CARB 31g; FIB 3g; CHOL 22mg; IRON 2.1mg; SOD 647mg; CALC 46mg

CHOCOLATE BREAD PUDDING

1⅔ cups skim milk, divided
3 tablespoons semisweet chocolate chips
1 (1-ounce) square unsweetened chocolate, chopped
½ cup sugar
½ teaspoon vanilla extract
2 large eggs, lightly beaten
4 cups (1-inch) cubed stale French bread (about 4 ounces)
Cooking spray

1. Preheat oven to 350°.
2. Combine 1 cup milk and chocolates in a microwave-safe bowl. Microwave at HIGH 3 minutes or until chocolate melts, stirring every minute.
3. Add remaining milk, sugar, vanilla, and eggs; stir well. Add bread cubes; toss well to coat. Let stand 10 minutes. Spoon mixture into an 8-inch square baking dish coated with cooking spray. Bake at 350° for 25 minutes or until set. YIELD: 9 servings.

POINTS: 3; **EXCHANGES:** 1½ Starch, ½ Fat; **PER SERVING:** CAL 145 (29% from fat); PRO 4.6g; FAT 4.4g (sat 2.1g); CARB 23.3g; FIB 0.5g; CHOL 48mg; IRON 0.8mg; SOD 121mg; CALC 75mg

MUSSELS EN BRODO

2 tablespoons extra-virgin olive oil
4 garlic cloves, minced
1 cup chopped fennel bulb
1 teaspoon fennel seeds
2 (14.5-ounce) cans diced tomatoes, undrained
¾ cup dry white wine
½ cup water
2 tablespoons lemon juice
1 tablespoon tomato paste
½ teaspoon salt
¼ teaspoon crushed red pepper
4 dozen mussels (about 4½ pounds), scrubbed and debearded
1 garlic clove, halved
4 (1-inch-thick) slices stale sourdough bread (about 5 ounces)

1. Heat oil in a large Dutch oven over medium-high heat until hot. Add minced garlic, and sauté 3 minutes. Add fennel and seeds; sauté 2 minutes. Add tomatoes and next 6 ingredients; bring to a boil. Reduce heat, and simmer 10 minutes. Add mussels, and bring to a boil. Cover, reduce heat, and simmer 10 minutes or until shells open. Remove from heat. Discard any unopened shells.
2. Preheat oven to 375°.
3. Rub garlic on both sides of bread slices; discard garlic. Place bread on baking sheet; bake at 375° for 5 minutes on each side or until toasted.
4. Place 1 toasted bread slice in each of 4 bowls; top evenly with mussels and tomato mixture. YIELD: 4 servings (serving size: 1 slice bread, 12 mussels, and 1¼ cups tomato mixture).

POINTS: 9; **EXCHANGES:** 3½ Veg, 3 Lean Meat, 1½ Starch, 1 Fat; **PER SERVING:** CAL 424 (28% from fat); PRO 33.7g; FAT 13g (sat 1.9g); CARB 43.8g; FIB 1.9g; CHOL 64mg; IRON 11.1mg; SOD 1,631mg; CALC 151mg

APPLE-CINNAMON PARFAITS

1 tablespoon butter or stick margarine
4 Golden Delicious apples (about 1½ pounds), peeled, cored, and cut into thin wedges
2 tablespoons brown sugar
¼ cup apple brandy or apple juice, divided
2 teaspoons lemon juice
1 teaspoon vanilla extract
¾ teaspoon ground cinnamon
¼ teaspoon ground nutmeg
¼ teaspoon salt
4 (1-ounce) slices stale cinnamon-raisin bread
1¼ cups frozen reduced-calorie whipped topping, thawed

1. Melt butter in a nonstick skillet over medium heat. Add apple, brown sugar, 2 tablespoons brandy, lemon juice, and next 4 ingredients; stir well. Cover and cook 4 minutes or until apples are tender, stirring occasionally. Remove from heat; let cool.
2. Brush remaining 2 tablespoons brandy evenly over both sides of bread; cut each slice into 6 cubes.
3. Arrange 3 bread cubes in the bottom of each of 4 wine or parfait glasses; top each with about 2 tablespoons whipped topping. Spread about ¼ cup apple mixture evenly over each parfait. Repeat layers, and top each parfait with 1 tablespoon whipped topping. YIELD: 4 servings.

POINTS: 5; **EXCHANGES:** 1½ Starch, 1½ Fruit, 1 Fat; **PER SERVING:** CAL 270 (24% from fat); PRO 3g; FAT 7.2g (sat 2.2g); CARB 46.8g; FIB 3.9g; CHOL 8mg; IRON 1.2mg; SOD 296mg; CALC 48mg

SAVORY SAUSAGE-BREAD CASSEROLE

1¼ cups drained chopped bottled roasted red bell peppers
1 cup skim milk
3 tablespoons red wine vinegar
½ teaspoon salt
2 large eggs, lightly beaten
6⅔ cups (1-inch) cubed stale French bread (about 8 ounces)
½ cup (2 ounces) shredded Asiago cheese, divided
½ pound fresh turkey breakfast sausage links
1 cup chopped onion
1 teaspoon dried oregano
½ teaspoon fennel seeds
⅛ teaspoon pepper
2 garlic cloves, minced
Cooking spray

1. Combine first 5 ingredients in a bowl; stir well. Add bread cubes and ¼ cup Asiago cheese; toss well to coat. Let mixture stand 30 minutes.
2. Preheat oven to 350°.
3. Remove turkey sausage from casings. Cook sausage, chopped onion, oregano, fennel seeds, pepper, and minced garlic in a nonstick skillet over medium-high heat until sausage is browned, stirring to crumble. Drain well. Add sausage mixture to bread mixture, and stir well.
4. Spoon into an 11- x 7-inch baking dish coated with cooking spray. Sprinkle with remaining ¼ cup cheese. Bake at 350° for 30 minutes. Let stand 10 minutes before serving. YIELD: 6 servings.

POINTS: 6; **EXCHANGES:** 1½ Starch, 1½ Med-fat Meat, ½ Veg; **PER SERVING:** CAL 256 (33% from fat); PRO 17g; FAT 9.4g (sat 1g); CARB 25.8g; FIB 1.8g; CHOL 104mg; IRON 2.2mg; SOD 1,210mg; CALC 228mg

PANE COTTO

6 cups (1-inch) cubed stale Italian bread (about 12 ounces)
½ cup dry white wine, divided
Cooking spray
1½ teaspoons olive oil
3 cups slivered onion
2 (10-ounce) packages frozen chopped spinach, unthawed
¼ cup chopped kalamata olives
¼ teaspoon salt
¼ teaspoon crushed red pepper
6 garlic cloves, minced
1 (6-ounce) package presliced provolone cheese slices

1. Place bread in a large bowl. Drizzle ¼ cup white wine over bread, tossing well to coat.
2. Coat a large nonstick skillet with cooking spray; add olive oil, and place over medium-high heat until hot. Add onion; sauté 5 minutes. Reduce heat to medium; sauté an additional 15 minutes or until golden brown. Remove onion from skillet and set aside.
3. Pour remaining ¼ cup wine into skillet. Add chopped spinach and next 4 ingredients; cover and cook over medium-high heat 8 minutes, stirring occasionally to break up spinach. Reduce heat to medium; add bread and onion. Cook, uncovered, 5 minutes, tossing gently. Top with provolone slices. Remove from heat; cover and let stand 5 minutes or until cheese melts. YIELD: 6 servings (serving size: about 1⅓ cups).

POINTS: 6; **EXCHANGES:** 1 Wh Milk, 1½ Veg, 1½ Starch; **PER SERVING:** CAL 321 (28% from fat); PRO 16.1g; FAT 10.1g (sat 5.2g); CARB 42.7g; FIB 5.6g; CHOL 20mg; IRON 3.8mg; SOD 819mg; CALC 354mg

Think Outside the Box

Seven flavorful pizza creations live up to America's innovative spirit.

American soldiers brought the concept of pizza back from Italy when they returned from World War II. But American pizzas have come a long way from the traditional Italian recipes. Our pizza is limited only by the imagination and what happens to be in the refrigerator. We offer seven quick, easy pizzas that embody that creative spirit.

FAJITA PIZZAS

6 ounces lean flank steak, thinly sliced
¾ cup green bell pepper strips
⅛ teaspoon salt
2 (10-inch) flour tortillas
Cooking spray
½ cup salsa
½ cup (2 ounces) shredded reduced-fat Mexican cheese blend (such as Sargento)

1. Preheat oven to 450°.
2. Place a small nonstick skillet over high heat until hot. Add steak, bell pepper, and salt; sauté 2 minutes or until steak is done.
3. Place 2 tortillas on a baking sheet. Coat both tortillas with cooking spray; top each with another tortilla. Spread salsa over top of each tortilla stack, leaving a ½-inch border. Divide beef mixture evenly between tortillas; sprinkle with cheese. Bake at 450° for 8 minutes or until cheese melts and edges of tortillas are crisp. YIELD: 2 servings.

POINTS: 9; **EXCHANGES:** 3 Lean Meat, 1½ Starch, 1 Wh Milk; **PER SERVING:** CAL 433 (34% from fat); PRO 32.6g; FAT 16.5g (sat 3.6g); CARB 37.6g; FIB 3.3g; CHOL 65mg; IRON 4.7mg; SOD 951mg; CALC 346mg

MEDITERRANEAN GARLIC PIZZA

1 (10-ounce) can refrigerated pizza crust dough
Cooking spray
6 tablespoons sun-dried tomato spread or sun-dried tomato paste
4 garlic cloves, thinly sliced
¾ cup (3 ounces) crumbled feta cheese with garlic and herbs
¼ cup chopped ripe olives

1. Preheat oven to 450°.
2. Unroll dough on a baking sheet coated with cooking spray; pat dough into a 10- x 8-inch rectangle. Spread sun-dried tomato spread over dough, leaving a ½-inch border.
3. Coat a small nonstick skillet with cooking spray, and place over medium heat until hot. Add garlic, and sauté 5 minutes or until browned (do not burn garlic or it will taste bitter). Sprinkle garlic, crumbled feta, and chopped olives evenly over tomato spread. Bake pizza at 450° for 12 minutes or until crust is lightly browned. YIELD: 4 servings.

POINTS: 7; **EXCHANGES:** 2 Starch, ½ Wh Milk, 1 Fat, ½ Veg; **PER SERVING:** CAL 297 (32% from fat); PRO 10g; FAT 10.4g (sat 3.3g); CARB 39.9g; FIB 1.2g; CHOL 19mg; IRON 8.3mg; SOD 967mg; CALC 133mg

PESTO PIZZA WITH SHRIMP, ASPARAGUS, AND PROSCIUTTO

Don't worry about using raw shrimp; it comes out perfectly cooked in the oven. If you can't find thin asparagus spears, use larger ones and cut them in half lengthwise. Substitute good-quality smoked ham for prosciutto.

1 (10-ounce) can refrigerated pizza crust dough
Cooking spray
¼ cup prepared pesto (such as Pesto Sanremo)
12 thin asparagus spears, cut into 2-inch pieces
½ pound medium shrimp, peeled and deveined
2 ounces very thinly sliced prosciutto, chopped

1. Preheat oven to 425°.
2. Unroll pizza crust dough on a large baking sheet coated with cooking spray; pat dough into a 14- x 9-inch rectangle. Bake at 425° for 5 minutes.
3. Spread prepared pesto over dough, leaving a ½-inch border. Top with asparagus spears, shrimp, and prosciutto. Bake pizza at 425° for 10 minutes or until shrimp are done and crust is lightly browned. YIELD: 6 servings.

POINTS: 5; **EXCHANGES:** 1½ Starch, 1 Lean Meat, 1 Fat, ½ Veg; **PER SERVING:** CAL 235 (32% from fat); PRO 14.1g; FAT 8.4g (sat 1.7g); CARB 27.2g; FIB 2.6g; CHOL 45mg; IRON 3.8mg; SOD 555mg; CALC 105mg

SMOKY HAM-AND-BEAN CORN BREAD PIZZAS

1 (10-ounce) package frozen chopped broccoli, thawed and drained
1⅔ cups diced lean smoked ham (about ½ pound)
1 (15-ounce) can navy beans, rinsed and drained
¼ teaspoon pepper
1 (11.5-ounce) can refrigerated corn bread twists dough
Cooking spray
1 cup shredded reduced-fat sharp cheddar cheese

1. Preheat oven to 425°.
2. Pat broccoli dry with paper towels. Combine broccoli, ham, beans, and pepper. Stir well; set aside.
3. Separate dough into 8 slices. Place 1 slice on a baking sheet coated with cooking spray, and roll into a 5½-inch circle. Repeat with remaining slices. Place ½ cup ham mixture onto each crust; sprinkle evenly with cheese. Bake at 425° for 9 minutes or until crusts are golden. YIELD: 8 servings.

POINTS: 6; EXCHANGES: 2 Starch, 1½ Very Lean Meat, 1 Fat; PER SERVING: CAL 266 (35% from fat); PRO 16.7g; FAT 10.5g (sat 3.6g); CARB 27.5g; FIB 2.5g; CHOL 24.5mg; IRON 2.5mg; SOD 940mg; CALC 164mg

FRENCH BREAD CAPRESE PIZZA

1 (16-ounce) loaf French bread
1½ cups tomato and basil pasta sauce (such as Barilla basilico)
2 tablespoons capers
1 (6-ounce) package presliced part-skim mozzarella cheese slices
24 fresh basil leaves

1. Preheat oven to 425°.
2. Cut bread loaf in half horizontally; spread pasta sauce evenly over cut sides of each piece of bread. Sprinkle capers evenly over sauce, and top evenly with cheese slices.
3. Place pizza on a baking sheet, and bake at 425° for 10 minutes or until cheese melts. Arrange basil leaves on top of cheese. Cut pizza into 12 equal portions. YIELD: 6 servings (serving size: 2 pieces).

POINTS: 6; EXCHANGES: 3 Starch, 1 Med-fat Meat; PER SERVING: CAL 316 (21% from fat); PRO 14.8g; FAT 7.4g (sat 3.5g); CARB 46.7g; FIB 3.3g; CHOL 17mg; IRON 2.1mg; SOD 1,015mg; CALC 247mg

ROASTED PEPPER, CHICKEN, AND GOAT CHEESE PIZZA

1 (12-ounce) bottle roasted red bell peppers, undrained
Cooking spray
1 cup thinly sliced shallots
1 (16-ounce) loaf French bread
2 (6-ounce) packages Italian-flavored ready-to-eat skinned, boned chicken breast strips (such as Louis Rich)
1 (3.5-ounce) package goat cheese, crumbled

1. Preheat oven to 425°.
2. Drain bell peppers, reserving liquid. Chop bell peppers; set aside.
3. Coat a medium nonstick skillet with cooking spray; place over medium-high heat until hot. Add shallots; sauté 5 minutes or until lightly browned. Reduce heat to medium; add bell peppers and reserved liquid. Cook 5 minutes or until most of liquid evaporates.

4. Cut bread loaf in half horizontally; place on a baking sheet. Spread shallot mixture evenly over cut sides of each piece of bread; top with chicken strips and goat cheese. Bake at 425° for 10 minutes. Cut into 6 equal portions. YIELD: 6 servings.

POINTS: 8; EXCHANGES: 3 Starch, 1 Lean Meat, 1 Med-fat Meat, ½ Veg; PER SERVING: CAL 388 (23% from fat); PRO 25.2g; FAT 10g (sat 4.7g); CARB 48.9g; FIB 3.9g; CHOL 50mg; IRON 3.9mg; SOD 1,101mg; CALC 122mg

BBQ CHICKEN-AND-CORN PIZZA

1 (1-pound) package Italian cheese-flavored pizza crust (such as Boboli)
½ cup barbecue sauce (such as Bull's-Eye original), divided
1 (4.69-ounce) package ready-to-eat roasted skinned, boned chicken breasts, chopped (such as Tyson)
½ cup fresh corn kernels (1 ear)
1¼ cups (5 ounces) shredded Monterey Jack cheese

1. Preheat oven to 450°.
2. Place crust on a baking sheet; spread ¼ cup sauce over crust. Combine remaining ¼ cup barbecue sauce and chicken in a bowl; stir well. Spoon chicken mixture over crust; top evenly with corn and cheese. Bake at 450° for 10 minutes or until cheese melts. YIELD: 6 servings.

POINTS: 8; EXCHANGES: 2 Starch, 1 L-F Milk, 1 Med-fat Meat; PER SERVING: CAL 366 (31% from fat); PRO 22.8g; FAT 12.5g (sat 6.1g); CARB 38.9g; FIB 2g; CHOL 44mg; IRON 2.6mg; SOD 862mg; CALC 263mg

The Four O'Clock Fix

Get a handle on your late-afternoon cravings.

You know the feeling: Those cravings kick in like clockwork each afternoon, and you need your four o'clock fix.

An afternoon snack isn't a bad thing—unless it's a pile of chips or a hunk of chocolate. We talked with experts to learn what causes afternoon cravings, how to control them, and how to use them to your advantage.

THE FIX FIXATION. Sometimes real hunger sparks snacking. "It's natural to feel hungry every four to five hours," says Chris Rosenbloom, Ph.D., R.D., associate professor of nutrition at Georgia State University.

Psychological factors also create cravings. According to John Foreyt, Ph.D., director of the Nutrition Research Clinic at Baylor College of Medicine, "When you came home from school, chances are you were greeted with an afternoon snack." He says, "we're conditioned to associate snacking with that time of day. It's a difficult habit to break." Afternoon eating also creates a diversion from stress or boredom.

DOES IT HELP OR HURT? No one thinks that loading up each afternoon will help you lose weight. But a sensible snack can help you stick with a weight-loss plan.

Research results are mixed about snacking's effect on weight control. Some people who snack eat less later, but for others, snacking triggers overeating. It depends on the individual, so you want to figure out how snacking affects you.

A snack can aid weight loss by providing fuel for an after-work exercise session. If you work out on an empty stomach, you may feel tired or skip the workout altogether. A small, high-carbohydrate snack is enough for a pre-exercise energy boost. Try a few graham crackers or half of a bagel with a glass of water.

CONQUER CRAVINGS. Make snacking a mindful activity, Foreyt says. For a few days, write down what you snack on, your hunger level, and how you feel. "You'll learn if you're eating from emotion or hunger," says Foreyt. "List alternatives, such as a brisk walk, to help you cope without food at that time of day."

The body absorbs carbohydrates such as grains, fruits, and vegetables, in 30 to 60 minutes. If you're hungry just before dinner, a few pretzels will suffice. If dinner is hours away, add protein and fat to keep you satisfied longer. A few crackers with a glaze of peanut butter should do the trick.

The Snack Finder

In their book *Snacking Habits for Healthy Living* (John Wiley & Sons, 1997) the American Dietetic Association (ADA) offers these ideas for snacks, all at 150 calories or less. Calorie counts are from *Bowes & Church's Food Values of Portions Commonly Used* by Jean A.T. Pennington, Ph.D. (Lippincott-Raven, 1997).

CHEWY	Calories
Chewing gum, 1 stick	10
Fig bars, 2	110
Fruit leather roll-ups, 2	110
Raisins, ¼ cup	115

CRUNCHY	Calories
Apple, 1 medium	80
Baby carrots, raw, 1 cup	60
Popcorn, microwave, light, 4 cups	100
Tortilla chips, baked, 1 ounce	110

SWEET	Calories
Angel food cake, 1/12 of 10" cake	140
Fruit cocktail, 1 cup	115
Pudding, ½ cup	150
Vanilla wafers, 8	140

SALTY	Calories
Potato chips, baked, 1 ounce	110
Pretzels, 1 ounce	110
Saltine crackers, 5	60

HOT	Calories
Herbal tea	0
Hot chocolate, made with water from mix, 6 ounces	105
Oatmeal, apple-and-cinnamon flavor, 1 packet	125
Soup, vegetable, 1 cup	140

COLD	Calories
Frozen banana, 1 medium	105
Low-fat frozen yogurt, ½ cup	110
Low-fat ice cream, ½ cup	120
Raspberries, 1 cup	60
Sorbet, ½ cup	110
Strawberries, 1 cup	45

THIRST-QUENCHING	Calories
Frozen juice bar, 1	75
Grape juice spritzer, 1 cup juice plus 1 cup sparkling water	130
Mineral, sparkling, or tap water	0
Popsicle, 2-ounce bar	75

Tomato Techniques

Make good use of juicy, vine-ripened tomatoes with these three recipes. Step-by-step tips at right show how to peel and seed them.

BLT PASTA SALAD

3⅔ cups cooked large elbow
    macaroni (about 8 ounces
    uncooked), cooked without
    salt or fat
  4 cups peeled seeded, coarsely
    chopped tomato (about 2½
    pounds)
  4 hickory-smoked bacon slices,
    cooked and crumbled
  3 cups prepackaged very thinly
    sliced iceberg lettuce (such as
    Fresh Express "Shreds")
  ½ cup fat-free mayonnaise
  ⅓ cup low-fat sour cream
  1 tablespoon Dijon mustard
  1 teaspoon sugar
  2 teaspoons cider vinegar
  ½ teaspoon salt
  ½ teaspoon pepper

1. Combine first 4 ingredients in a large bowl; toss gently. Combine mayonnaise and next 6 ingredients; stir well. Add dressing to salad; toss gently. Serve immediately. YIELD: 10 servings (serving size: 1 cup).

POINTS: 3; **EXCHANGES:** 1½ Starch, 1 Veg;
PER SERVING: CAL 149 (18% from fat);
PRO 4.7g; FAT 2.9g (sat 0.7g); CARB 26.2g;
FIB 1.4g; CHOL 5mg; IRON 0.7mg;
SOD 367mg; CALC 18mg

STEP-BY-STEP

1. Cut a shallow "X" at the opposite end from the stem on each tomato, using a small sharp paring knife.

2. Add tomatoes at once to a large pan of boiling water; begin timing immediately for 30 seconds or until the skin begins to split at "X."

3. Remove tomatoes from water, using a slotted spoon; transfer to a bowl of ice water immediately to halt the cooking process. Drain tomatoes when cool to the touch.

4. Using your fingers or a paring knife, peel the skin in strips, much like peeling a banana. The skin should peel easily, but should not remove much flesh with it.

5. Using a sharp chef's knife, cut each tomato in half crosswise.

6. Using your finger or the handle end of a small spoon, scoop out the seeds.

FRESH TOMATO CHUTNEY SANDWICHES

1 cup diced red bell pepper
½ cup water
¼ cup firmly packed brown sugar
¼ cup cider vinegar
2 tablespoons chopped onion
1 teaspoon mustard seeds
⅛ teaspoon salt
⅛ teaspoon ground red pepper
2 cups peeled, seeded, chopped tomato
4 (6-inch) pita bread rounds, cut in half
4 ounces thinly sliced fresh mozzarella cheese
2 cups trimmed arugula or torn curly leaf lettuce

1. Combine first 8 ingredients in a medium saucepan; bring to a boil. Reduce heat, and simmer, uncovered, 35 minutes or until thick, stirring occasionally. Remove from heat; stir in tomato. Let cool to room temperature.
2. Fill each pita half with ½ ounce cheese and ¼ cup arugula. Spoon ¼ cup tomato chutney into each pita half, using a slotted spoon. YIELD: 4 servings (serving size: 2 stuffed pita halves).

NOTE: Fresh mozzarella may be labeled "Italian style." It's softer than regular mozzarella and has a sweet, delicate flavor. Look for fresh mozzarella in Italian markets, cheese shops, and some supermarkets. You can substitute regular mozzarella but expect a change in flavor and texture.

POINTS: 7; EXCHANGES: 3 Starch, 1½ Veg, 1 Fat; PER SERVING: CAL 331 (21% from fat); PRO 12.5g; FAT 7.7g (sat 4g); CARB 54.8g; FIB 3.2g; CHOL 22mg; IRON 2.9mg; SOD 502mg; CALC 238mg

SEAFOOD GRILL WITH GARDEN TOMATO SAUCE

¾ pound mahimahi or other firm white fish fillet
3 tablespoons fresh lime juice
1 tablespoon olive oil
½ teaspoon pepper
¼ teaspoon salt
⅛ teaspoon chili powder
⅛ teaspoon garlic powder
18 large shrimp (about 9 ounces), peeled and deveined
3 cups peeled seeded, coarsely chopped tomato
½ cup chopped yellow squash
¼ cup chopped fresh banana peppers or pepperoncini peppers
¼ cup chopped onion
¼ cup chopped fresh cilantro
1 tablespoon fresh lime juice
½ teaspoon sugar
½ teaspoon chili powder
¼ teaspoon salt
¼ teaspoon pepper
⅛ teaspoon ground red pepper
Cooking spray

1. Cut fish into 6 portions. Combine next 6 ingredients in a zip-top plastic bag. Add fish and shrimp; seal bag. Refrigerate 30 minutes to 2 hours.
2. Combine tomato and next 10 ingredients; toss gently. Set aside.
3. Remove fish and shrimp from bag; discard marinade. Place on grill rack coated with cooking spray; grill 4 minutes on each side or until shrimp is done and fish flakes when tested with a fork. YIELD: 6 servings (serving size: 2 ounces fish, 2 ounces shrimp, and ½ cup tomato mixture).

POINTS: 3; EXCHANGES: 2½ Very Lean Meat, 1½ Veg, ½ Fat; PER SERVING: CAL 150 (23% from fat); PRO 20.9g; FAT 3.9g (sat 0.6g); CARB 8.5g; FIB 1.8g; CHOL 107mg, IRON 2.5mg; SOD 324mg; CALC 35mg

NUTRITION

Being Fiber Fit

Dietary fiber is an important component of a healthy diet. And many high-fiber foods are packed with beneficial vitamins and minerals. This slow-cooker recipe is an easy way to get a good start on the daily recommended intake of 25 to 30 grams of fiber.

PORK-AND-BLACK BEAN CHILI

1 pound lean boned pork loin roast
1 (16-ounce) jar thick-and-chunky salsa
2 (15-ounce) cans no-salt-added black beans, undrained
1 cup chpped yellow bell pepper
¾ cup chopped onion
1 teaspoon ground cumin
1 teaspoon chili powder
1 teaspoon dried oregano
¼ cup fat-free sour cream

1. Trim fat from pork; cut pork into 1-inch pieces. Combine pork and next 7 ingredients in a 4-quart electric slow cooker; stir well. Cover with lid; cook on low-heat setting for 8 hours or until pork is tender. Ladle chili into bowls; top with sour cream. YIELD: 4 servings (serving size: 2 cups chili and 1 tablespoon sour cream).

POINTS: 6; EXCHANGES: 4 Very Lean Meat, 2½ Starch, 1 Veg, ½ Fat; PER SERVING: CAL 379 (22% from fat); PRO 36.7g; FAT 9.4g; (sat 2.8g); CARB 45.4g; FIB 14.2g; CHOL 62mg; IRON 6mg; SOD 405mg; CALC 136mg

October

Retro Cakes

Think Mom spent hours baking those homemade cakes?
Take a closer look—you might be surprised.

Who has time to bake from scratch these days? Even in the 1950s, when women spent more time in the kitchen, cooks found ways to simplify. We revisit 10 cakes of that era, which may surprise you with their ease of preparation. You'll be able to say truthfully, "I made it from scratch." (Note: For successfully lightened cakes, it's critical to measure flour precisely. Turn to page 137 to learn the proper method for measuring flour.)

SOUR CREAM FUDGE CAKE WITH MOCHA GLAZE

The stronger coffee is brewed, the more intense the flavor is in this cake. You may also dissolve 1 1/2 teaspoons instant coffee granules in 1/4 cup hot water for strong coffee flavor.

Cooking spray
1 teaspoon all-purpose flour
2 (1-ounce) squares unsweetened chocolate, coarsely chopped
1 1/2 cups sifted cake flour
1 1/2 cups sugar
3 tablespoons unsweetened cocoa
1 teaspoon baking soda
1/4 teaspoon salt
1/4 cup butter or stick margarine, softened
1 (8-ounce) carton 30%-less-fat sour cream (such as Breakstone)
1/4 cup hot brewed coffee
1 teaspoon vanilla extract
1 large egg
Mocha Glaze

1. Preheat oven to 350°.
2. Coat a 13- x 9-inch baking pan with cooking spray, and dust with 1 teaspoon all-purpose flour; set aside.
3. Place coarsely chopped chocolate in the top of a double boiler. Cook over simmering water 5 minutes or until chocolate melts, stirring until smooth. Remove from heat; set aside.
4. Combine cake flour and next 4 ingredients in a large bowl. Add butter and sour cream; beat at low speed of a mixer 30 seconds or until blended. Beat at high speed 2 minutes. Add melted chocolate, coffee, vanilla, and egg; beat at low speed until blended. Beat at high speed 2 minutes.
5. Pour batter into prepared pan. Bake at 350° for 30 minutes or until a wooden pick inserted in center comes out clean.
6. Let cool completely in pan on a wire rack. Spread Mocha Glaze over cooled cake. YIELD: 15 servings.

POINTS: 6; EXCHANGES: 3 Starch, 1 Fat;
PER SERVING: CAL 245 (28% from fat);
PRO 2.9g; FAT 7.6g (sat 4.5g); CARB 43.4g;
FIB 0.1g; CHOL 29mg; IRON 1.6mg;
SOD 166mg; CALC 27mg

MOCHA GLAZE:

1 1/2 cups sifted powdered sugar
3 tablespoons unsweetened cocoa
3 tablespoons hot brewed coffee

1. Combine all ingredients in a small bowl; stir until smooth.
YIELD: about 2/3 cup.

BASIC WHITE LAYER CAKE

Cooking spray
1 1/3 cups 1% low-fat milk, divided
2 teaspoons vanilla extract
1 large egg
1 large egg yolk
2 1/3 cups sifted cake flour
1 1/4 cups sugar
1 tablespoon baking powder
1/2 teaspoon salt
6 tablespoons butter or stick margarine, softened
Rich Chocolate Frosting (page 137)

1. Preheat oven to 350°.
2. Coat 2 (9-inch) round cake pans with cooking spray; line bottoms of pans with wax paper. Coat wax paper with cooking spray; set aside.
3. Combine 1/3 cup milk, vanilla, egg, and egg yolk in a bowl; stir with a whisk until well blended. Set aside.
4. Combine flour and next 3 ingredients; stir. Add 1 cup milk and butter; beat at low speed until blended. Beat at medium 1 1/2 minutes. Add egg mixture in thirds, beating 20 seconds after each addition or until blended.
5. Pour batter into prepared pans. Bake at 350° for 23 minutes or until a wooden pick inserted in center comes out clean. Let cool in pans 10 minutes on wire racks; remove from pans. Let cool completely on racks.
6. Place 1 cake layer on a plate; spread with 1/4 cup Rich Chocolate Frosting. Top with second cake layer; spread 1/3 cup frosting over top. Spread remaining 3/4 cup frosting around cake sides.
YIELD: 16 servings.

POINTS: 6; EXCHANGES: 3 1/2 Starch, 1/2 Fat;
PER SERVING: CAL 267 (22% from fat);
PRO 3.3g; FAT 6.4g (sat 3.7g); CARB 50g;
FIB 0g; CHOL 40mg; IRON 1.5mg;
SOD 236mg; CALC 84mg

DATE-NUT CAKE WITH FRESH ORANGE GLAZE

Don't substitute prechopped dates here. They're coated with date sugar and do not perform well in this recipe. Use scissors to chop whole dates.

Cooking spray
- 1 tablespoon all-purpose flour
- 1 (10-ounce) package whole pitted dates, chopped
- 1 teaspoon baking soda
- 1 cup boiling water
- ¾ cup granulated sugar
- 1 tablespoon butter or stick margarine, softened
- ¼ cup chopped walnuts
- 1 teaspoon vanilla extract
- 2 large egg whites
- ⅓ cup chopped dried apricots
- 1½ cups all-purpose flour
- ¼ teaspoon salt
- ¾ cup sifted powdered sugar
- ½ teaspoon grated orange rind
- 1½ teaspoons fresh orange juice

1. Coat a 9- x 5-inch loafpan with cooking spray, and dust with 1 tablepoon flour; set aside.
2. Combine dates and baking soda. Pour boiling water over date mixture; stir well. Let stand 45 minutes.
3. Preheat oven to 325°.
4. Combine granulated sugar and butter in a large bowl; beat at medium speed of a mixer 1 minute. Add walnuts, vanilla, and egg whites; beat well. Add date mixture and apricots; beat well. Combine 1½ cups flour and salt; add to date mixture, beating until blended.
5. Pour batter into prepared pan. Bake at 325° for 1 hour and 15 minutes or until a wooden pick inserted in center comes out clean.

Let cool in pan 10 minutes on a wire rack; remove from pan. Let cool completely on wire rack.
6. Combine powdered sugar, rind, and orange juice, stirring well. Spoon glaze over cake. YIELD: 10 servings.

POINTS: 5; **EXCHANGES:** 2½ Starch, 1½ Fruit; **PER SERVING:** CAL 291 (11% from fat); PRO 4.2g; FAT 3.5g (sat 0.9g); CARB 63.9g; FIB 3.1g; CHOL 3mg; IRON 1.6mg; SOD 212mg; CALC 18mg

SOUR CREAM COFFEECAKE

Our test kitchens found that light butter works best in this tender cake. Avoid the temptation to substitute margarine. The end result will not be as good.

Cooking spray
- ¼ cup all-purpose flour
- ¼ cup firmly packed brown sugar
- 3 tablespoons finely chopped pecans
- ½ teaspoon ground cinnamon
- 1 tablespoon light stick butter (such as Land O' Lakes), melted
- 1 (8-ounce) carton fat-free sour cream, divided
- 1 teaspoon vanilla extract
- 1 large egg
- 1 large egg white
- 1⅔ cups sifted cake flour
- 1 cup granulated sugar
- 1 teaspoon baking soda
- ½ teaspoon baking powder
- ¼ teaspoon salt
- 7 tablespoons light butter (such as Land O' Lakes), softened

1. Preheat oven to 350°.
2. Coat a 9-inch springform pan with cooking spray; line bottom of pan with wax paper. Coat wax paper with cooking spray; set aside.

3. Combine all-purpose flour and next 3 ingredients in a bowl. Add 1 tablespoon melted butter; toss with a fork (streusel will be crumbly). Set aside.
4. Combine ¼ cup sour cream, vanilla, egg, and egg white in a small bowl; stir well with a whisk. Set sour cream-egg mixture aside.
5. Combine cake flour and next 4 ingredients in a bowl; stir well. Add remaining sour cream and 7 tablespoons butter; beat at low speed of a mixer until moist. Beat at medium speed 1½ minutes. Add sour cream-egg mixture in thirds, beating 10 seconds after each addition.
6. Pour batter into prepared pan. Sprinkle streusel evenly over batter to edges of pan. Bake at 350° for 35 minutes or until a wooden pick inserted in center comes out clean. Let cool completely on a wire rack. Remove sides of pan before serving. YIELD: 10 servings.

POINTS: 5; **EXCHANGES:** 3 Starch, ½ Fat; **PER SERVING:** CAL 248 (25% from fat); PRO 4.8g; FAT 7g (sat 3.5g); CARB 42.3g; FIB 0.3g; CHOL 37mg; IRON 1.6mg; SOD 243mg; CALC 21mg

HOT MILK CAKE

- ¾ cup 1% low-fat milk
- ⅓ cup butter or stick margarine
- 1¾ cups all-purpose flour
- 1¾ cups sugar
- 2 teaspoons baking powder
- ¼ teaspoon salt
- 2 teaspoons vanilla extract
- 2 large eggs, lightly beaten
- 2 large egg whites, lightly beaten
Cooking spray
Lemon Sauce
Fresh strawberries (optional)

1. Preheat oven to 325°.

2. Combine low-fat milk and butter in a small saucepan. Place over medium-low heat, and cook until butter melts, stirring occasionally.

3. Combine flour and next 3 ingredients in a large bowl; stir well. Add milk mixture, stirring well. Add vanilla, eggs, and egg whites; stir until well blended. Pour batter into a 13- x 9-inch baking pan coated with cooking spray.

4. Bake at 325° for 35 minutes or until a wooden pick inserted in center comes out clean. Let cool in pan at least 45 minutes on a wire rack. Serve warm or at room temperature with Lemon Sauce. Garnish with strawberries, if desired. YIELD: 15 servings (serving size: 1 slice cake and 4 teaspoons Lemon Sauce).

POINTS: 5; EXCHANGES: 2½ Starch, ½ Fat; PER SERVING: CAL 222 (22% from fat); PRO 3.3g; FAT 5.4g (sat 3.1g); CARB 40.5g; FIB 0.4g; CHOL 42mg; IRON 0.9mg; SOD 191mg; CALC 59mg

LEMON SAUCE:
 1 cup water
 ⅓ cup sugar
 1 tablespoon cornstarch
 ⅛ teaspoon salt
 2½ tablespoons fresh lemon juice
 1½ teaspoons butter or stick margarine

1. Combine first 4 ingredients in a small saucepan; stir with a whisk until well blended. Bring to a boil, and cook 2 minutes, stirring constantly. Pour into a bowl. Add lemon juice and butter, stirring until butter melts. YIELD: 1¼ cups.

TRADITIONAL MARBLE CAKE

The marble cake you're used to is most likely a mixture of vanilla and chocolate cake. But originally, the vanilla cake batter was swirled with ribbons of spiced batter. One taste will make you wonder why it ever changed.

Cooking spray
 1 tablespoon cake flour
 2 cups sugar
 ½ cup butter or stick margarine, softened
 2 large eggs
 2 large egg whites
 2¾ cups sifted cake flour
 2¾ teaspoons baking powder
 ½ teaspoon salt
 1 cup 1% low-fat milk
 1½ teaspoons vanilla extract
 2 teaspoons ground cinnamon
 ½ teaspoon ground cloves
 ½ teaspoon ground nutmeg

1. Preheat oven to 350°.

2. Coat a 10-inch tube pan with cooking spray, and dust with 1 tablespoon flour; set aside.

3. Combine sugar and butter in a bowl; beat at low speed of a mixer 2 minutes or until well blended. Add eggs and egg whites, one at a time, beating just until blended after each addition. Combine 2¾ cups flour, baking powder, and salt; stir well. Add flour mixture to creamed mixture, alternately with milk, beginning and ending with flour mixture. Add vanilla, beating until blended.

4. Remove 1 cup batter to a small bowl; stir in cinnamon, cloves, and nutmeg. Spoon remaining vanilla batter into prepared tube pan. Dollop spice batter over vanilla

batter. Swirl batters together with a knife.

5. Bake at 350° for 45 minutes or until a wooden pick inserted in center comes out clean. Let cool in pan 10 minutes on a wire rack; remove from pan. Let cool completely on wire rack. YIELD: 12 servings.

POINTS: 7; EXCHANGES: 3½ Starch, 1 Fat; PER SERVING: CAL 317 (26% from fat); PRO 4.5g; FAT 9g (sat 5.2g); CARB 55g; FIB 0.1g; CHOL 58mg; IRON 2.3mg; SOD 319mg; CALC 103mg

LEMON POPPY SEED CAKE

(pictured on page 135)

Cooking spray
 1½ tablespoons all-purpose flour
 1½ cups fat-free milk
 ⅔ cup vegetable oil
 2 tablespoons grated lemon rind
 1½ teaspoons vanilla extract
 ½ teaspoon almond extract
 2 large eggs
 1 large egg white
 3 cups all-purpose flour
 2¼ cups sugar
 2½ tablespoons poppy seeds
 1½ teaspoons baking powder
 ¾ teaspoon salt
Lemon Glaze

1. Preheat oven to 350°.

2. Coat a 10-inch Bundt pan with cooking spray, and dust with 1½ tablespoons flour.

3. Combine milk and next 6 ingredients in a bowl. Combine 3 cups flour and next 4 ingredients; add to milk mixture, beating at medium speed of a mixer 2 minutes.

continued

4. Pour batter into prepared pan. Bake at 350° for 54 minutes or until a wooden pick inserted in center comes out clean. Let cool in pan 10 minutes on a wire rack. Remove from pan; and place on wire rack. Brush Lemon Glaze evenly over warm cake; let cool completely. YIELD: 18 servings.

POINTS: 6; EXCHANGES: 3 Starch, 1 Fat; **PER SERVING:** CAL 281 (30% from fat); PRO 4g; FAT 9.4g (sat 1.7g); CARB 45.9g; FIB 0.7g; CHOL 25mg; IRON 1.3mg; SOD 160mg; CALC 73mg

LEMON GLAZE:
¼ cup sugar
¼ cup fresh lemon juice

1. Combine sugar and lemon juice in a small saucepan. Place over medium heat; cook 3 minutes or until sugar dissolves, stirring occasionally. YIELD: about 7 tablespoons.

WARM MOLASSES CAKE WITH CARAMEL GLAZE

⅔ cup firmly packed brown sugar
¼ cup butter or stick margarine, softened
1 large egg
½ cup molasses
2 cups all-purpose flour
1¾ teaspoons baking powder
¾ teaspoon ground cinnamon
½ teaspoon ground allspice
¼ teaspoon salt
½ cup fat-free milk
Cooking spray
Caramel Glaze

1. Preheat oven to 375°.
2. Combine brown sugar and butter in a large bowl; beat at medium speed of a mixer 5 minutes or until well blended. Add egg; beat well. Add molasses; beat well. Combine flour and next 4 ingredients; stir well. Add flour mixture to creamed mixture, alternately with milk, beginning and ending with flour mixture.
3. Pour batter into a 9-inch square baking pan coated with cooking spray. Bake at 375° for 27 minutes or until a wooden pick inserted in center comes out clean. Let cool in pan 45 minutes on a wire rack. Spread Caramel Glaze evenly over cake in pan. Serve warm or at room temperature. YIELD: 12 servings.

POINTS: 6; EXCHANGES: 3½ Starch, ½ Fat; **PER SERVING:** CAL 265 (22% from fat); PRO 3.2g; FAT 6.4g (sat 3.8g); CARB 49.7g; FIB 0.6g; CHOL 34mg; IRON 2.3mg; SOD 231mg; CALC 112mg

CARAMEL GLAZE:
⅔ cup firmly packed brown sugar
2 tablespoons butter or stick margarine
2 tablespoons fat-free milk
⅛ teaspoon salt

1. Combine all ingredients in a saucepan. Place over medium heat; cook until butter melts and mixture is smooth, stirring constantly with a whisk. Remove from heat; let cool slightly. Spread evenly over Warm Molasses Cake. YIELD: ⅔ cup.

APPLESAUCE CAKE

1¾ cups unsweetened applesauce
1¾ cups granulated sugar
9 tablespoons butter or stick margarine, softened
3 cups all-purpose flour
2 teaspoons baking powder
2 teaspoons ground cinnamon
½ teaspoon ground allspice
¼ teaspoon baking soda
¼ teaspoon salt
½ cup raisins
Cooking spray
2 teaspoons powdered sugar

1. Preheat oven to 325°.
2. Place applesauce in a microwave-safe bowl. Microwave at MEDIUM (50% power) 2½ minutes or until warm; set aside.
3. Combine granulated sugar and butter; beat at medium speed of a mixer 5 minutes or until well blended. Add warm applesauce; beat well. Combine flour and next 5 ingredients; stir well. Add to applesauce mixture; beat until well blended. Stir in raisins.
4. Pour batter into a 10-inch Bundt pan coated with cooking spray. Bake at 325° for 50 minutes or until a wooden pick inserted in center comes out clean. Let cool in pan 10 minutes on a wire rack; remove from pan. Let cool completely on wire rack. Sift powdered sugar over cooled cake. YIELD: 16 servings.

POINTS: 5; EXCHANGES: 2½ Starch, ½ Fruit, ½ Fat; **PER SERVING:** CAL 248 (24% from fat); PRO 2.5g; FAT 6.7g (sat 4.1g); CARB 45.6g; FIB 1.2g; CHOL 17mg; IRON 1.3mg; SOD 157mg; CALC 34mg

New Year, New Life

JOANNA KAY • **HEIGHT** 5'7" • **BEFORE** 260 LBS. • **AFTER** 166 LBS.

Hint: Find more healthful treats that satisfy your cravings for dessert. "I never had sorbet before, but now I love it—and Jello."

In December 1997, a friend asked 27-year-old Joanna Kay to be a bridesmaid in her wedding.

"There was no way I'd fit in the dress she picked; we had to buy a size 28 dress in the same color, so I could stand with the bridal party," Joanna says. That shopping trip, plus New Year's Eve and her upcoming 10-year high school reunion, made Joanna take stock of her life.

"I had a great job (as a high school guidance counselor) and a great apartment; everything was great except my weight. So, I made a New Year's resolution to lose it and was serious this time," she says.

Joanna went to Weight Watchers and set an ambitious goal to achieve her goal weight in a year. That day, she cleaned out the refrigerator and cupboards. "I wanted it to be hard to cheat. I'd have to get dressed, get in the car, and pay for something if I caved in to a craving," she says.

For the first time, Joanna was reading nutrition labels and buying low-fat, high-fiber foods. She established a Sunday grocery shopping routine: She made a list (also a first), spent more time in the produce section, then came home and chopped fruits and vegetables for the week. She put snacks in containers and wrote **POINT** values on the lids. Having a week of meals at her fingertips curbed the impulse to stop for a burger and fries after work.

Joanna also began walking an hour a day. "I'd walk with my portable stereo, and I told myself I could buy a new CD every week. That kept me going," she says. "I used to avoid going to the city with friends. I knew we'd walk a lot and I'd get tired. Now I like it, because I get my walking done and have fun, too."

By June, Joanna had lost 50 pounds but wanted to lose 75 pounds by December. She also went back to the bridal shop to see if she could wear the dress the other bridesmaids would wear at her friend's wedding. To her delight, she could.

"I told my friend right away," Joanna says. "She didn't care what I wore. She just wanted me to be there, even if I wore sweatpants. But it was an accomplishment for me, a really important moment."

By December, Joanna had dropped 75 pounds and then some, and now she is down to 166. "I can shop wherever I want," she says. "And I wear rings every day. I always wanted to, but I could never get them on my finger."

"I set a goal and achieved it. I think I've really been a good role model."

New clothes and jewelry offer motivation, but not as much as the teenagers Joanna counsels at work. "They have seen the transformation," she says. "I set a goal and achieved it. I think I've really been a good role model."

Cornmeal-Pecan
Pancakes, page 118

Lemon Poppy Seed Cake,
page 131

Very Berry Summer Fruit
Compote, page 99

Braised Beef With Prunes and
Caramelized Onions, page 138

Salmon With Moroccan
Tomato Relish, page 83

DEVIL'S FOOD CAKE

Cooking spray
  2 teaspoons cake flour
1¾ cups sugar
  ¾ cup light butter (such as
    Land O' Lakes), softened
  3 large eggs
2⅔ cups sifted cake flour
  ¾ cup unsweetened cocoa
  ¾ teaspoon baking soda
  ¾ teaspoon salt
  1 cup boiling water
  1 tablespoon vanilla extract
Rich Chocolate Frosting

1. Preheat oven to 350°.
2. Coat 2 (8-inch) round cake pans with cooking spray; line bottoms of pans with wax paper. Coat wax paper with cooking spray, and dust with 2 teaspoons flour; set aside.
3. Beat sugar and butter at medium speed of a mixer until well blended. Add eggs, 1 at a time, beating just until blended after each addition. Combine 2⅔ cups flour, cocoa, baking soda, and salt in a bowl. Add flour mixture to sugar mixture alternately with boiling water, beginning and ending with flour mixture. Add vanilla, and beat until blended.
4. Pour batter into prepared pans. Bake at 350° for 25 minutes or until a wooden pick inserted in center comes out with small crumbs attached. Let cool in pans 10 minutes on wire racks; remove from pans. Peel off wax paper; let cool completely on wire racks.
5. Place 1 cake layer on a serving plate; spread with about ¼ cup Rich Chocolate Frosting. Top with remaining cake layer; spread about ⅓ cup Rich Chocolate Frosting over top of cake. Spread remaining ¾ cup frosting around sides of cake. YIELD: 16 servings.

POINTS: 7; **EXCHANGES:** 4 Starch, ½ Fat;
PER SERVING: CAL 308 (21% from fat); PRO 4.9g; FAT 7.2g (sat 4.3g); CARB 57.6g; FIB 0.1g; CHOL 55mg; IRON 2.2mg; SOD 260mg; CALC 37mg

RICH CHOCOLATE FROSTING:

2¾ cups sifted powdered sugar
  3 tablespoons unsweetened cocoa
  ¼ teaspoon salt
  1 (1-ounce) square unsweetened
    chocolate
5½ tablespoons evaporated skim
    milk
  1 teaspoon vanilla extract

1. Combine first 3 ingredients in a small bowl; stir well, and set aside.
2. Place chocolate square in a microwave-safe bowl. Microwave at HIGH 1 to 1½ minutes or until very soft, stirring until smooth. Immediately add 3 tablespoons evaporated skim milk to melted chocolate, stirring with a whisk until blended. Gradually add sugar mixture to chocolate mixture, beating at low speed of a mixer until blended. Add remaining evaporated milk, beating until smooth. (If frosting is too stiff when remaining milk is incorporated, add an additional 1 to 2 tablespoons milk.) Stir in vanilla. Let frosting stand 5 minutes before spreading on cake. YIELD: about 1⅓ cups (serving size: about 4 teaspoons).
NOTE: This frosting sets up rapidly, so work quickly. For smoothest finish, do not respread frosting.

POINTS: 2; **EXCHANGES:** 1½ Starch;
PER SERVING: CAL 99 (10% from fat); PRO 0.9g; FAT 1.1g (sat 0.6g); CARB 22.2g; FIB 0g; CHOL 0mg; IRON 0.3mg; SOD 45mg; CALC 19mg

Spoon, Don't Scoop

Low-fat baking presents some extra challenges. Less fat means less room for error, particularly when measuring flour. *Weight Watchers Magazine's* Test Kitchens Director Kathleen Phillips offers advice on measuring correctly.

"If you dip your measuring cup into a flour canister, you can overmeasure as much as 2 tablespoons per cup," she explains. Instead, she suggests stirring the flour several times with a fork. Then, use a large spoon to spoon flour into the appropriate dry measuring cup until it's brimming over. Use a straight-edged spatula or knife to level the flour.

H O W   T O
Building a Braise

Braised dishes use a combination of dry heat and moist heat to tenderize food and produce a tasty sauce. Because you use a small amount of liquid, the food is both simmered and steamed, maximizing flavors and tenderizing meat. And, these one-pot meals maintain much of their nutrient values.

S T E P - B Y - S T E P

1. Heat oil in a large ovenproof Dutch oven over medium-high heat until very hot. Add meat, turning to sear on both sides.

2. Remove meat, leaving browned bits in pan to add flavor and color. Add onions, prunes, and seasonings; sauté to blend flavors.

3. Return meat to pan, placing over onion mixture. Pour wine-broth mixture over meat; bring to a simmer. Cover pan with tight-fitting lid and bake.

4. After braising, meat should be very tender and tear apart easily with two forks. This method is ideal for tougher cuts of meat.

BRAISED BEEF WITH PRUNES AND CARAMELIZED ONIONS

(pictured on page 135)

1 cup dry red wine
1 tablespoon Worcestershire sauce
2 teaspoons grated lemon rind
1 (2-pound) fresh beef brisket
½ teaspoon salt
¼ teaspoon pepper
1 tablespoon vegetable oil
1 pound small boiling onions (about 20), peeled
1 cup pitted prunes
¼ cup water
2 tablespoons tomato paste
½ teaspoon paprika
¼ teaspoon ground allspice
1⅓ cups beef broth, divided
1 teaspoon cornstarch
4½ cups hot cooked medium egg noodles (4½ cups uncooked), cooked without salt or fat

1. Preheat oven to 325°.
2. Combine first 3 ingredients in a small bowl; set aside.
3. Trim fat from brisket. Sprinkle salt and pepper over both sides.
4. Heat oil in an ovenproof Dutch oven over medium-high heat until very hot. Add brisket; cook 2 minutes on each side or until browned. Remove from pan; set aside. Reduce heat to medium. Add onions, prunes, and water; cook 8 minutes or until onions are golden, stirring frequently. Stir in tomato paste, paprika, and allspice. Return brisket to pan, placing over onion mixture. Pour wine mixture and 1¼ cups broth over brisket; bring to a simmer.
5. Cover pan with a tight-fitting lid; bake at 325° for 2½ hours or until

brisket is tender. Remove brisket from pan; keep warm. Combine remaining beef broth and cornstarch; stir well. Place pan over medium-high heat; bring liquid to a boil. Add cornstarch mixture, and cook 1 minute or until thick, scraping pan to loosen browned bits. Return brisket to pan; spoon sauce evenly over brisket. Serve over noodles. YIELD: 6 servings (serving size: about 2½ ounces meat, ¾ cup sauce, and ¾ cup noodles).

POINTS: 9; **EXCHANGES:** 3 Lean Meat, 2½ Starch, 1 Fruit, 1 Veg, ½ Fat; **PER SERVING:** CAL 455 (26% from fat); PRO 29.4g; FAT 13g (sat 3.9g); CARB 56.1g; FIB 6g; CHOL 102mg; IRON 5.2mg; SOD 553mg; CALC 58mg

FALL VEGETABLE BRAISE WITH WHITE BEANS

1 tablespoon olive oil
3½ cups (1-inch) peeled seeded cubed butternut squash (about 1½ pounds)
2 cups (1-inch-thick) sliced parsnip
2 cups finely chopped leek
4 large garlic cloves, minced
2 tablespoons chopped fresh or 2 teaspoons rubbed sage
1 teaspoon chopped fresh or ¼ teaspoon dried rosemary, crumbled
¼ teaspoon salt
¼ teaspoon freshly ground pepper
1 bay leaf
¾ cup canned vegetable broth
⅓ cup medium sherry
1 (19-ounce) can cannellini beans or other white beans, drained
2 tablespoons (½ ounce) grated fresh Parmesan cheese

1. Preheat oven to 325°.
2. Heat oil in a 4-quart ovenproof Dutch oven until very hot. Add squash and parsnip; sauté 5 minutes or until edges are browned (be careful not to burn vegetables). Remove vegetables from pan; set aside.
3. Reduce heat to medium. Add leek and garlic; sauté 2 minutes or until leek is tender. Stir in sage and next 4 ingredients. Return squash mixture to pan (do not stir). Pour broth and sherry over vegetables; bring to a simmer.
4. Cover pan with a tight-fitting lid; bake at 325° for 40 minutes. Stir in beans. Cover and bake an additional 10 minutes. Spoon into bowls; sprinkle with cheese. YIELD: 4 servings (serving size: about 1½ cups vegetable mixture and 1½ teaspoons cheese).
NOTE: To prepare squash, cut a slice from each end; peel skin to reach the flesh. Cut in half lengthwise; scrape out seeds with a small spoon.

POINTS: 6; **EXCHANGES:** 3 Starch, 1 Veg, 1 Fat; **PER SERVING:** CAL 301 (17% from fat); PRO 9.8g; FAT 5.8g (sat 1g); CARB 49.4g; FIB 3.7g; CHOL 3.25mg; IRON 4.2mg; SOD 831mg; CALC 202mg

5 INGREDIENTS
A Simpler Side

Slow down and enjoy these time-honored side dishes that you remember with affection.

There once was a simpler time, when a commute to work was 15 minutes and you enjoyed making home-cooked meals. Those relaxed days may be gone, but we've recaptured one of life's simplicities with these classic side dishes. Our recipes are lighter, yet just as satisfying as the classics.

NACHO ORDINARY MACARONI AND CHEESE

1 (8-ounce) package uncooked large elbow macaroni
5 ounces light processed cheese, cubed (such as Velveeta Light)
1 teaspoon taco seasoning
½ cup salsa
⅓ cup thinly sliced green onions (optional)

1. Cook macaroni in boiling water 9 minutes, omitting salt and fat. Drain and return macaroni to pan. Add cheese and taco seasoning, stirring until cheese melts. Stir in salsa. Sprinkle with green onions, if desired. YIELD: 8 servings (serving size: about ⅔ cup).

POINTS: 3; **EXCHANGES:** 1½ Starch, ½ Med-fat Meat; **PER SERVING:** CAL 150 (14% from fat); PRO 7.1g; FAT 2.4g (sat 1.4g); CARB 24.6g; FIB 1.2g; CHOL 9.4mg; IRON 1.4mg; SOD 355mg; CALC 109mg

PDQ LOADED MASHED POTATOES

Omit green onions, if desired.

2¼ cups 1% low-fat milk
1 (22-ounce) bag frozen mashed potatoes
½ cup light cream cheese, softened
⅓ cup thinly sliced green onions
¼ cup (2 ounces) shredded reduced-fat sharp Cheddar cheese
½ teaspoon salt
¼ teaspoon pepper

1. Heat milk over medium-high heat in a large heavy saucepan to 180° or until tiny bubbles form around edge of pan (do not boil). Add potatoes and cook 9 minutes, stirring constantly. Remove from heat; add cream cheese, stirring until smooth. Stir in onions and remaining ingredients. YIELD: 6 servings (serving size: 1 cup).

POINTS: 5; **EXCHANGES:** 1½ Starch, 1 Fat, ½ L-F Milk; **PER SERVING:** CAL 230 (34% from fat); PRO 9.1g; FAT 8.6g (sat 4.9g); CARB 27.7g; FIB 1.5g; CHOL 24mg; IRON 0.2mg; SOD 616mg; CALC 225mg

CARROTS IN MELTING HONEY-MUSTARD SAUCE

1 pound fresh baby-cut carrots
1 tablespoon brown sugar
1 tablespoon butter or stick margarine
1 tablespoon honey mustard
1 tablespoon frozen orange juice concentrate
¼ teaspoon salt
⅛ teaspoon pepper

1. Place carrots in a small saucepan, and cover with water; bring to a boil. Reduce heat, and simmer 8 minutes or just until carrots are tender. Drain well.
2. Return hot carrots to pan. Add sugar and remaining ingredients; stir well. Cook over medium-low heat until margarine melts and carrots are coated, stirring constantly.
YIELD: 4 servings (serving size: ¾ cup).

POINTS: 1; **EXCHANGES:** 2 Veg, ½ Starch, ½ Fat; **PER SERVING:** CAL 98 (28% from fat); PRO 1.4g; FAT 3.1g (sat 1.9g); CARB 17.2g; FIB 3.7g; CHOL 8mg; IRON 0.7mg; SOD 223mg; CALC 42mg

BRUSSELS SPROUTS GRATIN

1 pound fresh Brussels sprouts
Cooking spray
⅔ cup evaporated skim milk
½ teaspoon grated lemon rind
2 tablespoons fresh lemon juice
¼ teaspoon salt
¼ teaspoon pepper
1 large egg
½ cup (2 ounces) shredded fresh Parmesan cheese

1. Preheat oven to 375°.
2. Cut each Brussels sprout in half lengthwise. Place in a medium saucepan, and cover with water; bring to a boil. Reduce heat, and simmer 5 minutes or just until tender; drain well.
3 Arrange Brussels sprouts in a 9-inch quiche dish coated with cooking spray. Combine milk and next 5 ingredients in a bowl; stir with a whisk until well blended. Pour milk mixture over Brussels sprouts; sprinkle with cheese.

4. Bake at 375° for 35 minutes or until lightly browned. Serve immediately. YIELD: 4 servings.
NOTE: If fresh Brussels sprouts aren't available, substitute 1 (16-ounce) package frozen Brussels sprouts. Cook according to package directions.

POINTS: 2; **EXCHANGES:** 2 Veg, ½ Sk Milk, ½ Lean Meat, ½ Fat; **PER SERVING:** CAL 146 (27% from fat); PRO 12.6g; FAT 4.3g (sat 2.2g); CARB 17g; FIB 5.3g; CHOL 64mg; IRON 2.1mg; SOD 401mg; CALC 299mg

CRANBERRY-SWEET POTATO SKILLET

4 cups peeled diced sweet potato (about 2 large)
2 teaspoons butter or stick margarine
1 cup diced plum (2 medium)
1 (12-ounce) container cranberry-orange crushed fruit (such as Ocean Spray)
¼ teaspoon salt
¼ teaspoon ground red pepper
2 tablespoons chopped pecans, toasted

1. Place sweet potato in a large non-stick skillet, and cover with water; bring to a boil. Reduce heat, and simmer 7 minutes or until tender; drain well in a colander. Set aside.
2. Melt butter in skillet over medium heat. Add plum; cook 2 minutes. Stir in sweet potato, crushed fruit, salt, and pepper; cook 5 minutes or until thoroughly heated, stirring occasionally. Sprinkle with pecans.
YIELD: 5 servings (serving size: 1 cup).

POINTS: 5; **EXCHANGES:** 2 Starch, 2 Fruit, ½ Fat; **PER SERVING:** CAL 291 (14% from fat); PRO 2.3g; FAT 4.4g (sat 1.2g); CARB 60.8g; FIB 5.2g; CHOL 4mg; IRON 0.8mg; SOD 183mg; CALC 27mg

GARLICKY GREEN BEAN CASSEROLE

(pictured on page 158)

⅔ cup water
4 garlic cloves, minced
1 (16-ounce) package frozen cut
green beans
1 (10¾-ounce) can condensed
reduced-fat, reduced-salt cream
of mushroom soup, undiluted
1 cup coarsely crushed onion
melba toast (about 10
rectangular crackers), divided
¼ teaspoon salt
¼ teaspoon pepper
Butter-flavored cooking spray

1. Preheat oven to 350°.
2. Combine water and garlic in a
saucepan; bring to a boil, and cook 2
minutes. Add green beans, and
return to a boil. Cover, reduce heat,
and simmer 8 minutes or until
crisp-tender. Drain beans, reserving
cooking liquid. Set beans aside.
3. Return cooking liquid to pan;
bring to a boil, and cook 2 minutes
or until reduced to 2 tablespoons.
Add soup, stirring until smooth.
Add green beans, ½ cup melba toast,
salt, and pepper. Spoon mixture into
a 1-quart casserole dish coated with
cooking spray. Sprinkle remaining ½
cup melba toast evenly over casserole;
coat generously with cooking spray.
4. Bake, uncovered, at 350° for 25
minutes; let stand 5 minutes before
serving. YIELD: 4 servings (serving
size: about 1 cup).

POINTS: 2; **EXCHANGES:** 1½ Veg, ½ Starch,
½ Fat; **PER SERVING:** CAL 104 (14% from fat);
PRO 4g; FAT 1.6g (sat 0.5g); CARB 18.3g;
FIB 2.5g; CHOL 3mg; IRON 2mg;
SOD 544mg; CALC 58mg

SWEET-AND-SOUR CABBAGE AND APPLES

(pictured on page 157)

2 hickory-smoked bacon slices
2 medium Granny Smith apples,
each cut into 12 wedges
4 cups thinly sliced red cabbage
¼ cup balsamic vinegar
2 tablespoons sugar
¼ teaspoon salt
¼ teaspoon pepper

1. Cook bacon in a large nonstick
skillet over medium-high heat
until crisp. Remove bacon from skillet, reserving 1 tablespoon bacon fat
in skillet; crumble bacon, and
set aside.
2. Arrange apple wedges, cut side
down, in skillet; cook over
medium-high heat 3 minutes
(do not turn apples or they will
overcook). Reduce heat to
medium. Add cabbage; cover and
cook 5 minutes.
3. Add vinegar and next 3 ingredients; bring to a boil. Reduce heat,
and simmer, uncovered, 5 minutes or
until liquid almost evaporates, stirring occasionally. Sprinkle with
crumbled bacon. YIELD: 6 servings
(serving size: ⅔ cup).

POINTS: 2; **EXCHANGES:** ½ Starch, ½ Fruit,
½ Veg, ½ Fat; **PER SERVING:** CAL 104
(31% from fat); PRO 1.6g; FAT 3.7g (sat 1.3g);
CARB 17.9g; FIB 2.9g; CHOL 4mg;
IRON 0.5mg; SOD 143mg; CALC 31mg

CHEESY SPINACH AND MUSHROOMS

2 (10-ounce) packages frozen
chopped spinach
Cooking spray
1 cup chopped onion
1 (8-ounce) package presliced
fresh mushrooms
6 tablespoons spreadable
cheese with garlic and herbs
(such as Alouette), softened
2 tablespoons grated Parmesan
cheese

1. Cook spinach according to
microwave directions on package,
and drain (do not squeeze out excess
moisture). Set spinach aside.
2. Coat a large nonstick skillet with
cooking spray; place over medium-
high heat until hot. Add onion and
mushrooms, and sauté 5 minutes or
until tender.
3. Stir in spinach. Drop spreadable
cheese by heaping teaspoonfuls over
hot spinach mixture, stirring gently
until cheese melts. Sprinkle with
Parmesan cheese. YIELD: 4 servings
(serving size: ¾ cup).

POINTS: 2; **EXCHANGES:** 2 Veg, 1 Fat,
½ Very Lean Meat; **PER SERVING:** CAL 123
(49% from fat); PRO 7.4g; FAT 6.7g (sat 4g);
CARB 11.6g; FIB 5.5g; CHOL 24.5mg;
IRON 3.7mg; SOD 256mg; CALC 215mg

No Offense, Mom

Everyone thinks their mom makes the best meat loaf. As adults we appreciate the fact that meat loaf is easy to make and laden with flavor. To compete with your mother's classic, we made sure our recipes don't require too much time in the kitchen, and we packed them full of grown-up ingredients that reflect the healthful way you want to eat.

CHILI MEAT LOAF

1 cup chopped onion
¾ cup hickory-flavored barbecue sauce (such as KC Masterpiece), divided
½ cup dry breadcrumbs
1 tablespoon chili powder
½ teaspoon hot sauce
1 (16-ounce) can kidney beans, drained
2 large egg whites, lightly beaten
¾ pound lean ground pork
Cooking spray

1. Preheat oven to 375°.
2. Combine chopped onion, ½ cup barbecue sauce, breadcrumbs, and next 4 ingredients in a large bowl; stir well. Crumble pork over bean mixture, and stir just until blended. Shape mixture into a 7½- x 3½-inch loaf. Place in an 11- x 7-inch baking dish coated with cooking spray. Spread remaining ¼ cup barbecue sauce over top of loaf. Bake at 375° for 45 minutes or until an instant-read thermometer registers 160°. Let stand 5 minutes before slicing. YIELD: 6 servings.

POINTS: 6; **EXCHANGES:** 2½ Lean Meat, 2 Starch; **PER SERVING:** CAL 297 (29% from fat); PRO 22.1g; FAT 9.5g (sat 3g); CARB 30.1g; FIB 3.1g; CHOL 47mg; IRON 3.3mg; SOD 569mg; CALC 72mg

ALMOST CLASSIC MEAT LOAF

2 cups refrigerated shredded hash browns (such as Simply Potatoes)
1 cup Italian-seasoned breadcrumbs
1 cup chopped onion
½ cup ketchup
¼ cup Dijon mustard
2 teaspoons dried oregano
½ teaspoon salt
2 large eggs, lightly beaten
2 garlic cloves, minced
2 pounds lean ground beef
Cooking spray
⅓ cup ketchup

1. Preheat oven to 375°.
2. Combine first 9 ingredients in a bowl; stir mixture well. Crumble ground beef over potato mixture; stir just until blended. Shape mixture into an 8½- x 4½-inch loaf. Place loaf in an 11- x 7-inch baking dish coated with cooking spray.
2. Spread ⅓ cup ketchup over top of loaf. Bake at 375° for 1 hour and 15 minutes or until instant-read thermometer registers 160°. Let stand 5 minutes before slicing.
YIELD: 10 servings.

POINTS: 5; **EXCHANGES:** 3 Lean Meat, 1½ Starch; **PER SERVING:** CAL 246 (31% from fat); PRO 27.5g; FAT 8.4g (sat 3.6g); CARB 21.7g; FIB 1.3g; CHOL 115mg; IRON 3.8mg; SOD 912mg; CALC 41mg

ITALIANO MEAT LOAF

1 cup chopped onion
1 cup chopped green bell pepper
¾ cup Italian-seasoned breadcrumbs
¼ cup grated Parmesan cheese
2 teaspoons dried basil
½ teaspoon salt
¼ teaspoon pepper
1 (8-ounce) can tomato sauce
3 large egg whites, lightly beaten
2 garlic cloves, minced
1 cup cooked orzo (about ⅓ cup uncooked rice-shaped pasta), cooked without salt and fat
1 pound lean ground round
Cooking spray
3 cups fresh tomato and basil pasta sauce (such as Five Brothers)
Basil sprigs (optional)

1. Preheat oven to 375°.
2. Combine first 10 ingredients in a large bowl; stir well. Stir in orzo. Crumble beef over orzo mixture, and stir just until blended. Shape mixture into a 9- x 4½-inch loaf. Place loaf in an 11- x 7-inch baking dish coated with cooking spray.
3. Bake at 375° for 1 hour or until an instant-read thermometer registers 160°. Let stand 5 minutes before slicing. Cut into 6 slices; top each slice with ½ cup pasta sauce. Garnish with basil, if desired.
YIELD: 6 servings.

POINTS: 7; **EXCHANGES:** 2½ Med-fat Meat, 2 Veg, 1½ Starch, ½ Fat; **PER SERVING:** CAL 351 (34% from fat); PRO 27.2g; FAT 13.2g (sat 5g); CARB 35.5g; FIB 4.9g; CHOL 57mg; IRON 4.4mg; SOD 1433mg; CALC 150mg

GREEK LEMON-DILL MEAT LOAF

2 cups water
2 teaspoons lemon pepper, divided
1 cup uncooked long-grain rice
2 tablespoons olive oil
3 tablespoons all-purpose flour
1½ cups fat-free milk
1 teaspoon grated lemon rind
1 tablespoon fresh lemon juice
1½ teaspoons salt, divided
1 cup (4 ounces) crumbled feta cheese
1 cup chopped onion
¼ cup chopped fresh dill
1 (10-ounce) package frozen chopped spinach, thawed, drained, and squeezed dry
2 large egg whites, lightly beaten
2 pounds fresh ground turkey (white and dark meat)
Cooking spray

1. Preheat oven to 400°.
2. Combine water and 1 teaspoon lemon pepper in a saucepan; bring to a boil. Add rice; cover, reduce heat, and simmer 20 minutes or until rice is tender and liquid is absorbed. Remove from heat; let cool.
3. Heat oil in a saucepan over medium heat. Add remaining lemon pepper and flour; cook 4 minutes, stirring constantly. Gradually add milk, stirring with a whisk until blended. Cook 4 minutes or until sauce is slightly thick, stirring frequently. Stir in rind, lemon juice, and ¼ teaspoon salt. Remove from heat; let cool 5 minutes. Stir in cheese.
4. Combine rice, remaining 1¼ teaspoons salt, 1 cup cheese sauce, onion, and next 3 ingredients in a bowl; stir well. Crumble turkey over rice mixture; stir just until blended.

Shape mixture into an 11- x 6-inch loaf. Place loaf in 11- x 7-inch baking dish coated with cooking spray.
5. Bake at 400° for 1 hour and 10 minutes or until instant-read thermometer registers 160°. Let stand 5 minutes before slicing. Carefully reheat remaining cheese sauce in a small saucepan over low heat or microwave at MEDIUM (50% power) until warm. Cut loaf into 8 slices; top each slice with 1 tablespoon cheese sauce. YIELD: 8 servings.

POINTS: 6; EXCHANGES: 2 Med-fat Meat, 1½ Starch, ½ Veg; PER SERVING: CAL 289 (36% from fat); PRO 20.1g; FAT 11.4g (sat 4g); CARB 26.9g; FIB 1.8g; CHOL 56mg; IRON 3mg; SOD 721mg; CALC 200mg

MOROCCAN LAMB MEAT LOAF

1 cup finely chopped onion
⅓ cup golden raisins
¼ cup uncooked bulgur or cracked wheat
¼ cup chopped fresh mint
¼ cup coarsely chopped pimiento-stuffed olives
2 tablespoons lemon juice
1 teaspoon ground cumin
½ teaspoon salt
½ teaspoon ground coriander
¼ teaspoon ground red pepper
2 large egg whites, lightly beaten
1 pound lean ground lamb
Cooking spray

1. Preheat oven to 375°.
2. Combine first 11 ingredients in a bowl; stir well. Crumble lamb over onion mixture; stir just until blended. Shape mixture into an 8- x 4-inch loaf. Place loaf in 11- x 7-inch baking dish coated with cooking spray.

3. Bake at 375° for 45 minutes or until an instant-read thermometer registers 160°. Let stand 5 minutes before slicing. YIELD: 4 servings.

POINTS: 7; EXCHANGES: 4 Lean Meat, 1 Starch, ½ Fruit; PER SERVING: CAL 318 (30% from fat); PRO 32.2g; FAT 10.7g (sat 3.6g); CARB 23.7g; FIB 3.5g; CHOL 91mg; IRON 3.5mg; SOD 515mg; CALC 55mg

TEX-MEX TURKEY MEAT LOAF

2 cups (8 ounces) shredded reduced-fat sharp Cheddar cheese
1 cup chunky salsa
¼ cup canned chopped green chiles
1 (15-ounce) can black beans, rinsed and drained
1 pound fresh ground turkey breast
Cooking spray
Additional chunky salsa (optional)
Sliced green onions (optional)

1. Preheat oven to 375°.
2. Combine first 4 ingredients in a large bowl; stir well. Crumble turkey over bean mixture, and stir just until blended. Shape mixture into a 6½- x 4½-inch loaf. Place loaf in an 11- x 7-inch baking dish coated with cooking spray.
3. Bake at 375° for 55 minutes or until an instant-read thermometer registers 160°. Let stand 5 minutes before slicing. Serve with additional salsa, and garnish with green onions, if desired. YIELD: 5 servings.

POINTS: 6; EXCHANGES: 4 Very Lean Meat, 1 L-F Milk, ½ Starch; PER SERVING: CAL 306 (29% from fat); PRO 38.3g; FAT 9.9g (sat 5.5g); CARB 17.1g; FIB 3g; CHOL 78.4mg; IRON 2mg; SOD 925mg; CALC 431mg

November/December

Big Bird, Little Bird

When it comes to holiday dinners, one size does not fit all.

Tired of the usual turkey? There are plenty of other options for holiday dinners. Of course, we have a recipe for a traditional 12-pound turkey. But we also suggest fare for smaller gatherings. There's something for everyone because the holiday dinner should be as unique as your family.

DUCK BREAST WITH CHERRY-MANDARIN SAUCE

2 (11-ounce) cans mandarin oranges in light syrup, undrained
¾ cup fresh sweet cherries, pitted, halved, and divided
3 tablespoons light stick butter (such as Land O' Lakes), divided
2 tablespoons balsamic vinegar
2 tablespoons low-salt soy sauce
1 cup thinly sliced shallots
½ teaspoon freshly ground pepper
¼ teaspoon sea salt or salt
4 (4-ounce) skinned, boned fresh or frozen domestic duck breast halves, thawed
1 tablespoon coarsely chopped pistachios, toasted
Orange rind curls (optional)

1. Pour oranges and syrup into a large ovenproof skillet. Remove ½ cup oranges with a slotted spoon; set aside. Add ½ cup cherries, 1 tablespoon butter, vinegar, and soy sauce to skillet; bring to a boil. Reduce heat to medium; simmer, uncovered, 25 minutes. Strain fruit, reserving syrup mixture. Set fruit and syrup aside. Wipe skillet clean with paper towel.
2. Preheat oven to 350°.
3. Melt 1 tablespoon butter in skillet over medium heat. Add shallot; sauté 10 minutes or until golden. Spoon shallot into a bowl; set aside.

4. Sprinkle pepper and salt over duck. Melt remaining 1 tablespoon butter in skillet over medium-high heat. Add duck; cook 2 minutes on each side or until browned. Pour reserved syrup mixture over duck. Cover skillet with lid; bake at 350° for 15 minutes or until instant-read thermometer registers 160°. Remove duck from skillet; set aside, and keep warm.
5. Add ½ cup drained oranges, remaining cherries, and strained fruit mixture to skillet. Bring to a boil; reduce heat to medium, and simmer, uncovered, 10 minutes or until sauce is the consistency of thin syrup.
6. Spoon ¼ cup sauce onto each of 4 plates. Cut each duck breast diagonally into thin slices; arrange over sauce. Top evenly with browned shallot, and sprinkle evenly with pistachios. Garnish with orange rind curls, if desired. YIELD: 4 servings (serving size: 1 breast, ¼ cup sauce, 2 tablespoons browned shallot, and ¾ teaspoon pistachios.)
NOTE: If you don't have a skillet with an ovenproof handle, wrap the handle of the skillet and lid in foil to protect them in the oven.

POINTS: 7; **EXCHANGES:** 3 Med-fat Meat, 1 Fruit, 1 Veg; **PER SERVING:** CAL 302 (46% from fat); PRO 22.8g; FAT 15.3g (sat 6.7g); CARB 20.5g; FIB 1.8g; CHOL 91mg; IRON 3.4mg; SOD 505mg; CALC 41mg

SOUTHWESTERN CHICKEN WITH ROASTED PEPPER-CORN RELISH

1 poblano chile
1 anaheim chile
1 medium-size red bell pepper
½ small red onion, cut into thin wedges
1 garlic clove, unpeeled
3 limes, divided
1 (5-pound) roasting chicken
¼ cup chopped fresh cilantro, divided
1 teaspoon chili powder, divided
½ teaspoon salt, divided
Cooking spray
¼ cup yellow cornmeal (not cornmeal mix or self-rising)
1 (11-ounce) can vacuum-packed white shoepeg corn, drained

1. Cut chiles and bell pepper in half lengthwise; discard stems, seeds, and membranes. Place chile and pepper halves, skin side up, on a foil-lined baking sheet; flatten with hand. Add onion and garlic to baking sheet. Broil 15 minutes or until blackened. Place chiles and bell pepper in a zip-top plastic bag; seal bag, and let stand 15 minutes. Peel chiles, bell pepper, and garlic. Coarsely chop roasted vegetables; set aside.
2. Preheat oven to 350°.
3. Remove rind from 1 lime using a vegetable peeler, making sure not to get any of the white pithy part of the rind. Cut peeled lime into 6 slices; set aside.
4. Remove and discard giblets and neck from chicken. Rinse chicken under cold water; pat dry. Trim excess fat. Starting at neck cavity,

(continued)

loosen skin from breast and drumsticks by inserting fingers and gently pushing between skin and meat.

5. Combine 2 tablespoons cilantro, ½ teaspoon chili powder, and ¼ teaspoon salt; rub under loosened skin over breast and drumsticks. Place lime slices under loosened skin. Cut 1 lime in half, and place in body cavity. Tie ends of legs together with cord. Lift wing tips up and over back; tuck under chicken.

6. Place chicken, breast side up, on a broiler pan coated with cooking spray. Pierce skin several times with a meat fork. Combine remaining ½ teaspoon chili powder and cornmeal in a bowl; stir well. Rub cornmeal mixture over chicken. Insert meat thermometer into meaty part of thigh, making sure not to touch bone. Bake at 350° for 1 hour and 55 minutes or until meat thermometer registers 180°. Cover chicken loosely with foil; let stand 15 minutes.

7. Squeeze juice from remaining lime; set aside. Coat a large nonstick skillet with cooking spray, and place over medium heat until hot. Add corn; sauté 6 minutes or until corn is lightly browned. Stir in roasted vegetable mixture, remaining ¼ teaspoon salt, and lime juice; sauté 1 minute or until thoroughly heated. Remove from heat; stir in remaining 2 tablespoons cilantro. Discard skin before serving; serve relish with chicken. YIELD: 8 servings (serving size: about 3 ounces chicken and about ⅓ cup relish).

POINTS: 4; **EXCHANGES:** 3½ Very Lean Meat, 1 Veg, ½ Starch; **PER SERVING:** CAL 201 (20% from fat); PRO 27.9g; FAT 4.4g (sat 1g); CARB 14.2g; FIB 1.5g; CHOL 82mg; IRON 2.6mg; SOD 419mg; CALC 13mg

PLUM-GLAZED TURKEY AND VEGETABLES

⅔ cup red plum jam
½ cup apple cider
1 tablespoon cornstarch
2 teaspoons grated lemon rind
2 tablespoons fresh lemon juice
¾ teaspoon dry mustard
½ teaspoon salt
1 cup sliced plums
1 (5-pound) whole turkey breast
Cooking spray
4 medium sweet potatoes (about 2 pounds), peeled and each cut into eight pieces
6 large shallots, peeled and quartered

1. Preheat oven to 350°.

2. Combine first 7 ingredients in a medium saucepan; stir well. Bring to a boil; cook 1 minute or until thick and bubbly, stirring constantly. Remove from heat; stir in plums. Reserve ½ cup plum mixture in a bowl to brush over cooked turkey.

3. Starting at neck cavity, loosen skin from breast, gently pushing fingers between skin and meat. Spread ½ cup plum mixture over breast meat under skin. Place on a broiler pan coated with cooking spray. Insert meat thermometer into turkey breast, making sure not to touch bone. Bake at 350° for 45 minutes.

4. Combine ⅔ cup plum mixture, sweet potatoes, and shallots in a bowl; toss well to coat. Arrange sweet potato mixture around turkey on broiler pan. Bake at 350° an additional 1 hour and 45 minutes or until thermometer registers 170° and vegetables are tender (cover turkey loosely with foil to prevent overbrowning, if necessary).

5. Place turkey on a platter; spoon sweet potato mixture around turkey. Brush reserved ½ cup plum mixture over turkey and sweet potato mixture. Discard skin before serving turkey. YIELD: 12 servings (serving size: 3 ounces turkey and ½ cup sweet potato mixture).

POINTS: 5; **EXCHANGES:** 3 Very Lean Meat, 1½ Starch, 1½ Fruit; **PER SERVING:** CAL 294 (4% from fat); PRO 28.2g; FAT 1.2g (sat 0.3g); CARB 43g; FIB 3.5g; CHOL 72mg; IRON 2.2mg; SOD 185mg; CALC 42mg

CORNISH HENS WITH PORT WINE SAUCE

2 (1½-pound) Cornish hens
½ teaspoon sea salt or salt, divided
½ teaspoon freshly ground pepper, divided
Cooking spray
1 tablespoon stick butter
¼ cup minced shallots
2 garlic cloves, minced
¾ cup chicken broth
½ cup port or other sweet red wine
⅓ cup dried tart cherries
¼ cup black cherry juice (such as R.W. Knudsen Family)
1 teaspoon chopped fresh thyme

1. Preheat oven to 350°.

2. Remove and discard giblets and necks from hens. Rinse hens under cold water; pat dry. Trim excess fat. Starting at neck cavities, loosen skin from breasts and drumsticks by inserting fingers and gently pushing between skin and meat.

3. Rub ¼ teaspoon salt and ¼ teaspoon pepper over breasts and drumsticks under loosened skin of hens. Place hens, breast side up, on a broiler pan coated with cooking spray. Bake at 350° for 55 minutes or until juices run clear. Cover hens loosely with foil; let stand 10 minutes. Discard skin. Split hens in half lengthwise; set aside, and keep warm.

4. Melt butter in a medium saucepan over medium-high heat. Add shallot and garlic; sauté 3 minutes. Add remaining ¼ teaspoon salt, ¼ teaspoon pepper, broth, and next 4 ingredients; bring to a boil. Reduce heat, and simmer, uncovered, 30 minutes or until sauce is reduced to ½ cup. Spoon sauce over Cornish hens. YIELD: 4 servings (serving size: 1 hen half and 2 tablespoons sauce).

POINTS: 5; EXCHANGES: 3 Lean Meat, 1 Fruit; PER SERVING: CAL 221 (30% from fat); PRO 21.6g; FAT 7.4g (sat 2.7g); CARB 16.6g; FIB 1g; CHOL 101mg; IRON 1.7mg; SOD 571mg; CALC 39mg

BAKED QUAIL WITH MUSHROOMS AND WILD RICE

 1 (6-ounce) package wild rice (about 1 cup uncooked)
Cooking spray
 ½ cup all-purpose flour
 ½ teaspoon sea salt or salt
 ½ teaspoon freshly ground pepper
 8 (4-ounce) semiboned quail, skinned, or 2 (16-ounce) packages frozen semiboned quail, thawed and skinned
 2 tablespoons olive oil, divided
 ½ cup chopped red onion
 1 (8-ounce) package sliced fresh mushrooms
 3 cups one-third-less salt chicken broth
 ¾ cup dry sherry
 ⅔ cup seedless red grapes, halved

1. Sprinkle rice in a 13- x 9-inch baking dish coated with cooking spray; set aside.

2. Combine flour, salt, and pepper in a pie plate or shallow dish; stir well. Dredge quail in flour mixture, reserving remaining flour mixture. Heat 1½ tablespoons oil in a large skillet over medium heat. Add quail; cook 2 minutes on each side or until browned. Place quail on top of rice; set aside.

3. Heat ½ teaspoon oil in skillet over medium-high heat. Add onion and mushrooms; sauté 3 minutes or until tender. Spoon over quail.

4. Preheat oven to 350°.

5. Place remaining 1 teaspoon oil in skillet; add reserved flour mixture, stirring with a whisk. Place skillet over medium heat, and cook 1 minute, stirring constantly. Gradually add chicken broth and sherry, stirring with a whisk until well blended. Bring to a boil, stirring constantly. Reduce heat, and simmer 10 minutes or until slightly thick, stirring occasionally. Pour gravy over quail mixture; top with grapes. Cover and bake at 350° for 1 hour and 15 minutes or until rice is tender.
YIELD: 4 servings (serving size: 2 quail and about ¾ cup rice mixture).

POINTS: 10; EXCHANGES: 3½ Lean Meat, 3 Starch, 1 Veg, ½ Fat; PER SERVING: CAL 462 (25% from fat); PRO 34.7g; FAT 12.6g (sat 2.5g); CARB 53.2g; FIB 3.7g; CHOL 0mg; IRON 7.3mg; SOD 822mg; CALC 36mg

CHICKEN ROULADE WITH MUSHROOM DUXELLE AND TARRAGON CREAM SAUCE

(pictured on page 159)

 1 tablespoon light stick butter (such as Land O' Lakes), divided
 1 (8-ounce) package crimini or button mushrooms, sliced
 1 tablespoon chopped shallots (about 1 small)
 2 garlic cloves, chopped
 ½ cup dry white wine
 ¾ pound skinned, boned chicken breast halves
 10 sheets frozen phyllo dough, thawed
Cooking spray
 ½ cup fresh spinach leaves
 ¾ cup (3 ounces) crumbled feta cheese
 2 tablespoons all-purpose flour
 1 cup 1% low-fat milk
 ½ cup one-third-less salt chicken broth
 2 teaspoons chopped fresh or ½ teaspoon dried tarragon
 ½ teaspoon sea salt or salt
 ½ teaspoon freshly ground pepper
Additional freshly ground pepper (optional)

1. Preheat oven to 375°.

2. Melt 2 teaspoons butter in a large nonstick skillet over medium-high heat. Add mushrooms, shallot, and garlic; sauté 3 minutes or until mushrooms are tender. Add wine; bring to a boil. Reduce heat, and simmer, uncovered, 5 minutes or until most of liquid evaporates. Remove from heat; let cool.

3. Place each chicken breast half between 2 sheets of heavy-duty

(continued)

plastic wrap; flatten to ¼-inch thickness, using a meat mallet or rolling pin. Set aside.

4. Place 1 phyllo sheet on a large baking sheet coated with cooking spray (cover remaining dough to keep from drying); lightly coat phyllo with cooking spray. Repeat procedure with remaining phyllo and cooking spray, forming a stack of phyllo.

5. Place chicken breasts along 1 long edge of phyllo stack, leaving a 1-inch border around edges. Place spinach leaves over chicken; top with mushroom mixture and feta cheese. Fold over short edges of phyllo to cover 1 inch of chicken mixture on each end. Fold over long edge of phyllo to cover 1 inch of chicken mixture, and roll up jelly-roll fashion. Lightly coat top of roulade with cooking spray.

6. Bake at 375° for 30 minutes or until an instant-read thermometer inserted in center registers 160°. Let stand 10 minutes.

7. Place flour in a saucepan. Gradually add milk and chicken broth, stirring with a whisk until blended. Stir in remaining teaspoon butter, tarragon, salt, and pepper. Place over medium heat, and cook 8 minutes or until sauce is thick and coats the back of a spoon.

8. Cut roulade into 6 slices. Spoon 3½ tablespoons sauce on each of 6 plates; place roulade slices on sauce. Sprinkle with additional pepper, if desired. Serve immediately.

YIELD: 6 servings.

POINTS: 6; **EXCHANGES:** 2 Very Lean Meat, 1½ Starch, 1½ Fat, ½ Veg; **PER SERVING:** CAL 270 (30% from fat); PRO 21g; FAT 9.1g (sat 4.5g); CARB 25g; FIB 0.8g; CHOL 58mg; IRON 2.5mg; SOD 687mg; CALC 163mg

GARLIC-RUBBED HEN WITH SUN-DRIED TOMATO SAUCE AND POLENTA

(pictured on page 154)

While the hen bakes, prepare the tomato sauce and polenta so the whole dish is ready at the same time.

1 (5-pound) hen
4 garlic cloves, minced
¾ teaspoon sea salt or salt, divided
Cooking spray
2 tablespoons olive oil, divided
1 cup chopped green onions
3½ cups one-third-less salt chicken broth (such as Swanson Natural Goodness), divided
¼ cup sun-dried tomato sprinkles
1 (14½-ounce) can stewed tomatoes with basil, garlic, and oregano, undrained and chopped
1 cup water, divided
1 (0.35-ounce) package dried porcini mushrooms
1 cup yellow cornmeal (not cornmeal mix or self-rising)
¼ cup (1 ounce) shredded fresh Parmesan cheese
Oregano sprigs (optional)

1. Preheat oven to 350°.
2. Remove and discard giblets and neck from hen. Rinse hen under cold water; pat dry. Trim excess fat. Starting at neck cavity, loosen skin from breast and drumsticks by inserting fingers and gently pushing between skin and meat.
3. Combine garlic and ½ teaspoon salt. Rub garlic mixture under loosened skin over breast and drumsticks and into body cavity. Lift wing tips up and over back; tuck under hen.

4. Place hen, breast side up, on a broiler pan coated with cooking spray. Insert meat thermometer into meaty part of thigh, making sure not to touch bone. Bake at 350° for 1 hour and 30 minutes or until thermometer registers 180°. Cover hen loosely with foil; let stand 10 minutes. Discard skin; remove meat from bones.

5. Heat 1 tablespoon oil in a large nonstick skillet over medium-high heat. Add green onions; sauté 2 minutes. Add ½ cup chicken broth, sun-dried tomatoes, and stewed tomatoes; bring to a boil. Reduce heat, and simmer, uncovered, 10 minutes or until slightly thick.

6. Bring ½ cup water to a boil in a medium saucepan; stir in mushrooms. Remove from heat; let stand 15 minutes. Remove mushrooms from saucepan with a slotted spoon, and coarsely chop. Return mushrooms to water in pan. Add remaining ½ cup water, 3 cups broth, and ¼ teaspoon salt; bring to a boil. Gradually add cornmeal, stirring constantly with a whisk. Reduce heat to medium, and cook 15 minutes or until thick, stirring frequently. Remove from heat; stir in remaining 1 tablespoon oil and cheese.

7. Spoon polenta onto plates; top evenly with sliced hen. Spoon tomato sauce over hen and polenta. Garnish with oregano, if desired.

YIELD: 8 servings (serving size: ½ cup polenta, about 3 ounces hen, and ¼ cup tomato sauce).

POINTS: 6; **EXCHANGES:** 4 Very Lean Meat, 1 Starch, 1 Fat; **PER SERVING:** CAL 270 (30% from fat); PRO 31g; FAT 8.9g (sat 2.1g); CARB 18.9g; FIB 2.7g; CHOL 83.9mg; IRON 2.9mg; SOD 898mg; CALC 70mg

SAVORY HOLIDAY TURKEY WITH SWEET ONION GRAVY

(pictured on page 157)

1 (12-pound) fresh or frozen
    whole turkey, thawed
1 tablespoon chopped fresh
    rosemary
1 tablespoon chopped fresh thyme
2 teaspoons freshly ground
    pepper, divided
½ teaspoon sea salt or salt
Cooking spray
4½ cups chicken broth
¾ cup chopped carrot
¾ cup chopped celery
1 whole clove
1½ tablespoons peanut or
    vegetable oil
4 cups chopped sweet onion
½ cup all-purpose flour

1. Preheat oven to 325°.
2. Remove giblets and neck from
turkey; discard. Rinse turkey under
cold water; pat dry. Trim excess fat.
Starting at neck cavity, loosen skin
from breast and drumsticks by
inserting fingers and gently pushing
between skin and meat.
3. Combine rosemary, thyme, 1 teaspoon pepper, and salt. Rub herb
mixture under loosened skin over
breast and drumsticks and into body
cavity. Tie ends of legs to tail with
cord. Lift wing tips up and over
back; tuck under turkey.
4. Place turkey on a broiler pan
coated with cooking spray. Insert
meat thermometer into meaty part
of thigh, making sure not to touch
bone. Bake at 325° for 3 hours or
until thermometer registers 180°.
Cover turkey loosely with foil; let

stand 10 minutes. Set pan and drippings aside.
5. Pour chicken broth in a medium
saucepan. Add remaining 1 teaspoon
pepper, carrot, celery, and clove;
bring to a boil. Cover, reduce heat,
and simmer 45 minutes. Strain broth
mixture, reserving liquid; discard
solids. Set broth mixture aside.
6. Pour pan drippings into a small
heavy-duty zip-top plastic bag; seal
bag. Snip off 1 small corner of the
bag; drain drippings into bowl,
stopping before the fat layer reaches
the opening. Reserve drippings; discard fat.
7. Heat oil in a large saucepan over
medium-high heat. Add onion; sauté
9 minutes or until lightly browned
and tender. Sprinkle flour over
onion mixture, stirring well. Add
reserved drippings and broth mixture; bring to a boil. Reduce heat,
and cook over medium heat until
slightly thick and bubbly, stirring
occasionally with a whisk. Discard
skin from turkey. Serve gravy with
turkey. YIELD: 18 servings (serving
size: 3 ounces turkey and about ⅓
cup gravy).

POINTS: 4; **EXCHANGES:** 2 Very Lean Meat,
2 Lean Meat, ½ Starch; **PER SERVING:**
CAL 204 (28% from fat); PRO 28.6g; FAT 6.4g
(sat 1.9g); CARB 6.2g; FIB 1g; CHOL 70mg;
IRON 2.2mg; SOD 332mg; CALC 39mg

WEEKNIGHTS

Turkey: Take Two

Some traditions are worth keeping.
Eating the same old turkey sandwich
is not one of them. We can help put
variety in the holiday leftovers.

TURKEY BREAST WITH APPLE-SAGE SAUCE

2 tablespoons all-purpose flour
1 tablespoon water
¼ cup 33%-less-fat sour cream
    (such as Breakstone)
1 teaspoon vegetable oil
1 cup quartered fresh mushrooms
1 cup coarsely chopped Golden
    Delicious apple
½ cup finely chopped onion
1 teaspoon sugar
1 cup apple juice
1 cup one-third-less salt chicken
    broth (such as Swanson Natural
    Goodness)
1 teaspoon finely chopped fresh
    sage
½ teaspoon salt
¾ pound sliced cooked turkey
    breast
4 cups hot cooked long-grain
    rice, cooked without salt or fat

1. Combine flour and water in a
bowl; stir with a whisk until blended.
Stir in sour cream; set aside.
2. Heat oil in a nonstick skillet over
medium-high heat. Add mushrooms;
sauté 2 minutes. Add apple, onion,

(continued)

and sugar; sauté 4 minutes or until onion is lightly browned. Add apple juice and next 3 ingredients; bring to a boil. Reduce heat; simmer 15 minutes or until reduced to 1½ cups. Reduce heat to medium-low. Stir in sour cream mixture; cook 1 minute or until thick, stirring constantly.

3. Add turkey to sauce; cook 2 minutes or until thoroughly heated. Serve turkey and sauce over rice. YIELD: 4 servings (serving size: 3 ounces turkey, ½ cup sauce, and 1 cup rice).

POINTS: 9; EXCHANGES: 3½ Starch, 3 Very Lean Meat, ½ Fruit, ½ Fat; PER SERVING: CAL 431 (9% from fat); PRO 32.2g; FAT 4.3g (sat 1.9g); CARB 63.4g; FIB 2.2g; CHOL 78mg; IRON 4mg; SOD 507mg; CALC 60mg

TURKEY GREMOLATA

Gremolata is a sprightly mixture of lemon zest, parsley, and garlic that adds zing to leftover turkey.

2 tablespoons grated lemon rind
2 tablespoons minced fresh parsley
5 garlic cloves, minced and divided
Cooking spray
2 cups coarsely chopped red bell pepper
1 cup coarsely chopped onion
2 (14½-ounce) cans one-third-less salt chicken broth
5 thyme sprigs
3 cups chopped cooked dark turkey
¼ teaspoon salt
1 tablespoon all-purpose flour
2 tablespoons water
4 cups hot cooked basmati rice, cooked without salt or fat

1. Combine lemon rind, parsley, and 2 garlic cloves; stir well. Set aside.

2. Coat a nonstick skillet with cooking spray; place over medium-high heat until hot. Add remaining garlic, bell pepper, and onion; sauté 5 minutes. Add broth and thyme; bring to a boil. Stir in turkey and salt. Cover, reduce heat to medium-low; simmer 30 minutes. Increase heat to medium-high; cook, uncovered, 15 minutes.

3. Reduce heat to medium-low. Combine flour and water, stirring until blended. Add to turkey mixture; simmer 5 minutes or until thick, stirring occasionally. Spoon over rice; sprinkle with gremolata. YIELD: 4 servings (serving size: ¾ cup turkey mixture and 1 cup rice).

POINTS: 8; EXCHANGES: 3½ Starch, 3 Very Lean Meat, 1 Veg; PER SERVING: CAL 423 (15% from fat); PRO 33.4g; FAT 7.2g (sat 2.3g); CARB 54.5g; FIB 2.4g; CHOL 74mg; IRON 5.1mg; SOD 841mg; CALC 69mg

ENCHILADAS SUIZAS

¾ cup 33%-less-fat sour cream
¼ cup fat-free milk
1 tablespoon finely chopped fresh cilantro
1 to 2 tablespoons seeded minced jalapeño pepper
1 tablespoon fresh lime juice
3 garlic cloves, minced and divided
½ teaspoon salt, divided
Cooking spray
1 cup chopped onion
1 (14½-ounce) can one-third-less salt chicken broth
2 cups diced cooked white and dark turkey
2 teaspoons ground cumin
12 (6-inch) corn tortillas
1 (16-ounce) jar tomatillo salsa
Cilantro sprigs (optional)

1. Preheat oven to 350°.

2. Combine first 5 ingredients in a small bowl. Add 1 garlic clove and ¼ teaspoon salt; stir well, and set aside.

3. Coat a large nonstick skillet with cooking spray; place over medium-high heat until hot. Add onion; sauté 5 minutes or until golden. Add remaining 2 garlic cloves; sauté 1 minute. Add remaining ¼ teaspoon salt, chicken broth, turkey, and cumin. Reduce heat, and simmer, uncovered, 12 minutes or until most of liquid evaporates.

4. Heat tortillas according to package directions. Spread about 2 tablespoons turkey mixture down center of each tortilla; roll up. Place enchiladas, seam side down, in a 13- x 9-inch baking dish. Spread salsa over enchiladas. Cover and bake at 350° for 20 minutes. Drizzle sour cream mixture over enchiladas before serving. Garnish with cilantro sprigs, if desired. YIELD: 6 servings (serving size: 2 enchiladas).

POINTS: 5; EXCHANGES: 2 Starch, 2 Lean Meat; PER SERVING: CAL 280 (21% from fat); PRO 20.5g; FAT 6.6g (sat 3g); CARB 32.7g; FIB 4g; CHOL 47mg; IRON 2.2mg; SOD 949mg; CALC 201mg

HEAVENLY HASH AND EGGS

2 cups peeled diced baking potato
(about 1 pound)
1 teaspoon butter or stick
margarine
Butter-flavored cooking spray
1 cup diced onion
1 cup diced celery
2 garlic cloves, minced
2 cups diced cooked white and
dark turkey
2 teaspoons poultry seasoning
¼ cup 2% reduced-fat milk
2 tablespoons chopped fresh chives
1½ teaspoons chopped fresh thyme
½ teaspoon salt
½ teaspoon pepper
5 large eggs, poached
Cracked black pepper (optional)

1. Place potato in a large saucepan,
and cover with water. Bring to a
boil, and cook 7 minutes or just
until tender. Drain; set aside.
2. Melt butter in a large nonstick
skillet coated with cooking spray over
medium-high heat. Add onion, celery,
and garlic; sauté 10 minutes or until
tender and golden. Add potato,
turkey, and poultry seasoning; sauté 5
minutes. Reduce heat to medium; stir
in milk and next 4 ingredients. Cook
2 minutes or until thoroughly heated,
stirring frequently.
3. Spoon hash onto plates; top with
poached eggs. Sprinkle with cracked
pepper, if desired. YIELD: 5 servings
(serving size: 1 cup hash and 1 egg).

POINTS: 6; **EXCHANGES:** 3 Lean Meat,
1½ Starch; **PER SERVING:** CAL 272
(30% from fat); PRO 25.2g; FAT 9.2g (sat 3.2g);
CARB 21.4g; FIB 2.3g; CHOL 259mg;
IRON 2.5mg; SOD 379mg; CALC 85mg

ASIAN ANGEL HAIR SALAD

When you're pinched for time,
substitute 1 cup packaged shredded
carrot for the julienne-cut carrot.

3 cups coarsely chopped bok choy
1 cup julienne-cut or preshredded
carrot
1 cup fresh snow peas
½ cup hoisin sauce
¼ cup rice vinegar
¼ cup low-salt soy sauce
1 tablespoon minced garlic
1 tablespoon peeled minced fresh
ginger
1 tablespoon dark sesame oil
4 cups hot cooked angel hair pasta
(about 8 ounces uncooked
pasta), cooked without salt or fat
2 cups diced cooked white and
dark turkey
1 cup diagonally sliced green
onions
4 teaspoons sesame seeds, toasted

1. Cook first 3 ingredients in boiling
water 1 minute. Drain; rinse under
cold water. Drain well; let cool.
2. Combine hoisin sauce and
next 5 ingredients in a large bowl;
stir well. Add bok choy mixture,
pasta, turkey, and green onions;
toss well. Spoon mixture evenly
onto 8 plates; sprinkle with sesame
seeds. Serve at room temperature or
chilled. YIELD: 8 servings (serving
size: 1 cup salad and ½ teaspoon
sesame seeds).

POINTS: 5; **EXCHANGES:** 2 Starch,
1 Very Lean Meat, 1 Fat, ½ Veg;
PER SERVING: CAL 256 (19% from fat);
PRO 15.9g; FAT 5.3g (sat 1.1g); CARB 34.3g;
FIB 3.2g; CHOL 28mg; IRON 2.8mg;
SOD 496mg; CALC 66mg

TURKEY-ORZO SOUP WITH BLACK-EYED PEAS

Serve this soup immediately;
left standing, the orzo absorbs liquid
and the soup gets very thick.

2 teaspoons olive oil
1 cup sliced leek
¾ cup peeled diced turnip
½ cup diced celery
2 garlic cloves, minced
2 (14½-ounce) cans one-third-
less salt chicken broth (such as
Swanson Natural Goodness)
1 (15.8-ounce) can black-eyed
peas, rinsed and drained
1 (14.5-ounce) can stewed
tomatoes with basil, garlic, and
oregano, undrained and chopped
1 cup chopped cooked white and
dark turkey
½ cup uncooked orzo
(rice-shaped pasta)
¾ teaspoon dried marjoram
½ teaspoon salt
¼ teaspoon freshly ground pepper
¼ cup (1 ounce) shredded fresh
Parmesan cheese

1. Heat oil in a saucepan over
medium-high heat. Add leek and
next 3 ingredients; sauté 12 minutes.
Add broth, peas, and tomatoes; bring
to a boil. Reduce heat, and simmer
10 minutes. Add turkey and next 4
ingredients; simmer 10 minutes.
Ladle into bowls; sprinkle with
cheese. YIELD: 4 servings (serving size:
2 cups soup and 1 tablespoon cheese).

POINTS: 7; **EXCHANGES:** 2½ Veg,
2 Lean Meat, 2 Starch; **PER SERVING:**
CAL 339 (18% from fat); PRO 26.2g; FAT 6.6g
(sat 1.8g); CARB 44.4g; FIB 3.3g;
CHOL 34mg; IRON 4mg; SOD 1,524mg;
CALC 144mg

5 INGREDIENTS
Sweet Standbys

Life doesn't always call ahead. When you need an all-purpose dish for short-notice occasions, sweet breads come to the rescue. Our recipes use convenience products such as canned biscuits and breadsticks to give you an easy start. Topped with gooey sauce, these warm breads save the day when you need a dessert, breakfast dish, or snack. Your guests will never know that it isn't an old favorite baked especially for them.

PEANUTTY CHOCOLATE CHIP-BANANA MUFFINS

 1 (14-ounce) package banana quick bread mix (such as Pillsbury)
 ¼ cup semisweet chocolate minichips
 ¾ cup mashed banana
 ¾ cup water
 ⅓ cup reduced-fat chunky peanut butter
 3 large egg whites
Cooking spray

1. Preheat oven to 400°.
2. Combine bread mix and chips in a medium bowl; make a well in center of mixture. Combine banana and next 3 ingredients; stir with a whisk until blended. Add to dry ingredients, stirring just until moist.
3. Divide batter among 16 muffin cups coated with cooking spray.
4. Bake at 400° for 20 minutes or until muffins spring back when touched lightly in center. Remove muffins from pans immediately; place on a wire rack. YIELD: 16 servings.

POINTS: 3; **EXCHANGES:** 1½ Starch, ½ Fat; **PER SERVING:** CAL 155 (24% from fat); PRO 3.7g; FAT 4.1g (sat 1g); CARB 26g; FIB 0.9g; CHOL 0mg; IRON 0.8mg; SOD 190mg; CALC 1.8mg

PUMPKIN-RAISIN-NUT BREAD

 1 (15.4-ounce) package nut quick bread mix (such as Pillsbury)
 ½ cup raisins
 ¾ cup canned unsweetened pumpkin
 ½ cup water
 ¼ cup egg substitute
 1 teaspoon pumpkin pie spice
Cooking spray

1. Preheat oven to 350°.
2. Combine bread mix and raisins in a medium bowl; make a well in center of mixture. Combine pumpkin and next 3 ingredients; stir well. Add to dry ingredients, stirring just until moist.
3. Spoon batter into an 8½- x 4-inch loaf pan coated with cooking spray. Bake at 350° for 45 minutes or until a wooden pick inserted in center comes out clean. Let cool in pan 10 minutes on a wire rack; remove from pan. Let cool on wire rack. YIELD: 12 servings.

POINTS: 3; **EXCHANGES:** 2 Starch; **PER SERVING:** CAL 173 (19% from fat); PRO 3.8g; FAT 3.6g (sat 0.5g); CARB 32.1g; FIB 1.8g; CHOL 0mg; IRON 1.5mg; SOD 189mg; CALC 29mg

DRIED CHERRY SCONES

 ½ cup sugar, divided
 2¾ cups reduced-fat biscuit and baking mix (such as Bisquick)
 ¼ cup chilled light stick butter (such as Land O' Lakes), cut into small pieces
 ½ cup dried sweet cherries
 1 (8-ounce) carton cherry vanilla fat-free yogurt (such as Dannon Light)
Cooking spray
 1 tablespoon light stick butter, melted

1. Preheat oven to 400°.
2. Reserve 1 tablespoon sugar to sprinkle over top of scones; set aside. Combine remaining sugar and baking mix in a bowl; stir well. Cut in ¼ cup butter with a pastry blender or 2 knives until mixture resembles coarse meal. Add cherries; toss well. Add yogurt, stirring just until moist (dough will be sticky).
3. Turn dough out onto a lightly floured surface. Knead dough with floured hands 4 or 5 times. Pat dough into a 9-inch circle on a baking sheet coated with cooking spray. Cut dough into 10 wedges with a lightly floured knife, cutting into, but not through, dough. Sprinkle reserved sugar over dough.
4. Bake at 400° for 18 minutes or until golden. Remove from oven, and brush with melted butter. YIELD: 10 servings.

POINTS: 5; **EXCHANGES:** 2 Starch, ½ Fruit, ½ Fat; **PER SERVING:** CAL 220 (21% from fat); PRO 3.5g; FAT 5.2g (sat 2.4g); CARB 40.7g; FIB 0.9g; CHOL 11mg; IRON 1.3mg; SOD 429mg; CALC 72mg

Enjoying the Ride

HAL BREY • **HEIGHT** 6'1" • **BEFORE** 304 LBS. • **AFTER** 198 LBS.

Philosophy: Success is in the journey, not the destination.
It's a process; it just goes on and on.

Lifting 70 pounds of potatoes, Hal Brey marveled at how far he and his wife, Deb, had come. Their Weight Watchers leader had asked them to bring a charity food donation that weighed as many pounds as they had lost. Hal had lost 50 pounds and Deb had lost 20—and hauling the heavy sacks of potatoes showed him how successful they were.

Hal decided to lose weight after an allergic reaction to medication sent him to the hospital. "Heart-related illness runs in my family," says Hal. "So I'm thinking, 'I'm too young to have a heart attack.' " When a doctor suggested Weight Watchers, Hal agreed to try it.

> *"Men want to do it themselves. It's like the guy who needs a map . . . but won't ask for directions."*

"I'm a junior," Hal says, "but I was never 'Little Hal.' " He had wanted to lose weight for years but diets didn't work. He lost about 60 pounds on three different occasions, but gained it back each time.

More than 100 pounds lighter today, Hal credits his success to a lifestyle change. "This isn't a diet," he says. "Sometimes you make good choices, and sometimes you make not-so-good choices. But they are still choices you have to make."

Hal takes Deb, who has lost 80 pounds, out to dinner at least four times a week, and he eats lunch out every day. Using a journal keeps him on track. He chooses a salad or skinless chicken breast at restaurants.

Hal is a believer in breakfast. "I think it's *the* meal," he says. Breakfast used to be biscuits and gravy, hash browns, corned beef hash, and poached eggs. Now he starts his day with something nutritious, such as a bran muffin. He also bikes and walks for exercise.

Hal thinks some men have a difficult time seeking help with weight loss because they fear being seen as weak. "Men want to do it themselves," Hal explains. "It's like the guy who needs a map to know where he's going, but won't ask for directions." That's too bad, says Hal, who believes the support from Deb and others in their group was crucial to his weight loss success.

"I believe you find motivation in yourself," he explains. "It's like going to church. When you're around people who like to go to church, you want to go to church, too. When you're around people who are working at losing weight, it becomes easier for you to lose weight."

153

Garlic-Rubbed Hen With
Sun-Dried Tomato Sauce
and Polenta, page 148

Garlicky Acorn Squash and Wild
Rice Stuffing, page 163

Toasted Oat
Scones, page 119

Spinach-Walnut
Manicotti, page 77

Savory Holiday Turkey With Sweet
Onion Gravy, page 149

Sweet-and-Sour Cabbage and
Apples, page 141

Garlicky Green Bean Casserole, page 141

Sticky Caramel-Pecan Rolls, page 161

Blueberry Pie With Amaretti Streusel, page 100

Chicken Roulade With Mushroom
Duxelle and Tarragon Cream
Sauce, page 147

Better Than Ever

CAMILLA STEVENSON • **HEIGHT** 5'5" • **BEFORE** 170 LBS. • **AFTER** 140 LBS.

Philosophy: I can cope with whatever life gives me because I am physically, mentally, and emotionally strong.

The eyes may be windows to the soul, but Camilla Stevenson believes the body tells all. After years of caring for everyone but herself, Camilla was 30 pounds heavier, and her body was crying out for help.

Camilla's struggles started when the her husband 's death left her a 36-year-old single mother of Stephanie, 8, and Ashley, 5. Camilla was substitute teaching and caring for ailing parents. "I wanted to be two parents to my daughters, and my parents needed help," she says. When her father died, Camilla didn't have the energy to grieve.

Her girls were in high school when Camilla needed a hysterectomy. After surgery, she rushed back to caring for her mother. "I spent four nights at my house and three at hers," Camilla says. "I ate junk because I was on the go. I ate to take my mind off things."

Finally, Ashley begged Camilla to reform her habits and lose weight. "She was beside herself with worry," Camilla recalls.

Aware that she needed to get control of her life, Camilla says, "I had no idea where to start." Stephanie suggested she try a personal trainer, someone who could teach her the fundamentals of exercise.

With the help of Helen Moock, a trainer at a nearby gym. Camilla began walking or running regularly and lifting weights for an hour a week. She also learned to reach for healthful foods. "I moved away from potato chips and toward fruits, vegetables, and oatmeal," she says. "I couldn't believe how delicious oatmeal was."

Camilla was losing pounds and inches when the other shoe dropped. A routine mammogram led to a diagnosis of breast cancer. "Initially, the news devastated me, but I'd come so far, I wouldn't let it lick me," she says. "I'd dealt with so much, I knew I could handle anything."

Despite complications and her doctor's skepticism, Camilla was lifting weights again within a few weeks. "My trainer gave me motivation and confidence, and she helped me realize that no matter what, I would be okay," says Camilla.

"I knew I could handle anything."

Soon after, Camilla reached her goal weight of 140 pounds. Five months later, she ran the "Race for the Cure," a fundraiser for breast cancer. Camilla knows she has everything to be thankful for. "Of course your problems don't go away," she says. "It's all a matter of how you look at them."

CREAM CHEESE-FILLED MONKEY BREAD

1 (2-pound) package frozen white
   bread dough
½ cup (4 ounces) block-style
   cream cheese
⅓ cup sugar, divided
1¼ teaspoons ground cinnamon,
   divided
Cooking spray
½ cup reduced-calorie
   maple-flavored pancake syrup

1. Thaw bread dough in refrigerator
according to package directions.
2. Combine cream cheese, 1 tablespoon sugar, and ¼ teaspoon
cinnamon in a bowl. Stir well;
set aside. Combine remaining
sugar and cinnamon; stir well, and
set aside.
3. Cut each loaf of dough into
24 equal portions. Flatten each
portion into a 2½-inch circle.
Spoon ½ teaspoon cream cheese
mixture into center of each circle.
Gather dough around cheese
mixture, forming a ball; pinch
edges of dough together to seal.
Roll each dough ball in cinnamon-
sugar mixture. Layer balls in a
12-cup Bundt pan coated with
cooking spray. Sprinkle any remaining cinnamon-sugar mixture over
dough; pour syrup over dough.
Cover and let rise in a warm
place (85°), free from drafts, 40 minutes or until doubled in bulk.
4. Preheat oven to 350°.
5. Bake at 350° for 28 minutes
or until lightly browned. Immediately loosen edges of bread with
a knife. Place a serving plate,
upside down, on top of pan; invert
bread onto plate. Remove pan;

drizzle remaining syrup over bread.
YIELD: 16 servings (serving size: 3 balls).

POINTS: 4; EXCHANGES: 2 Starch, ½ Fat;
PER SERVING: CAL 174 (22% from fat);
PRO 5g; FAT 4.2g (sat 1.6g); CARB 29.4g;
FIB 0g; CHOL 8mg; IRON 1.3mg;
SOD 281mg; CALC 37mg

STICKY CARAMEL-PECAN ROLLS

(pictured on page 158)

¼ cup fat-free caramel-flavored
   sundae syrup
Cooking spray
1 (8-ounce) can refrigerated
   reduced-fat crescent dinner rolls
¼ cup firmly packed brown sugar
2 tablespoons finely chopped pecans
½ teaspoon ground cinnamon

1. Preheat oven to 375°.
2. Spoon 1½ teaspoons syrup into
each of 8 muffin cups coated with
cooking spray; set aside.
3. Unroll dough; separate into 4 rec-
tangles. Combine brown sugar,
pecans, and cinnamon. Sprinkle
sugar mixture evenly over each rectangle; press gently into dough.
Beginning at 1 long edge, roll up
jelly-roll fashion. Pinch ends of
dough to seal. Cut each roll into 6
slices. Place 3 slices, cut sides down,
in prepared muffin cups. Bake at
375° for 14 minutes. Run a knife
around edges of cups; invert onto a
platter. YIELD: 8 servings.

POINTS: 4; EXCHANGES: 1½ Starch, 1 Fat;
PER SERVING: CAL 172 (30% from fat);
PRO 2.2g; FAT 5.8g (sat 0.1g); CARB 26.9g;
FIB 0.2g; CHOL 0mg; IRON 1mg;
SOD 260mg; CALC 13mg

APRICOT-ALMOND BRAID

1 (1-pound) loaf frozen white
   bread dough, thawed
Cooking spray
1 (3-ounce) block cream cheese,
   softened
½ cup apricot preserves
3 tablespoons sliced almonds,
   divided
1 large egg white, lightly beaten

1. Thaw bread dough in refrigerator
according to package directions.
2. Cover a large baking sheet with
heavy-duty foil; coat foil with cooking spray. Press dough into a 12- x
8-inch rectangle on prepared baking
sheet. Spread cream cheese lengthwise down center third of dough.
Spread preserves over cream cheese;
sprinkle with 2 tablespoons
almonds.
3. Make diagonal cuts, 1 inch apart,
on opposite sides of filling to within
½ inch of filling. Fold strips alternately over filling from each side,
overlapping at an angle. Cover; let
rise in a warm place (85°), free from
drafts, 40 minutes or until puffy.
4. Preheat oven to 350°.
5. Brush egg white over loaf; sprinkle with remaining 1 tablespoon
almonds. Bake at 350° for 22
minutes or until lightly browned.
YIELD: 12 servings.

POINTS: 4; EXCHANGES: 2 Starch, ½ Fat;
PER SERVING: CAL 171 (26% from fat);
PRO 4.6g; FAT 4.9g (sat 1.7g); CARB 27.8g;
FIB 0.4g; CHOL 8mg; IRON 0.3mg;
SOD 218mg; CALC 40mg

CRANBERRY-APPLE BREAKFAST RING

1 (1-pound) loaf frozen white
    bread dough, thawed
Cooking spray
½ cup whole-berry cranberry sauce
⅓ cup light apple pie filling,
    chopped
¼ cup chopped pecans, divided
½ cup sifted powdered sugar
1 tablespoon water

1. Thaw bread dough in refrigerator according to package directions.
2. Pat dough into a 16- x 8-inch rectangle on a baking sheet coated with cooking spray. Set aside.
3. Combine cranberry sauce and pie filling; stir well. Spread fruit mixture down 1 long edge of dough, leaving a ½-inch margin around edges. Sprinkle 3 tablespoons pecans over fruit mixture. Beginning at edge with fruit mixture, roll up jelly-roll fashion; pinch seam to seal (do not seal ends of roll). Bring ends of roll together to form a ring; pinch ends together to seal. Cut two-thirds through dough from outer edge at 1-inch intervals. Cover; let rise in a warm place (85°), free from drafts, 1 hour or until doubled in bulk.
4. Preheat oven to 375°.
5. Bake at 375° for 22 minutes or until golden brown. Combine powdered sugar and water; stir with a whisk until smooth. Drizzle glaze over warm bread. Sprinkle with remaining pecans. YIELD: 12 servings.

POINTS: 4; **EXCHANGES:** 2 Starch, ½ Fruit;
PER SERVING: CAL 182 (12% from fat);
PRO 4.6g; FAT 2.5g (sat 0.1g); CARB 35.9g;
FIB 0.3g; CHOL 3.5mg; IRON 1.5mg;
SOD 351mg; CALC 30mg

Tough Skin, Tender Heart

Despite the virtues of long shelf life, delicious taste, and nutritional value, winter squash are often passed over for vegetables that appear simpler to prepare. But, with a sharp knife and a meat mallet (even a hammer will do), you can tap into what might become a favorite vegetable. Butternut and acorn are the most common varieties of winter squash. Unlike their summer cousins, these squash have firm, orange-colored flesh protected by a thick skin. Thanks to this tough outer layer, the vegetable can be stored in a cool, dark place at room temperature for a month or more.

CHOCOLATE-TOPPED BUTTERNUT SQUASH FLAN

1 butternut squash (about 1
    pound)
¾ cup sugar
3 large eggs
½ cup firmly packed dark brown
    sugar
2 cups evaporated skim milk
½ teaspoon vanilla extract
⅛ teaspoon salt
¼ cup (1 ounce) grated sweet dark
    chocolate (such as Ghirardelli)

1. Preheat oven to 350°.
2. Cut squash in half lengthwise, and discard seeds and membrane. Place squash halves, cut sides down, in a baking dish. Bake at 350° for 45 minutes or until tender. Use a spoon to scoop 1⅓ cups squash pulp from halves. Place 1⅓ cups squash in a food processor; process until puréed. Set aside. Reserve remaining squash for another use.
3. Place sugar in a small heavy saucepan over medium-high heat; cook until sugar dissolves, stirring constantly. Reduce heat to medium; continue cooking until golden, stirring frequently. Immediately pour into an 8-inch round cake pan, tipping quickly until caramelized sugar coats bottom of cake pan.
4. Place eggs in a large bowl; stir with a whisk. Stir in brown sugar. Add milk, vanilla, and salt; stir well. Add ¾ cup puréed squash; stir until well blended.
5. Pour squash mixture into prepared pan. Place pan in a shallow roasting pan; add hot water to roasting pan to a depth of 1 inch. Bake at 350° for 50 minutes or until a knife inserted in center comes out clean. Remove cake pan from water; let cool completely on a wire rack. Cover surface of flan with plastic wrap; chill 8 hours.
6. Loosen edges of flan with a knife or rubber spatula. Place a large plate upside down on top of cake pan; invert flan onto plate. Drizzle any remaining syrup over flan. Cut into wedges; place on chilled dessert plates. Top with grated chocolate. YIELD: 8 servings.

POINTS: 5; **EXCHANGES:** 3 Starch;
PER SERVING: CAL 230 (13% from fat);
PRO 7.6g; FAT 3.3g (sat 1.4g); CARB 44g;
FIB 0.3g; CHOL 85mg; IRON 1mg;
SOD 142mg; CALC 217mg

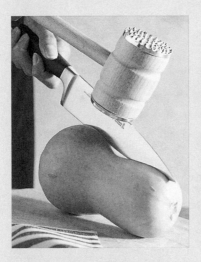

1. Place squash on a cutting board. Using a mallet, gently tap the sharp end of a large knife into the squash. Cut squash in half.

2. Scrape seeds and membranes from squash. Bake squash in a baking dish, cut sides down, at 350° for 45 minutes or until tender, or microwave at HIGH about 8 minutes, turning dish every 2 minutes.

3. Use a spoon to scoop squash pulp from each half. Use pulp as directed in recipe.

GARLICKY ACORN SQUASH AND WILD RICE STUFFING

(pictured on page 154)

1 medium acorn squash (about 1¼ pounds)
1 teaspoon stick margarine
½ cup chopped onion
3 garlic cloves, minced
1 (14½-ounce) can chicken broth
¾ cup dried sweetened cranberries
½ cup orange juice
1 teaspoon minced fresh rosemary
⅛ teaspoon salt
¼ teaspoon pepper
1 (6-ounce) package long-grain-and-wild rice mix
3 tablespoons chopped walnuts, toasted

1. Preheat oven to 350°.
2. Cut squash in half lengthwise, and discard seeds and membrane. Place squash halves, cut sides down, in a baking dish. Bake at 350° for 45 minutes or until tender. Use a spoon to scoop 1¾ cups squash pulp from halves in 1-inch chunks; set aside. Reserve remaining squash for another use.
3. Melt margarine in a saucepan over medium-high heat. Add onion and garlic. Reduce heat to medium; sauté 3 minutes or until tender. Add chicken broth and next 5 ingredients; bring to a boil. Stir in rice mix and 1 tablespoon of contents from seasoning packet. Bring to a boil; cover, reduce heat, and simmer 25 minutes or until liquid is absorbed. Remove from heat; stir in 1¾ cups squash and walnuts. Cover; let stand 5 minutes.
YIELD: 7 servings (serving size: about ¾ cup).
NOTE: Stir remaining seasoning mix into plain rice as it cooks to spice up a side dish for another meal.

POINTS: 4; **EXCHANGES:** 2 Starch, ½ Fruit; **PER SERVING:** CAL 193 (14% from fat); PRO 4.6g; FAT 3g (sat 0.3g); CARB 38.1g; FIB 2.6g; CHOL 0mg; IRON 1.5mg; SOD 184mg; CALC 46mg

One day's menu provides at least two servings of milk and at least five servings of fruits and/or vegetables.

	MONDAY	TUESDAY	WEDNESDAY	THURSDAY
BREAKFAST	**oatmeal,** 1 cup, with 2 tablespoons raisins and 1 teaspoon brown sugar **blueberry fat-free yogurt,** 8 ounces **orange juice,** ½ cup	**Egg-and-Potato Burrito** (Combine 1 egg, 1 egg white, and 1 tablespoon *each of* skim milk and pimiento. Sauté ¾ cup diced potato and ¼ cup chopped onion in a nonstick skillet coated with cooking spray over medium heat until tender; add egg mixture. Cook until firm, stirring. Sprinkle with 2 tablespoons shredded sharp cheddar cheese and a dash *each of* salt and pepper. Spoon onto an 8-inch fat-free flour tortilla; roll up. [*POINTS:* 8]) **skim milk,** 1 cup	**kiwifruit,** 1 **strawberry fat-free yogurt,** 8 ounces	**Cranberry Oatmeal** (Combine 1 cup cooked oatmeal, 2 tablespoons *each of* dried cranberries and skim milk, 2 teaspoons brown sugar, and a dash of cinnamon; stir well. [*POINTS:* 4]) **orange juice,** ½ cup
LUNCH	**Cranberry-Chicken Salad** (Combine 1 tablespoon *each of* dried cranberries, chopped celery, light mayonnaise, and plain fat-free yogurt with 2 ounces drained canned chunk white chicken in water; spoon onto a lettuce leaf. [*POINTS:* 4]) **skim milk,** 1 cup **saltines,** 6	**Broccoli-Rice Toss** (Combine 1 cup steamed small broccoli florets, ¾ cup cooked brown rice, 1 tablespoon *each of* lemon juice and chopped walnuts, and 2 ounces julienne-cut cooked turkey breast; toss well. [*POINTS:* 6]) **vanilla fat-free yogurt,** 8 ounces	**Turkey-and-Havarti Sandwich** (Spread 2 teaspoons light mayonnaise and 1 teaspoon Dijon mustard over 2 slices whole-wheat bread; place 2 ounces thinly sliced cooked turkey breast, ¾ ounce shredded Havarti cheese, 2 tomato slices, and 2 lettuce leaves on 1 bread slice. Top with remaining bread slice. [*POINTS:* 9]) **grapes,** 1 cup **skim milk,** 1 cup	**Twice-Baked Potato** (Cut a ¼-inch slice off the top of a large baked potato; scoop out pulp, leaving a ¼-inch-thick shell. Combine potato pulp, ⅓ cup chopped cooked broccoli florets, 3 tablespoons shredded sharp cheddar cheese, 1 tablespoon *each of* chopped green onions, fat-free ranch dressing, plain fat-free yogurt, and a dash *each of* salt and pepper. Stuff potato shell with mixture; bake at 350° for 15 minutes or until thoroughly heated. [*POINTS:* 6]) **skim milk,** 1 cup
DINNER	**Salmon with Fennel-Dill Relish** (Heat 1 teaspoon olive oil in a nonstick skillet over medium-high heat. Add ⅓ cup chopped onion, 3 tablespoons chopped fennel, and ⅛ teaspoon salt; sauté 5 minutes. Stir in 2 teaspoons chopped fresh dill. Serve over 3 ounces broiled salmon. [*POINTS:* 4]) **Spinach Sauté** (Heat ½ teaspoon olive oil in a nonstick skillet over medium heat. Add ¼ cup *each of* sliced mushrooms and onion; sauté 3 minutes. Add 1½ cups torn fresh spinach; sauté until spinach wilts. Toss with 1 tablespoon fat-free red wine vinaigrette. [*POINTS:* 1]) **cooked brown rice,** ½ cup	**Chicken-Tomato Bake** (Combine ⅓ cup drained canned diced tomatoes, 3 tablespoons *each of* chopped onion and fennel, ⅛ teaspoon dried Italian seasoning, 1 minced garlic clove, and a dash *each of* salt and pepper; spoon over 1 [4-ounce] skinned, boned chicken breast half. Cover and bake at 350° for 25 minutes. Sprinkle with 1 tablespoon grated Parmesan cheese; bake, uncovered, 10 minutes or until done. Serve over 1 cup cooked linguine. [*POINTS:* 6]) **grapes,** 1 cup	**Pork-Potato Sauté** (Heat 1 teaspoon olive oil over medium-high heat. Add ½ cup chopped onion, ⅛ teaspoon *each of* salt and pepper, and 1 minced garlic clove; sauté 3 minutes. Add 3 ounces cubed pork loin; sauté 3 minutes. Add 1 cup cubed potato, 1 cup broccoli florets, ¼ cup fat-free chicken broth or water, ¼ teaspoon curry powder, and a dash of dried crushed red pepper; cook over medium heat until potato is tender. [*POINTS:* 7])	**Chicken With Caramelized Onions** (Heat 1 teaspoon olive oil over medium-high heat. Sauté 1 cup thinly sliced onion 10 minutes, stirring frequently; add 3 tablespoons water, 1 tablespoon balsamic vinegar, and a dash *each of* salt, pepper, and thyme. Cook 5 minutes, stirring frequently. Remove and set aside. Sprinkle 1 [4-ounce] skinned, boned chicken breast half with a dash *each of* salt, garlic powder, and pepper; cook over medium heat 5 minutes on each side or until done. Top with onion mixture. [*POINTS:* 4]) **green salad,** 2 cups, with 2 tablespoons fat-free red wine vinaigrette
SNACK	**carrot sticks,** 1 cup	**Sunshine Smoothie** (Place ¾ cup orange juice, ¼ cup strawberry sorbet, 2 teaspoons grenadine, and 4 ice cubes in a blender; process until smooth. [*POINTS:* 3])	**bagel,** ½ small, with 2 tablespoons fat-free cream cheese and ½ cup sliced strawberries	**banana,** 1 medium, with 1 tablespoon peanut butter **skim milk,** 1 cup
POINTS	***POINTS*** for the day: 22 **Exchanges:** 5 Starch, 2½ Fruit, 2 Sk Milk, 2½ Fat, 2 Very Lean Meat, 3 Lean Meat, 3 Veg	***POINTS*** for the day: 28 **Exchanges:** 1 Med-fat Meat, 5½ Very Lean Meat, 6½ Starch, ½ Hi-fat Meat, 2 Sk Milk, 3 Veg, 1 Fat, ½ Lean Meat, 2½ Fruit	***POINTS*** for the day: 25 **Exchanges:** 2½ Fruit, 2 Sk Milk, 2 Fat, 5 Starch, ½ Hi-fat Meat, 3 Veg, 3 Lean Meat, 2 Very Lean Meat	***POINTS*** for the day: 23 **Exchanges:** 5 Starch, 3 Fruit, 3 Veg, 1 Hi-fat Meat, 2 Sk Milk, 2 Fat, 3 Very Lean Meat

	FRIDAY	SATURDAY	SUNDAY
BREAKFAST	**bran flakes,** 1 cup, with 1 sliced banana **skim milk,** 1 cup	**Strawberry-Yogurt Gulp** (Combine 1 cup sliced fresh strawberries, ½ cup skim milk, and 8 ounces vanilla fat-free yogurt in a blender; process until smooth. [*POINTS:* 4])	**orange juice,** ½ cup **toasted waffle,** 1 (4-inch) frozen, with 1 tablespoon maple syrup and 1 tablespoon dried cranberries **skim milk,** 1 cup
LUNCH	**Bean-and-Cheese Burrito** (Microwave ½ cup fat-free refried beans until warm; spread over an 8-inch fat-free flour tortilla. Top with ⅓ cup thinly sliced romaine lettuce and 3 tablespoons *each of* shredded sharp cheddar cheese, chopped plum tomato, and salsa; roll up. [*POINTS:* 5]) **skim milk,** 1 cup	**Peanut Butter-Banana Sandwich** (Spread 1 tablespoon peanut butter over 1 slice whole-wheat bread; top with 1 sliced banana, 2 teaspoons honey, and another slice bread. [*POINTS:* 9]) **cucumber spears,** 1 cup, with 1 tablespoon fat-free ranch dressing **skim milk,** 1 cup	**Tuna-Spinach Roll-Up** (Combine 4 ounces drained canned tuna with 2 tablespoons *each of* finely chopped carrot and fennel, 1 tablespoon *each of* celery, diced pimiento, light mayonnaise, and plain fat-free yogurt, and 2 teaspoons chopped fresh dill; spread over an 8-inch fat-free flour tortilla. Top with ½ cup torn fresh spinach and ¼ cup sliced cucumber; roll up. [*POINTS:* 6]) **skim milk,** 1 cup **kiwifruit,** 1
DINNER	**grilled filet mignon,** 3 ounces **Couscous-Walnut Pilaf** (Combine ½ cup boiling water, ⅓ cup uncooked couscous, 1 tablespoon *each of* chopped walnuts and green onions, 1 teaspoon lemon juice, and a dash of salt. Cover and let stand 5 minutes; fluff with a fork. [*POINTS:* 3]) **steamed broccoli florets,** 1 cup **steamed carrots,** 1 cup	**Maple-Glazed Pork Chop** (Dredge 1 [4-ounce] boned loin pork chop in 1 tablespoon dry breadcrumbs. Heat ½ teaspoon olive oil in a nonstick skillet over medium heat; add chop. Cook 2 minutes on each side. Add 3 tablespoons apple cider and ½ cup sliced apple; simmer 10 minutes or until done. Add 1 tablespoon maple syrup, 1 teaspoon Dijon mustard, and a dash *each of* salt and pepper; stir well. Cook 5 minutes or until thick. [*POINTS:* 7]) **steamed carrots,** 1 cup **cooked brown rice,** 1 cup	**Zucchini Pasta With Havarti** (Sauté 1 cup sliced zucchini and 1 minced garlic clove in a nonstick skillet over medium heat 3 minutes; stir in 1 tablespoon *each of* lemon juice and chopped walnuts and a dash *each of* salt and pepper. Toss with 1 cup cooked penne pasta and 3 tablespoons shredded Havarti cheese. [*POINTS:* 5]) **green salad,** 2 cups, with 2 tablespoons fat-free red wine vinaigrette
SNACK	**Strawberry Waffle à la Sorbet** (Toast 1 [4-inch] frozen waffle; top with ½ cup sliced fresh strawberries, ¼ cup strawberry sorbet, and 2 tablespoons fat-free whipped topping. [*POINTS:* 5])	**bagel,** ½ small, with 1 tablespoon cream cheese	**baked tortilla chips,** 1 ounce, with ¼ cup salsa
POINTS	**POINTS** for the day: 28 **Exchanges:** 9 Starch, 1½ Fruit, 2 Sk Milk, 3 Veg, 1 Hi-fat Meat, 3 Lean Meat, 2 Fat	**POINTS** for the day: 28 **Exchanges:** 3 Fruit, 2½ Sk Milk, 1½ Fat, ½ Hi-fat Meat, 7 Starch, 2 Veg, 3 Lean Meat	**POINTS** for the day: 25 **Exchanges:** 2½ Fruit, 7 Starch, 3 Fat, 2 Sk Milk, 4 Very Lean Meat, 4 Veg, 1 Hi-fat Meat

One day's menu provides at least two servings of milk and at least five servings of fruits and/or vegetables.

	MONDAY	TUESDAY	WEDNESDAY	THURSDAY
BREAKFAST	**Broccoli-Cheddar Omelet** (Combine 2 large egg whites, 1 large egg, 2 tablespoons skim milk, and a dash *each of* salt and pepper. Cook in a small nonstick skillet coated with cooking spray over medium heat 4 minutes or until set {do not stir}; top with ⅓ cup steamed chopped broccoli and 3 tablespoons shredded sharp cheddar cheese. Fold in half. [*POINTS:* 5]) **skim milk,** 1 cup **cantaloupe,** 1 cup, cubed	**cooked oatmeal,** 1 cup, with 2 tablespoons raisins and 1 tablespoon honey **skim milk,** 1 cup **orange juice,** ½ cup	**Banana-Peach Smoothie** (Combine 1 [8¼-ounce] can sliced peaches in juice, undrained, 1 [8-ounce] carton vanilla fat-free aspartame-sweetened yogurt, ½ cup skim milk, and 1 banana in a blender; process until smooth. [*POINTS:* 7])	**Egg and Cheese Sandwich** (Combine 1 large egg and 1 tablespoon skim milk; cook in a nonstick skillet until set, stirring frequently. Spoon over 1 slice toasted whole-wheat bread; top with 1 tablespoon shredded sharp cheddar cheese, a dash *each of* salt and pepper, and another slice of toasted bread. [*POINTS:* 7]) **orange juice,** ½ cup **skim milk,** 1 cup
LUNCH	**tomato soup,** 1½ cups, canned **saltines,** 6 **skim milk,** 1 cup **carrot sticks,** 1 cup	**Beef-and-Blue Sandwich** (Spread 2 teaspoons light mayonnaise and 1 teaspoon Dijon mustard over 2 slices whole-wheat bread. Layer 2 ounces thinly sliced roast beef, 2 tomato slices, 2 lettuce leaves, and 3 tablespoons crumbled blue cheese between bread slices. [*POINTS:* 9]) **grapes,** 1 cup	**Pimiento Cheese-Veggie Sandwich** (Combine ¼ cup shredded sharp cheddar cheese, 4 teaspoons *each of* light mayonnaise and diced pimiento; spread over 1 slice whole-wheat bread. Top with 2 lettuce leaves, 2 tomato slices, a dash *each of* salt and pepper, and another slice of bread. [*POINTS:* 9]) **celery sticks,** 1 cup	**cheese pizza,** ⅛ of 12-inch thin-crust pizza **green salad,** 2 cups, with 1 tablespoon fat-free Italian dressing **skim milk,** 1 cup
DINNER	**Tuna-Pasta Toss** (Melt ½ teaspoon margarine in a nonstick skillet over medium heat. Sauté 1 tablespoon chopped onion 2 minutes. Stir in 3 tablespoons skim milk, 2 tablespoons grated Parmesan cheese, 3 ounces drained canned albacore tuna in water, and a dash *each of* salt and pepper; toss with 1 cup hot cooked penne pasta. [*POINTS:* 8]) **steamed asparagus spears,** 1 cup	**Chicken-and-Asparagus Salad** (Cut 1 [4-ounce] skinned, boned chicken breast half into thin strips; toss with 1 teaspoon Dijon mustard and a dash *each of* salt and pepper. Heat ½ teaspoon olive oil in a nonstick skillet over medium heat until hot. Add chicken; sauté 6 minutes. Add 1 tablespoon *each of* sliced green onions and water, 1 teaspoon white wine vinegar, and ½ teaspoon *each of* Dijon mustard and olive oil to skillet. Spoon chicken and sauce over 1½ cups sliced romaine lettuce; top with ½ cup steamed asparagus spears. [*POINTS:* 4])	**Baked Pesto Salmon** (Brush 2 teaspoons prepared pesto over 1 [4-ounce] skinned salmon fillet; bake at 350° for 20 minutes or until fish flakes easily when tested with a fork. [*POINTS:* 5]) **steamed green beans,** 1 cup **cooked brown rice,** 1 cup	**grilled pork chop,** 3 ounces **Smashed Sweet Potatoes** (Combine 1 cup mashed cooked sweet potato, 2 tablespoons skim milk, 1 tablespoon chopped pecans, 1 teaspoon *each of* brown sugar and margarine, and a dash of salt; stir well. [*POINTS:* 6]) **steamed broccoli,** 1 cup
SNACK	**Cinnamon Toast** (Spread 1 teaspoon margarine over 1 slice whole-wheat bread; sprinkle with 1 tablespoon sugar and cinnamon to taste. Broil 2 minutes. [*POINTS:* 4])	**saltines,** 6, with 2 teaspoons peanut butter **skim milk,** 1 cup	**rice cakes,** 2 large **skim milk,** 1 cup	**cantaloupe,** 1 cup, cubed
POINTS	***POINTS*** for the day: 28 **Exchanges:** 6 Starch, 6 Veg, 3½ Lean Meat, 2½ Sk Milk, 2½ Fat, 2 Med-fat Meat, 1 Fruit	***POINTS*** for the day: 26 **Exchanges:** 5½ Starch, 5 Fat, 4 Veg, 3½ Fruit, 2 Sk Milk, 2 Lean Meat, 2 Very Lean Meat, 1 Med-fat Meat	***POINTS*** for the day: 28 **Exchanges:** 5 Starch, 4½ Fruit, 4½ Veg, 3 Lean Meat, 2½ Sk Milk, 2½ Fat, 1 Med-fat Meat	***POINTS*** for the day: 27 **Exchanges:** 6 Starch, 4 Med-fat Meat, 2½ Veg, 2 Sk Milk, 2 Fruit, 2 Fat, ½ Lean Meat

	FRIDAY	SATURDAY	SUNDAY
BREAKFAST	**bran flakes,** 1 cup **skim milk,** 1 cup **banana,** 1	**toasted whole-wheat bread,** 1 slice, with 1 tablespoon jelly **skim milk,** 1 cup **cantaloupe,** 1 cup, cubed	**bran flakes,** 1 cup **skim milk,** 1 cup **orange juice,** ¾ cup
LUNCH	**Turkey-Spinach Sandwich** (Spread 2 teaspoons light mayonnaise over 2 slices whole-wheat bread. Layer 2 ounces thinly sliced cooked turkey, ½ cup fresh spinach leaves, 2 tomato slices, and 3 tablespoons crumbled blue cheese between bread slices. [*POINTS:* 9]) **skim milk,** 1 cup	**Turkey-Pasta Salad** (Combine 1 cup cooked penne pasta, 1 ounce julienne-cut cooked turkey breast, 2 tablespoons sliced green onions, 1 tablespoon plain fat-free yogurt, 2 teaspoons light mayonnaise, and a dash *each of* salt and pepper; toss well. [*POINTS:* 5]) **carrot sticks,** 1 cup **orange juice,** 1 cup	**Stuffed Sweet Potato** (Cut a ¼-inch slice off the top of a large baked sweet potato; scoop out pulp, leaving a ¼-inch-thick shell. Combine pulp, 2 tablespoons skim milk, 1 tablespoon *each of* raisins and brown sugar, 1 teaspoon *each of* bourbon and margarine, and a dash of salt. Stuff mixture into potato shell; bake at 350° for 10 minutes or until thoroughly heated. [*POINTS:* 6]) **steamed broccoli florets,** 1 cup **skim milk,** 1 cup
DINNER	**Shrimp-Potato Hash** (Heat 1 teaspoon olive oil in a nonstick skillet over medium heat. Add ½ cup slivered onion and ½ teaspoon minced garlic; sauté 5 minutes. Add 1 cup peeled cubed cooked potato, 2 tablespoons water, and ⅛ teaspoon Italian seasoning; sauté 6 minutes. Add ½ cup cubed zucchini and 3 ounces peeled medium shrimp; sauté 4 minutes or until shrimp is done. [*POINTS:* 5])	**Chicken à la King** (Melt 1 teaspoon margarine in a nonstick skillet. Add 3 ounces cubed skinned, boned chicken breast and 1 tablespoon chopped onion; sauté 4 minutes. Add ¼ cup sliced fresh mushrooms; sauté 1 minute. Stir in 1 tablespoon flour; cook 1 minute, stirring constantly. Gradually add ½ cup skim milk, stirring constantly. Add 2 tablespoons frozen green peas and a dash *each of* salt, pepper, and paprika; cook until thick, stirring constantly. Serve over 1 slice toasted whole-wheat bread. [*POINTS:* 7]) **steamed green beans,** 1 cup	**Pesto-Cheese Tortellini** (Cook ¾ cup fresh cheese tortellini according to package directions; drain, reserving 1 tablespoon cooking water. Combine reserved cooking water, 2 teaspoons prepared pesto, and cooked tortellini; toss well. [*POINTS:* 7]) **spinach salad,** 2 cups torn fresh spinach, with 2 tablespoons fat-free red wine vinaigrette **steamed carrots,** 1 cup, with 1 teaspoon *each of* margarine and honey
SNACK	**strawberry fat-free aspartame-sweetened yogurt,** 8 ounces **rice cakes,** 2 large	**strawberry fat-free aspartame-sweetened yogurt,** 8 ounces	**banana,** 1
POINTS	**POINTS** for the day: 24 **Exchanges:** 5½ Starch, 3½ Sk Milk, 3½ Veg, 3 Very Lean Meat, 3 Fat, 2 Fruit	**POINTS** for the day: 21 **Exchanges:** 5½ Veg, 4½ Starch, 3½ Fruit, 3 Sk Milk, 3 Very Lean Meat, 1 Fat	**POINTS** for the day: 24 **Exchanges:** 6½ Starch, 5 Veg, 4 Fruit, 2 Sk Milk, 3 Fat

One day's menu provides at least two servings of milk and at least five servings of fruits and/or vegetables.

	MONDAY	TUESDAY	WEDNESDAY	THURSDAY
BREAKFAST	**cooked oatmeal,** 1 cup, with 2 tablespoons raisins and 1 tablespoon honey **skim milk,** 1 cup **orange juice,** ½ cup	**bran flakes,** 1 cup **skim milk,** 1 cup **fresh strawberries,** 1 cup	**skim milk,** 1 cup **bagel,** 1 small, with 2 tablespoons fat-free cream cheese **fresh strawberries,** 1 cup	**cooked oatmeal,** 1 cup, with 2 tablespoons raisins and 1 tablespoon brown sugar **orange juice,** 1 cup **skim milk,** 1 cup
LUNCH	**fast food hamburger,** 1 small **green salad,** 2 cups, with 1 tablespoon fat-free ranch dressing	**Tuna Salad** (Combine 4 ounces drained canned tuna in water with 1 tablespoon chopped celery, 2 teaspoons light mayonnaise, and 1 teaspoon Dijon mustard; stir well. Spoon into a tomato. [*POINTS:* 4]) **saltines,** 9	**Greek Salad** (Combine 2 teaspoons white wine vinegar, 1 teaspoon olive oil, ½ teaspoon *each* of Dijon mustard and honey, and a dash *each of* salt and pepper; toss with 2 cups sliced romaine lettuce, 1 quartered tomato, and 6 large black olives. Sprinkle with 3 tablespoons crumbled feta cheese. [*POINTS:* 4]) **French bread,** 1 (1-ounce) slice	**Pita Pizza** (Spread 2 tablespoons tomato sauce over 1 small pita bread round; sprinkle with 2 tablespoons *each of* grated Parmesan cheese and chopped black olives. Top with ¼ cup diced tomato and 1 tablespoon crumbled feta cheese. Bake at 350° for 5 minutes or until cheese melts. [*POINTS:* 4]) **skim milk,** 1 cup **grapes,** 1 cup
DINNER	**broiled pork chop,** 3 ounces **Apple-Almond Sauté** (Melt 1 teaspoon margarine in a nonstick skillet. Add ¼ cup sliced onion; sauté 3 minutes. Add 1 sliced Granny Smith apple and 1 tablespoon slivered almonds; sauté 5 minutes. Stir in 1 tablespoon maple syrup; sauté 2 minutes. [*POINTS:* 4]) **steamed spinach,** 1 cup	**Mediterranean Chicken Pita** (Broil a 4-ounce skinned, boned chicken breast half 5 minutes on each side or until done, basting frequently with 2 tablespoons fat-free Italian dressing. Cut into ¼-inch-wide strips. Spread 2 tablespoons prepared hummus onto 1 small pita bread round; arrange chicken strips, 1 lettuce leaf, and 2 tomato slices down center of pita. Sprinkle with 2 tablespoons crumbled feta cheese; roll up. [*POINTS:* 5]) **carrot sticks,** 1 cup **skim milk,** 1 cup	**baked salmon fillet,** 3 ounces **Roasted Mushroom-Rice Pilaf** (Combine 1 cup quartered fresh mushrooms, 1 tablespoon balsamic vinegar, 1 teaspoon olive oil, and a dash of dried Italian seasoning; bake at 425° for 20 minutes or until tender. Toss with 1 cup cooked brown rice. [*POINTS:* 5]) **steamed asparagus,** 1 cup	**Pork Tenderloin With Mango Relish** (Combine ⅓ cup chopped fresh mango, 1 tablespoon chopped onion, and 2 teaspoons lime juice; toss well. Serve with 2 ounces roasted pork tenderloin. [*POINTS:* 3]) **green salad,** 2 cups sliced romaine lettuce, with 2 tablespoons fat-free Italian dressing **French bread,** 2 (1-ounce) slices
SNACK	**vanilla fat-free aspartame-sweetened yogurt,** 8 ounces	**baked tortilla chips,** 1½ ounces **avocado,** ¼, mashed	**Mango-Banana Smoothie** (Combine 1 banana and ½ cup chopped fresh mango, 8 ounces vanilla fat-free aspartame-sweetened yogurt, and ½ cup skim milk in a blender; process until smooth. [*POINTS:* 6])	**blueberry fat-free aspartame-sweetened yogurt,** 8 ounces
POINTS	***POINTS*** for the day: 23 **Exchanges:** 6 Starch, 4 Fruit, 4 Veg, 2 Sk Milk, 5 Med-fat Meat, 2 Fat, 1 Free	***POINTS*** for the day: 24 **Exchanges:** 7½ Starch, 1 Fruit, 3 Veg, 2 Sk Milk, 7 Very Lean Meat, ½ Med-fat Meat, 3 Fat, 2 Free	***POINTS*** for the day: 27 **Exchanges:** 5½ Starch, 4 Fruit, 6 Veg, 2½ Sk Milk, 3 Lean Meat, 1 Med-fat Meat, 3 Fat, 2 Free	***POINTS*** for the day: 22 **Exchanges:** 6½ Starch, 4½ Fruit, 3 Veg, 3 Sk Milk, 3 Lean Meat, ½ Med-fat Meat, 1 Fat, 1 Free

7-DAY MENU PLANNER

APRIL

	FRIDAY	SATURDAY	SUNDAY
BREAKFAST	**Smoked Salmon-Egg Scramble** (Combine 1 large egg and 1 tablespoon skim milk; cook 30 seconds in a nonstick skillet. Stir in 1 ounce chopped smoked salmon; cook until set, stirring frequently. Spoon over ½ small bagel. [*POINTS:* 5]) **skim milk,** 1 cup **orange juice,** ½ cup	**bagel,** 1 small, with 1 tablespoon fat-free cream cheese and 1 ounce smoked salmon **skim milk,** 1 cup **grapes,** 1 cup	**Scrambled Egg-Bagel Sandwich** (Combine 1 large egg and 1 tablespoon skim milk; cook in a nonstick skillet until set, stirring frequently. Spoon over ½ small bagel; top with remaining bagel half. [*POINTS:* 5]) **orange juice,** ½ cup
LUNCH	**Roasted Vegetable Sandwich** (Combine ½ cup *each of* quartered onion, sliced yellow squash, and sliced zucchini, and 2 tablespoons balsamic vinegar in a baking dish coated with cooking spray; toss well. Bake at 400° for 20 minutes or until lightly browned. Spoon onto 1 [1-ounce] slice French bread; sprinkle with 3 tablespoons crumbled feta cheese. Top with another slice of bread. [*POINTS:* 6]) **skim milk,** 1 cup	**Roast Beef Sandwich** (Spread 2 teaspoons light mayonnaise and 1 teaspoon Dijon mustard over 1 side of *each of* 2 [1-ounce] slices French bread. Layer 2 ounces thinly sliced lean delistyle roast beef, 2 tomato slices, 1 onion slice, and 1 lettuce leaf between bread slices. [*POINTS:* 7]) **baked tortilla chips,** 1 ounce **celery sticks,** 1 cup	**Peanut Butter-Banana Pita Pocket** (Spread 1 tablespoon peanut butter in 1 small pita bread; stuff with 1 sliced banana, and drizzle with 1 teaspoon honey. [*POINTS:* 5]) **carrot sticks,** 1 cup **skim milk,** 1 cup
DINNER	**Steak with Mushroom Sauce** (Melt 1 teaspoon margarine in a nonstick skillet over medium-high heat. Add ¾ cup sliced fresh mushrooms and 2 tablespoons chopped shallot; sauté 4 minutes. Add ¼ cup *each of* dry red wine and fat-free beef broth; cook 5 minutes. Place mushroom-wine mixture in a bowl. Sprinkle a 4-ounce filet mignon steak with a dash *each of* salt and pepper; add to skillet. Cook 3 minutes on each side or until desired degree of doneness. Remove from skillet. Add mushroom mixture, ½ teaspoon cornstarch, and a dash of dried thyme to skillet. Boil 1 minute, stirring constantly. [*POINTS:* 6]) **steamed green beans,** 1 cup **mashed cooked potatoes,** ½ cup	**Cajun Grilled Snapper** (Combine 1 teaspoon *each of* melted margarine and lemon juice; brush over an 8-ounce snapper fillet; sprinkle with ¼ teaspoon Cajun seasoning. Grill 6 minutes on each side or until fish flakes easily when tested with a fork. [*POINTS:* 5]) **grilled corn on the cob,** 1 small **grilled zucchini squash,** 1 cup **skim milk,** 1 cup	**broiled lamb chop,** 3 ounces **Feta Mashed Potatoes** (Combine 1 cup mashed cooked potato, 2 tablespoons *each of* fat-free sour cream, skim milk, feta cheese, and a dash *each of* salt and pepper; stir well. [*POINTS:* 4]) **green salad,** 2 cups sliced romaine lettuce, 2 tomato wedges, and 2 tablespoons fat-free Italian dressing
SNACK	**prepared hummus,** ¼ cup **pita bread,** 1 small	**banana,** 1, with 2 teaspoons peanut butter	**blueberry fat-free aspartame-sweetened yogurt,** 8 ounces
POINTS	***POINTS*** for the day: 25 **Exchanges:** 7½ Starch, 4 Lean Meat, 2 Med-fat Meat, 1 Fruit, 4½ Veg, 2 Sk Milk, 1 Fat	***POINTS*** for the day: 28 **Exchanges:** 5 Starch, 3 Fruit, 4 Veg, 2 Sk Milk, 9 Lean Meat, 2 Fat, 1 Free	***POINTS*** for the day: 24 **Exchanges:** 8 Starch, 3 Fruit, 4 Veg, 2 Sk Milk, 3 Lean Meat, 1½ Med-fat Meat, 1 Fat, 2 Free

169

One day's menu provides at least two servings of milk and at least five servings of fruits and/or vegetables.

	MONDAY	TUESDAY	WEDNESDAY	THURSDAY
BREAKFAST	**cooked oatmeal,** 1 cup, with 2 tablespoons raisins and 1 tablespoon honey **cantaloupe,** 1 cup, cubed **orange juice,** 1 cup	**Strawberry-Banana Smoothie** (Combine ¾ cup strawberries, ⅓ cup skim milk, ½ banana, and 8 ounces vanilla fat-free aspartame-sweetened yogurt in a blender; process until smooth. [*POINTS:* 5])	**orange juice,** ½ cup **meatless breakfast patty,** 1 **cooked oatmeal,** 1 cup, with 1 tablespoon honey	**cooked oatmeal,** 1 cup, with 2 tablespoons raisins and 1 tablespoon honey **orange juice,** ½ cup **skim milk,** 1 cup
LUNCH	**tomato soup,** canned, 1½ cups **skim milk,** 1 cup **saltines,** 6	**Couscous-Vegetable Salad** (Combine 2 tablespoons chopped dried tomatoes [not packed in oil] with 2 tablespoons hot water; let stand 10 minutes. Combine 1 cup cooked couscous, ¼ cup *each of* diced cucumber, diced red bell pepper, and chopped drained canned artichoke hearts, dried tomatoes, 2 tablespoons chopped fresh parsley, and 1 teaspoon olive oil; toss well, and serve on a lettuce leaf. [*POINTS:* 4]) **skim milk,** 1 cup	**Tabbouleh-Filled Tomato** (Combine ¼ cup *each of* bulgur and boiling water in a small bowl; cover and let stand 20 minutes or until water is absorbed. Stir in ⅓ cup diced cucumber, 2 tablespoons fresh parsley, 1 tablespoon lemon juice, 1 teaspoon olive oil, 2 ounces diced roasted chicken breast, and a dash of salt. Cut a tomato into 4 wedges, cutting to but not through bottom; fill tomato with tabbouleh. [*POINTS:* 5]) **skim milk,** 1 cup	**Chef's Salad** (Top 2 cups sliced romaine lettuce with 2 ounces julienne-cut turkey breast, 2 tomato slices, and ¼ cup *each of* shredded carrot and sliced cucumber; serve with 2 tablespoons fat-free Italian dressing. [*POINTS:* 2]) **saltines,** 6
DINNER	**Roasted Chicken and Artichoke Linguine** (Heat 1 teaspoon olive oil over medium heat; add ¼ cup *each of* diced red bell pepper and chopped onion. Sauté 3 minutes; add 2 ounces chopped roasted chicken breast, ½ cup chopped drained canned artichoke hearts, and ⅛ teaspoon dried Italian seasoning. Toss with 1 cup cooked linguine. [*POINTS:* 6]) **steamed asparagus,** 1 cup	**Roasted Chicken Pizza** (Spread ¼ cup tomato purée over a 4-ounce Italian cheese-flavored pizza crust [such as Boboli]. Top with ⅓ cup *each of* thinly sliced fresh spinach and sliced fresh mushrooms, 2 tablespoons chopped onion, and 1 ounce chopped roasted chicken breast; sprinkle with 3 tablespoons grated Parmesan cheese. Bake at 450° for 6 minutes or until cheese melts. [*POINTS:* 9]) **grapes,** 1 cup	**Main-Dish Squash Casserole** (Combine 1 large egg, 1 [1-ounce] slice chopped French bread, and 1½ teaspoons margarine; stir well. Add 1½ cups chopped cooked yellow squash, and a dash *each of* salt and pepper. Spoon into a small baking dish coated with cooking spray; sprinkle with 3 tablespoons shredded cheddar cheese, and bake at 350° for 30 minutes. [*POINTS:* 8])	**Sun-Dried Tomato Pizza** (Combine 3 tablespoons chopped dried tomatoes [not packed in oil] with 3 tablespoons hot water; let stand 10 minutes. Stir dried tomatoes into 3 tablespoons tomato purée, and spread over a 4-ounce Italian cheese-flavored pizza crust [such as Boboli]. Top with ¼ cup *each of* diced yellow squash and chopped drained canned artichoke hearts; sprinkle with 3 tablespoons grated Parmesan cheese. Bake at 450° for 6 minutes or until cheese melts. [*POINTS:* 8]) **apple slices,** 1 cup
SNACK	**baked tortilla chips,** 1 ounce, with ¼ cup salsa **skim milk,** 1 cup	**Ice Cream Parfait** (Layer ½ cup *each of* vanilla fat-free ice cream and sliced fresh strawberries, and 3 tablespoons crumbled graham crackers in a parfait glass. [*POINTS:* 5])	**cantaloupe,** 1 cup, cubed **vanilla fat-free aspartame-sweetened yogurt,** 8 ounces	**Pimiento-and-Cheese Spread** (Combine 2 tablespoons shredded sharp cheddar cheese and 2 teaspoons *each of* diced pimiento and light mayonnaise; serve spread with 1 cup celery sticks. [*POINTS:* 2]) **skim milk,** 1 cup
POINTS	***POINTS*** for the day: 24 **Exchanges:** 9 Starch, 4 Fruit, 3 Veg, 2 Sk Milk, 2 Lean Meat, 1 Fat, 1 Free	***POINTS*** for the day: 24 **Exchanges:** 8½ Starch, 3½ Fruit, 4 Veg, 2½ Sk Milk, 2 Lean Meat, 1 Fat, 1 Free	***POINTS*** for the day: 23 **Exchanges:** 5½ Starch, 2 Fruit, 4½ Veg, 2 Sk Milk, 3 Lean Meat, 2 Med-fat Meat, 2½ Fat	***POINTS*** for the day: 24 **Exchanges:** 7½ Starch, 3 Fruit, 5½ Veg, 2 Sk Milk, 2 Lean Meat, 1½ Med-fat Meat, 1½ Fat, 1 Free

FRIDAY	SATURDAY	SUNDAY	
Egg-Sausage Burrito (Combine 1 egg, 1 egg white, and 1 tablespoon skim milk; cook 30 seconds in a nonstick skillet. Stir in 1 cooked, crumbled meatless breakfast patty; cook until set. Spoon onto an 8-inch fat-free flour tortilla; roll up. [*POINTS:* 7]) **skim milk,** 1 cup **orange juice,** 1 cup	**Fruit-Cheese Roll-Up** (Spread ⅓ cup fat-free cottage cheese over an 8-inch fat-free flour tortilla; top with ⅔ cup sliced strawberries and 1 tablespoon sugar. Roll up. [*POINTS:* 6])	**Yogurt-Topped Fruit** (Combine 1 cup sliced strawberries and 1 sliced banana in a bowl. Combine 8 ounces blueberry fat-free aspartame-sweetened yogurt and 1 teaspoon honey; spoon over fruit. [*POINTS:* 5])	**BREAKFAST**
Spinach-Stuffed Potato (Split a large baked potato, and stuff with ½ cup chopped fresh spinach, 3 tablespoons shredded cheddar cheese, 1 tablespoon fat-free sour cream, and a dash *each of* salt and pepper. Bake at 350° for 10 minutes or until cheese melts. [*POINTS:* 5])	**vegetarian vegetable soup,** canned, 1 cup **saltines,** 6 **grapes,** 1 cup **skim milk,** 1 cup	**Turkey-Spinach Roll-Up** (Spread 2 teaspoons light mayonnaise over an 8-inch fat-free flour tortilla; layer 2 ounces deli sliced turkey breast, ½ cup torn spinach, and 2 tablespoons shredded cheddar cheese. Roll up. [*POINTS:* 5]) **skim milk,** 1 cup	**LUNCH**
chicken sandwich, grilled, fast-food (*POINTS:* 8) **green salad,** 2 cups, with 2 tablespoons fat-free ranch dressing	**Beef-and-Vegetable Kabobs** (Cut a 4-ounce filet mignon steak into 1-inch pieces. Combine steak, ¼ cup *each of* red bell pepper squares, onion chunks, small mushrooms, and cherry tomatoes, 1 tablespoon balsamic vinegar, 1 teaspoon olive oil, ¼ teaspoon soy sauce, and a dash of dried Italian seasoning; marinate in refrigerator 1 hour. Thread on skewers and grill or broil 6 minutes or until steak is done. [*POINTS:* 6]) **cooked couscous,** ½ cup, with ½ teaspoon margarine **skim milk,** 1 cup	**baked flounder fillet,** 6 ounces **steamed broccoli,** 1 cup **steamed carrots,** 1 cup **French bread,** 2 (1-ounce) slices	**DINNER**
cucumber spears, 1 cup	**skim milk,** 1 cup **celery sticks,** 1 cup, with 2 teaspoons peanut butter	**baked tortilla chips,** 1 ounce, with ¼ cup salsa **skim milk,** 1 cup	**SNACK**
POINTS for the day: 27 **Exchanges:** 6 Starch, 2 Fruit, 3½ Veg, 2 Sk Milk, 1 Very Lean Meat, 5 Lean Meat, 2 Med-fat Meat, 2 Free	**POINTS** for the day: 26 **Exchanges:** 5½ Starch, 2 Fruit, 4 Veg, 3 Sk Milk, 1 Very Lean Meat, 3 Lean Meat, 2½ Fat	**POINTS** for the day: 26 **Exchanges:** 5½ Starch, 3 Fruit, 4½ Veg, 3 Sk Milk, 6 Very Lean Meat, 2 Lean Meat, ½ Med-fat Meat, 1 Fat, 1 Free	**POINTS**

One day's menu provides at least two servings of milk and at least five servings of fruits and/or vegetables.

	MONDAY	TUESDAY	WEDNESDAY	THURSDAY
BREAKFAST	**Fruit Smoothie** (Combine 1 banana, ½ cup fresh strawberries, 8 ounces vanilla fat-free aspartame-sweetened yogurt, and ½ cup skim milk in a blender; process until smooth. [*POINTS:* 6])	**Waffle With Blueberries** (Toast 1 [4-inch] frozen multigrain waffle; top with ½ teaspoon margarine, 1 tablespoon maple syrup, and 1 cup fresh blueberries. Sprinkle with a dash *each of* ground nutmeg and cinnamon. [*POINTS:* 6])	**skim milk,** 1 cup **whole-wheat toast,** 1 slice, with 1 tablespoon jelly **fresh strawberries,** 1 cup	**cooked oatmeal,** 1 cup, with 2 tablespoons raisins and 1 tablespoon brown sugar **orange juice,** 1 cup **skim milk,** 1 cup
LUNCH	**Broccoli-Carrot Stir-fry** (Heat 1 teaspoon sesame oil in a nonstick skillet. Add ⅓ cup *each of* chopped broccoli, julienne-cut carrot, and diced red bell pepper; stir-fry 5 minutes. Add 2 tablespoons chopped green onions, 1 teaspoon soy sauce, and a dash of pepper. [*POINTS:* 1]) **cooked brown rice,** 1 cup **skim milk,** 1 cup	**Turkey-Vegetable Sandwich** (Spread 2 teaspoons light mayonnaise over 2 slices whole-wheat bread, layer 2 ounces thinly sliced deli turkey breast, ¼ cup sliced cucumber, 2 tomato slices, and 1 lettuce leaf between bread slices. [*POINTS:* 7]) **skim milk,** 1 cup	**Vegetable Pasta Sauté** (Heat 1 teaspoon olive oil in a nonstick skillet over medium heat. Add ⅓ cup chopped onion and 1 garlic clove, minced; sauté 3 minutes. Add ⅓ cup *each of* diced red bell pepper, chopped tomato, and chopped broccoli; sauté 5 minutes. Stir in 2 teaspoons lemon juice and a dash *each of* salt, dried Italian seasoning, and pepper; toss with 1 cup cooked penne pasta. [*POINTS:* 4]) **grapes,** 1 cup **skim milk,** 1 cup	**cheese pizza,** 1 slice, ⅛ of 12-inch pizza [*POINTS:* 4] **green salad,** 2 cups, with 2 tablespoons fat-free Italian dressing **skim milk,** 1 cup
DINNER	**broiled chicken breast,** 3 ounces **Mashed Sweet Potatoes** (Combine 1 cup mashed cooked sweet potato, 2 tablespoons *each of* fat-free sour cream and skim milk, 1 tablespoon brown sugar, 1 teaspoon bourbon, and a dash of salt; stir well. [*POINTS:* 5]) **green salad,** 2 cups sliced romaine lettuce, with 4 tomato wedges and 2 tablespoons fat-free Italian dressing	**Shrimp-Fried Rice** (Heat 1 teaspoon sesame oil in a nonstick skillet over medium-high heat. Add 3 tablespoons egg substitute; stir-fry 30 seconds. Add 2 ounces peeled shrimp and 1 cup chilled cooked brown rice; stir-fry 4 minutes. Add ¼ cup frozen green peas, thawed, 2 tablespoons chopped green onions, 1 teaspoon soy sauce, and a dash of pepper; stir-fry until heated. [*POINTS:* 7]) **steamed broccoli florets,** 1 cup	**Cajun Breaded Pork Chop** (Combine 1½ teaspoons Dijon mustard and ⅛ teaspoon Cajun seasoning; spread over both sides of 1 [6-ounce] lean center-cut pork chop. Press 1½ tablespoons dry breadcrumbs onto both sides of chop; cook over medium-high heat in a nonstick skillet coated with cooking spray 6 minutes on each side. [*POINTS:* 5]) **steamed green beans,** 1 cup **mashed potatoes,** ½ cup	**grilled flank steak,** 3 ounces **Sunflower-Raisin Couscous** (Combine ½ cup boiling water and ⅓ cup uncooked couscous; cover and let stand 5 minutes. Add 2 tablespoons raisins and 2 teaspoons sunflower seeds; toss well. [*POINTS:* 5]) **steamed broccoli florets,** 1 cup **sliced tomato,** 1, with 1 teaspoon olive oil and a dash *each of* salt and pepper
SNACK	**orange juice,** ½ cup **saltines,** 6, with 2 teaspoons peanut butter	**banana,** 1 **skim milk,** 1 cup	**Swiss Melt** (Top 1 whole-wheat bread slice with 3 tablespoons shredded Swiss cheese; broil until cheese melts. [*POINTS:* 4]) **tomato juice,** 1 cup	**blueberry fat-free aspartame-sweetened yogurt,** 8 ounces
POINTS	**POINTS** for the day: 25 **Exchanges:** 7 Starch, 4 Fruit, 3 Veg, 2½ Sk Milk, 3 Very Lean Meat, ½ Hi-fat Meat, 1 Fat, 1 Free	**POINTS** for the day: 25 **Exchanges:** 7 Starch, 3½ Fruit, 2½ Veg, 2 Sk Milk, 4½ Very Lean Meat, 3 Fat	**POINTS** for the day: 24 **Exchanges:** 7 Starch, 3 Fruit, 4½ Veg, 2 Sk Milk, 4½ Lean Meat, 1 Hi-fat Meat, 1 Fat	**POINTS** for the day: 27 **Exchanges:** 7 Starch, 4 Fruit, 4 Veg, 3 Sk Milk, 3 Lean Meat, 1 Med-fat Meat, 2 Fat, 1 Free

	FRIDAY	SATURDAY	SUNDAY
BREAKFAST	**Ham and Eggs** (Combine 1 large egg and 1 tablespoon skim milk; cook 30 seconds in a nonstick skillet. Stir in 1 ounce chopped cooked ham; cook until egg is set. [*POINTS:* 4]) **whole-wheat toast,** 1 slice, with 1 tablespoon jelly **skim milk,** 1 cup **orange juice,** ½ cup	**Banana Waffles** (Toast 2 [4-inch] frozen multigrain waffles; top with 1 teaspoon margarine, ½ banana, sliced, and 2 tablespoons maple syrup). **orange juice,** ½ cup	**bran flakes,** 1 cup **skim milk,** 1 cup **fresh blueberries,** 1 cup
LUNCH	**Chef Salad** (Top 2 cups torn romaine lettuce with 1 ounce julienne-cut deli turkey breast, 2 tomato slices, and ¼ cup *each of* fat-free croutons, shredded carrot, and sliced cucumber. Serve with 3 tablespoons fat-free ranch dressing. [*POINTS:* 4]) **skim milk,** 1 cup **saltines,** 6	**Potato-and-Broccoli Soup** (Heat ½ teaspoon olive oil in a nonstick saucepan. Add ¼ cup chopped onion; sauté 3 minutes. Add ¾ cup peeled cubed potato; sauté 5 minutes. Add ¾ cup chopped broccoli florets and ⅓ cup water; cook until tender. Stir in 1 cup skim milk and ⅛ teaspoon *each of* salt and pepper; cook until thoroughly heated. [*POINTS:* 5]) **grapes,** 1 cup	**Couscous-Tuna Salad** (Combine ½ cup boiling water, ⅓ cup uncooked couscous, 1 tablespoon *each of* raisins and chopped green onions, and 1 teaspoon *each of* olive oil and red wine vinegar in a bowl. Cover and let stand 5 minutes. Add ½ cup chopped cucumber and 2 ounces drained, canned water-packed tuna; toss well. [*POINTS:* 6]) **grapes,** 1 cup **tomato juice,** 1 cup
DINNER	**Seared Lemon-Garlic Tuna** (Combine 1 tablespoon lemon juice, 1 teaspoon olive oil, and 1 garlic clove, minced; brush over 1 [4-ounce] tuna steak. Sprinkle with a dash *each of* salt and pepper. Grill 3 minutes on each side or until desired degree of doneness. [*POINTS:* 3]) **Sautéed Spinach** (Heat ½ teaspoon olive oil in a nonstick skillet. Add 1 garlic clove, minced, and 2 cups torn fresh spinach; sauté 3 minutes or until spinach wilts. Toss with 2 teaspoons fresh lemon juice and a dash of salt. [*POINTS:* 1]) **cooked linguine,** 1 cup, with 1 teaspoon lemon juice and ½ teaspoon olive oil	**Spinach-Swiss Omelet** (Combine 2 large egg whites, 1 large egg, 2 tablespoons skim milk, and a dash *each of* salt and pepper. Cook in a small nonstick skillet coated with cooking spray over medium heat 4 minutes or until set (do not stir); top with ⅓ cup *each of* torn fresh spinach and diced red bell pepper, and 3 tablespoons *each of* shredded Swiss cheese and chopped green onions. Fold omelet in half. [*POINTS:* 5]) **skim milk,** 1 cup	**Ham-Pineapple Sandwich** (Spread 2 teaspoons light mayonnaise and 1 teaspoon Dijon mustard over 2 slices whole-wheat bread; layer 2 ounces thinly sliced deli ham, 2 drained canned unsweetened pineapple slices, and 2 lettuce leaves between bread slices. [*POINTS:* 9]) **baked potato chips,** 1 ounce **skim milk,** 1 cup
SNACK	**apple,** 1	**cucumber spears,** 1 cup **skim milk,** 1 cup	**carrot sticks,** 1 cup, with 2 tablespoons fat-free ranch dressing
POINTS	**POINTS** for the day: 25 **Exchanges:** 6 Starch, 2 Fruit, 5 Veg, 2 Sk Milk, 4 Very Lean Meat, 1 Lean Meat, 1 Med-fat Meat, 2 Fat, 1½ Free	**POINTS** for the day: 26 **Exchanges:** 5½ Starch, 4 Fruit, 2½ Veg, 3 Sk Milk, 2 Very Lean Meat, 1 Med-fat Meat, ½ Hi-fat Meat, 3½ Fat	**POINTS** for the day: 25 **Exchanges:** 8½ Starch, 5 Fruit, 4 Veg, 2 Sk Milk, 4 Very Lean Meat, 1½ Fat, 1 Free

One day's menu provides at least two servings of milk and at least five servings of fruits and/or vegetables.

	MONDAY	TUESDAY	WEDNESDAY	THURSDAY
BREAKFAST	**cooked oatmeal,** 1 cup, with 2 tablespoons raisins and 1 tablespoon brown sugar **skim milk,** 1 cup **orange juice,** ½ cup	**bran flakes,** 1 cup **skim milk,** 1 cup **strawberries,** 1 cup	**Honeydew-Banana Smoothie** (Combine 1 banana and 1 cup chopped fresh honeydew melon, 8 ounces vanilla fat-free aspartame-sweetened yogurt, and ¼ cup skim milk in a blender; process until smooth. [*POINTS:* 6])	**cooked oatmeal,** 1 cup, with 2 tablespoons raisins and 1 tablespoon honey **skim milk,** 1 cup **orange juice,** 1 cup
LUNCH	**fast-food hamburger,** 1 small [*POINTS:* 5] **green salad,** 2 cups, with 1 tablespoon fat-free Italian dressing **apple,** 1	**Roast Beef-and-Vegetable Salad** (Combine 2 cups sliced romaine lettuce, ½ cup *each of* julienne-cut red bell pepper, sliced yellow squash, diced tomato, and sliced mushrooms, and 2 tablespoons fat-free balsamic vinaigrette; toss well. Top with 6 large kalamata olives and 1 ounce julienne-cut deli roast beef. [*POINTS:* 3]) **toasted rye bread,** 1 slice, with 1 teaspoon margarine **skim milk,** 1 cup	**Grilled Feta Sandwich** (Layer 6 tablespoons crumbled feta cheese, 1 thin onion slice, separated into rings, and 1 tablespoon chopped fresh basil over 1 slice rye bread; top with another slice of bread. Spread 1 teaspoon margarine over bread slices. Heat a nonstick skillet coated with cooking spray over medium heat; add sandwich. Cook 3 minutes; turn and cook an additional 3 minutes or until cheese melts and bread begins to brown. [*POINTS:* 9]) **carrot sticks,** 1 cup	**Carrot-Raisin Salad** (Combine ¾ cup grated carrot, 2 tablespoons raisins, 1 tablespoon fat-free mayonnaise, and a dash *each of* salt and pepper. [*POINTS:* 1]) **rye bread,** 1 slice **apple,** 1, with 1 tablespoon peanut butter **skim milk,** 1 cup
DINNER	**Tuna With Kalamata Olive Tapenade** (Combine 9 large pitted chopped kalamata olives, 1 tablespoon chopped fresh basil, ½ garlic clove, and ½ teaspoon olive oil in a food processor; process until smooth. Grill 1 [4-ounce] tuna steak 15 minutes; top with olive mixture. [*POINTS:* 5]) **Vegetable Sauté** (Heat ½ teaspoon olive oil in a nonstick skillet. Add ½ cup *each of* sliced red bell pepper, fresh mushrooms, and yellow squash, ¼ cup chopped onion, and 1 garlic clove, chopped; sauté 2 minutes. Stir in 2 teaspoons balsamic vinegar and a dash *each of* salt and pepper. [*POINTS:* 1]) **French bread,** 1 ounce	**Red Beans and Rice** (Brown 2 ounces lean turkey kielbasa and ⅓ cup diced onion over medium heat in a skillet; stir in ½ cup tomato sauce, ¼ teaspoon *each of* Cajun seasoning, hot pepper sauce, and white vinegar. Bring to a boil; stir in ⅔ cup drained canned red beans. Spoon over 1 cup cooked brown rice. [*POINTS:* 8]) **boiled okra,** 1 cup **baked apple,** 1, with dash of nutmeg	**Pasta Marinara** (Heat 1 teaspoon olive oil in a nonstick skillet. Sauté ⅔ cup diced yellow squash and 1 garlic clove, chopped, 4 minutes. Add 1 cup fat-free marinara sauce; cook over medium heat 5 minutes. Stir in 2 tablespoons chopped kalamata olives; spoon over 1 cup cooked linguine. Sprinkle with 3 tablespoons grated Parmesan cheese. [*POINTS:* 7]) **green salad,** 2 cups sliced romaine lettuce, 1 quartered tomato, and 2 tablespoons fat-free balsamic vinaigrette **skim milk,** 1 cup	**Pork-and-Pepper Stir-Fry** (Combine 4 ounces cubed pork tenderloin, 1 tablespoon orange juice, and 1 teaspoon soy sauce; stir-fry over medium heat in a nonstick skillet 4 minutes or until browned. Remove pork from skillet. Add ½ cup *each of* sliced onion and red and green bell peppers; stir-fry 2 minutes. Add 2 tablespoons orange juice, 1 teaspoon *each of* soy sauce, rice vinegar, and honey, and a dash of black pepper to skillet. Return pork to skillet; bring to a boil. Serve over 1 cup cooked brown rice. [*POINTS:* 9]) **steamed broccoli,** 1 cup
SNACK	**vanilla fat-free aspartame-sweetened yogurt,** 8 ounces	**popcorn,** 94%-fat-free microwave-popped, 1 bag	**vanilla fat-free ice cream,** ½ cup, with ½ cup sliced strawberries	**blueberry fat-free aspartame-sweetened yogurt,** 8 ounces
POINTS	*POINTS* for the day: 23 **Exchanges:** 5 Starch, 3 Fruit, 3½ Veg, 2 Sk Milk, 3 Very Lean Meat, 2 Med-fat Meat, 2 Fat, 1 Free	*POINTS* for the day: 23 **Exchanges:** 9 Starch, 3 Fruit, 5½ Veg, 2 Sk Milk, 2½ Very Lean Meat, 2 Lean Meat, 2 Fat, 3 Free	*POINTS* for the day: 28 **Exchanges:** 5 Starch, 3½ Fruit, 7 Veg, 1½ Sk Milk, 1½ Lean Meat, 1½ Med-fat Meat, 3 Fat, 1 Free	*POINTS* for the day: 27 **Exchanges:** 9 Starch, 4½ Fruit, 3½ Veg, 3 Sk Milk, 1 Very Lean Meat, 3 Lean Meat

	FRIDAY	SATURDAY	SUNDAY
BREAKFAST	**Egg Bagel** (Combine 1 large egg and 1 tablespoon skim milk; cook in a non-stick skillet over medium heat until set. Spoon over ½ small bagel. [*POINTS:* 4]) **orange juice,** ½ cup	**bran flakes,** 1 cup **skim milk,** 1 cup **strawberries,** 1 cup	**bagel,** 1 small, with 1 tablespoon *each of* fat-free cream cheese and chopped onion, 1 teaspoon capers, and 1 ounce smoked salmon **skim milk,** 1 cup **orange juice,** ½ cup
LUNCH	**Reuben Sandwich** (Spread 2 table-spoons fat-free Thousand Island dressing over 2 slices rye bread; top 1 slice with 2 ounces thinly sliced lean roast beef and ¼ cup drained canned sauer-kraut. Sprinkle with 2 tablespoons shredded Swiss cheese; top with remaining slice of bread. Broil 1 minute; turn, and broil an additional 1 minute or until bread browns and cheese melts. [*POINTS:* 9]) **skim milk,** 1 cup **carrot sticks,** 1 cup	**Couscous With Smoked Salmon** (Heat 1 teaspoon olive oil in a nonstick skillet over medium heat. Add 1 table-spoon chopped onion and 1 garlic clove, chopped; sauté 4 minutes. Add ⅓ cup *each of* diced red bell pepper, carrot, and tomato; sauté 4 minutes. Stir in 2 ounces chopped smoked salmon, 1 tea-spoon *each of* capers, white wine vine-gar, and lemon juice, and a dash *each of* salt and pepper; toss with 1 cup cooked couscous. [*POINTS:* 7])	**Egg Salad in Tomato** (Combine 1 hard-cooked egg, chopped, 1 table-spoon fat-free mayonnaise, and ½ tea-spoon Dijon mustard; stir well. Cut a medium tomato into 4 wedges, cutting to, but not through, bottom. Spoon egg salad into tomato. [*POINTS:* 2]) **carrot sticks,** 1 cup
DINNER	**Feta-and-Shrimp Pasta Toss** (Heat 1 teaspoon olive oil in a nonstick skillet. Sauté 2 tablespoons chopped onion and 1 garlic clove, minced, 5 minutes; add ¼ cup dry white wine. Bring to a boil; reduce heat, and simmer until reduced by half. Add 4 ounces peeled, deveined shrimp; sauté 3 minutes or until done. Stir in 1 cup cooked penne pasta, 2 tablespoons *each of* chopped fresh basil and crumbled feta cheese, 1 teaspoon capers, and a dash *each of* salt and pepper. [*POINTS:* 7]) **green salad,** 2 cups sliced romaine lettuce, 1 quartered tomato, and 2 table-spoons fat-free balsamic vinaigrette	**Kielbasa and Kraut** (Sauté 2 ounces lean turkey kielbasa, ½ cup *each of* sliced onion and apple, and a dash of caraway seeds in a nonstick skillet over medium heat 5 minutes. Add ⅓ cup *each of* fat-free chicken broth and rinsed, drained canned sauerkraut. Bring to a boil; reduce heat, and simmer 5 minutes. Sprinkle with 1 tablespoon shredded Swiss cheese. [*POINTS:* 3]) **steamed new potatoes,** 1 cup **skim milk,** 1 cup	**grilled sirloin steak,** 3 ounces **Mushroom-Spinach Sauté** (Melt 1 teaspoon margarine in a nonstick skillet over medium-high heat; add ½ cup sliced fresh mushrooms, 2 tablespoons chopped onion, and 1 garlic clove, minced. Sauté 4 minutes; add 1 table-spoon white wine. Cook 1 minute or until liquid evaporates. Stir in 2 cups torn fresh spinach and a dash *each of* salt and pepper; sauté 1 minute or until spinach wilts. [*POINTS:* 1]) **French bread,** 2 ounces
SNACK	**cappuccino fat-free aspartame-sweetened yogurt,** 8 ounces	**banana,** 1, with 2 teaspoons peanut butter	**Strawberries and Cream** (Serve 1 cup sliced fresh strawberries with ⅓ cup frozen reduced-calorie whipped topping and 4 animal crackers. [*POINTS:* 3]) **skim milk,** 1 cup
POINTS	**POINTS** for the day: 28 **Exchanges:** 5 Starch, 2 Fruit, 2½ Veg, 2 Sk Milk, 5 Very Lean Meat, 2½ Med-fat Meat, 1½ Fat, 1 Free	**POINTS** for the day: 22 **Exchanges:** 7 Starch, 3½ Fruit, 2½ Veg, 2 Sk Milk, 2 Very Lean Meat, 2 Lean Meat, ½ Hi-fat Meat, 1½ Fat, 1 Free	**POINTS** for the day: 24 **Exchanges:** 6½ Starch, 2 Fruit, 4½ Veg, 2 Sk Milk, 1½ Very Lean Meat, 3 Lean Meat, 2 Fat

One day's menu provides at least two servings of milk and at least five servings of fruits and/or vegetables.

	MONDAY	TUESDAY	WEDNESDAY	THURSDAY
BREAKFAST	**cooked oatmeal,** 1 cup, with ¼ cup raisins and 1 tablespoon brown sugar **orange juice,** ½ cup **skim milk,** 1 cup	**Yogurt-Topped Fruit** (Combine 1 banana, sliced, and ½ cup frozen blueberries, thawed, in a bowl. Top with 8 ounces vanilla fat-free aspartame-sweetened yogurt, and 1 teaspoon honey. Sprinkle with 3 tablespoons toasted wheat germ. [*POINTS:* 6])	**cooked oatmeal,** 1 cup, with ¼ cup raisins and 1 tablespoon brown sugar **orange juice,** 1 cup **skim milk,** 1 cup	**Fruit Smoothie** (Combine ½ cup *each of* skim milk, frozen blueberries, sliced banana, and 8 ounces vanilla fat-free aspartame-sweetened yogurt in a blender; process until smooth. Sprinkle with 1 teaspoon toasted wheat germ. [*POINTS:* 4])
LUNCH	**bean burrito,** fast food [*POINTS:* 6] **carrot sticks,** 1 cup **apple,** 1	**Hopping John** (Heat 1 teaspoon olive oil in a nonstick skillet over medium heat. Add ⅓ cup chopped onion and 1 garlic clove, minced; sauté 5 minutes. Add 1 teaspoon white wine vinegar and ⅛ teaspoon *each of* dried oregano and hot sauce; stir well. Add ⅓ cup drained canned black-eyed peas and ¼ cup lean chopped ham. Toss with 1 cup cooked brown rice. [*POINTS:* 8]) **fresh torn spinach,** 1 cup, with 1 tablespoon fat-free Italian dressing **skim milk,** 1 cup	**Chef Salad** (Top 2 cups sliced romaine lettuce with ½ cup julienne-cut lean ham, 1 tomato, sliced, and ¼ cup *each of* fat-free croutons, shredded carrot, and sliced cucumber. Serve with 3 tablespoons fat-free Italian dressing. [*POINTS:* 4]) **saltines,** 6 **strawberry cheesecake fat-free aspartame-sweetened yogurt,** 8 ounces	**Lentil and Feta Salad** (Combine ⅓ cup *each of* cooked lentils and chopped red bell pepper, 2 tablespoons chopped green onions, 2 teaspoons lemon juice, 1 teaspoon olive oil, and a dash of dried thyme. Sprinkle with 3 tablespoons crumbled feta cheese. [*POINTS:* 4]) **grapes,** 1 cup
DINNER	**roasted skinned boned chicken breast,** 3 ounces **Tomato-Corn Couscous** (Combine 1 cup cooked couscous, ⅓ cup *each of* chopped fresh tomato and drained canned whole-kernel corn, 1 tablespoon chopped fresh cilantro, 1 teaspoon olive oil, and a dash *each of* salt and pepper. [*POINTS:* 5]) **steamed spinach,** 1 cup	**Honey Mustard Pork Chop** (Combine 2 teaspoons *each of* Dijon mustard and honey, 1 teaspoon olive oil, and a dash *each of* dried thyme, salt, and pepper. Brush mustard mixture over both sides of 1 [4-ounce] lean boned pork chop. Place in a baking dish; bake at 450° for 15 minutes or until done. [*POINTS:* 6]) **mashed cooked sweet potato,** ⅔ cup, with 1 teaspoon margarine and ½ teaspoon brown sugar **steamed broccoli,** 1 cup	**Broiled Grouper** (Place 1 [8-ounce] grouper fillet on a broiler pan; broil 6 minutes on each side or until fish flakes easily when tested with a fork, basting occasionally with 2 tablespoons fat-free Italian dressing. Serve with lemon wedges. [*POINTS:* 3]) **steamed carrots,** 1 cup, with 1 teaspoon honey **cooked brown rice,** 1 cup	**grilled flank steak,** 3 ounces **baked potato,** 8 ounces, with 2 tablespoons *each of* dried chives and fat-free sour cream **steamed broccoli,** 1 cup
SNACK	**apple pie à la mode fat-free aspartame-sweetened yogurt,** 8 ounces, with 2 tablespoons toasted wheat germ	**chocolate graham crackers,** 2 sheets, with ⅓ cup frozen reduced-calorie whipped topping, thawed	**Peanut Butter-Banana Toast** (Toast 1 slice high-fiber bread; spread with 1 tablespoon peanut butter, and top with 1 banana, sliced. [*POINTS:* 5])	**vanilla sugar-free instant pudding** (prepared with skim milk), 1 cup, topped with 1 banana, sliced, and ⅓ cup frozen reduced-caloried whipped topping, thawed
POINTS	**POINTS** for the day: 25 **Exchanges:** 8 Starch, 4½ Fruit, 4 Veg, 2 Sk Milk, 3 Very Lean Meat, 1 Lean Meat, 2 Fat	**POINTS** for the day: 28 **Exchanges:** 7 Starch, 3 Fruit, 4 Veg, 2 Sk Milk, 4 Very Lean Meat, 2½ Fat, 1 Free	**POINTS** for the day: 30 **Exchanges:** 8½ Starch, 6 Fruit, 5½ Veg, 2 Sk Milk, 8½ Very Lean Meat, ½ Hi-fat Meat, 2 Free	**POINTS** for the day: 24 **Exchanges:** 5½ Starch, 4½ Fruit, 2½ Veg, 1½ Sk Milk, ½ Very Lean Meat, 3 Lean Meat, 1 Med-fat Meat, 1 Fat, 1 Free

FRIDAY	SATURDAY	SUNDAY	
bran flakes, 1 cup **skim milk,** 1 cup **orange juice,** ½ cup	**pancakes,** 2 (4-inch), topped with ½ cup frozen blueberries, thawed, and 1 tablespoon maple syrup **skim milk,** 1 cup **orange juice,** 1 cup	**bran flakes,** 1 cup, topped with 1 cup frozen blueberries **skim milk,** 1 cup	**BREAKFAST**
Grilled Chicken Salad (Top 2 cups sliced romaine lettuce with 3 ounces thinly sliced grilled chicken breast, 2 tomato slices, ¼ cup *each of* fat-free croutons, shredded carrot, and sliced cucumber, 3 large ripe olives, and 1 tomato, cut into wedges. Serve with 3 tablespoons fat-free ranch dressing. [*POINTS:* 8]) **skim milk,** 1 cup	**Turkey Burger** (Spread 1 tablespoon ketchup and 1 teaspoon Dijon mustard over cut sides of a 1½-ounce hamburger bun. Layer 1 [3-ounce] cooked lean ground turkey breast patty, 2 lettuce leaves, and 1 onion slice between bun halves. [*POINTS:* 6]) **vegetarian baked beans,** ½ cup **Italian tomatoes,** drizzle 1½ tablespoons fat-free Italian dressing over 1 tomato, sliced **grapes,** 1 cup	**French Onion Soup** (Heat 1 teaspoon olive oil in a small saucepan over medium heat. Add ¾ cup thinly sliced onion; sauté 15 minutes. Add 1 cup beef broth; bring to a boil. Reduce heat, and simmer 15 minutes. Spoon into a bowl; top with 1 [1-ounce] slice French bread, and sprinkle with ¾ ounce shredded Swiss cheese and freshly ground pepper. [*POINTS:* 5]) **carrot sticks,** 1 cup **cherry vanilla fat-free aspartame-sweetened yogurt,** 8 ounces	**LUNCH**
Mediterranean Tuna and Linguine (Combine ¼ cup chopped sun-dried tomatoes [not packed in oil] and 3 tablespoons boiling water; set aside. Heat ½ teaspoon olive oil over medium heat in a nonstick skillet. Add 2 tablespoons chopped onion and 1 garlic clove, minced; sauté 3 minutes. Stir in sun-dried tomatoes, 3 ounces drained canned tuna in water, 1 tablespoon chopped kalamata olives, and 1 teaspoon capers; sauté 3 minutes. Add 3 tablespoons feta cheese and a dash *each of* salt and pepper. Toss with 1 cup cooked linguine. [*POINTS:* 8]) **French bread,** 1 (1-ounce) slice	**grilled pork tenderloin,** 3 ounces **steamed broccoli,** 1 cup **cooked couscous,** 1 cup, tossed with 1 tablespoon mango chutney	**Sloppy Joe** (Cook 4 ounces lean ground turkey breast, ¼ cup chopped onion, and 1 minced garlic clove over medium-high heat until browned, stirring to crumble. Stir in ½ cup tomato sauce and ½ teaspoon chili powder; cook until thoroughly heated. Serve on a 1½-ounce hamburger bun. [*POINTS:* 6]) **vegetarian baked beans,** ½ cup **green salad,** 2 cups sliced romaine lettuce, 2 tomato wedges, and 2 tablespoons fat-free Italian dressing	**DINNER**
cucumber spears, 1 cup, with 2 tablespoons fat-free ranch dressing **skim milk,** 1 cup	**skim milk,** 1 cup **carrot sticks,** 1 cup, with 2 tablespoons fat-free ranch dressing	**chocolate graham crackers,** 2 sheets, with ⅓ cup frozen reduced-calorie whipped topping, thawed	**SNACK**
POINTS for the day: 27 **Exchanges:** 5½ Starch, 1 Fruit, 6 Veg, 3 Sk Milk, 6 Very Lean Meat, 1 Med-fat Meat, 2 Fat, 2 Free	*POINTS* for the day: 30 **Exchanges:** 7½ Starch, 3½ Fruit, 3½ Veg, 2 Sk Milk, 4 Very Lean Meat, 3 Lean Meat, 2½ Free	*POINTS* for the day: 22 **Exchanges:** 6½ Starch, 1 Fruit, 5½ Veg, 2 Sk Milk, 1 Very Lean Meat, 3 Lean Meat, 1 Med-fat Meat, 1 Fat, 1 Free	**POINTS**

7-DAY MENU PLANNER

One day's menu provides at least two servings of milk and at least five servings of fruits and/or vegetables.

	MONDAY	TUESDAY	WEDNESDAY	THURSDAY
BREAKFAST	**high-fiber whole-wheat bread,** 1 slice, toasted, with 1 tablespoon peanut butter **banana,** 1 **fat-free milk,** 1 cup	**whole-grain frozen waffles,** 2 (4-inch), toasted, with 1 tablespoon maple syrup **fat-free milk,** 1 cup **orange juice,** ½ cup	**Egg-and-Cheese Sandwich** (Combine 1 large egg and 3 tablespoons shredded reduced-fat sharp Cheddar cheese; stir well. Cook in a nonstick skillet over medium heat until set, stirring occasionally. Spread between 2 slices high-fiber whole-wheat bread. [*POINTS:* 4]) **fat-free milk,** 1 cup	**strawberry fat-free aspartame-sweetened yogurt,** 8 ounces, with 2 tablespoons toasted wheat germ **banana,** 1 **orange juice,** ½ cup
LUNCH	**Spinach-Egg Sandwich** (Spread 2 teaspoons light mayonnaise over 2 slices high-fiber whole-wheat bread. Layer 1 sliced hard-cooked large egg and ½ cup fresh spinach leaves between bread slices. [*POINTS:* 5]) **carrot sticks,** 1 cup **grapes,** 1 cup	**Tuna Sandwich** (Combine ½ cup drained canned tuna in water, 4 teaspoons light mayonnaise, ¼ teaspoon dried dill, and a dash of pepper; stir well. Spread on 1 slice high-fiber whole-wheat bread; top with ¼ cup fresh spinach leaves, 2 slices tomato, and another slice of bread. [*POINTS:* 7]) **kosher dill pickle,** 1 **carrot sticks,** 1 cup **gingersnaps,** 2	**Southwestern vegetable soup,** (1 [16-ounce] can]such as Campbell's Healthy Request], with 3 tablespoons shredded reduced-fat Cheddar cheese. [*POINTS:* 6]) **saltines,** 6 **prepackaged coleslaw,** 1 cup, with 2 tablespoons fat-free Catalina dressing **grapes,** 1 cup	**Spinach-Ham Salad** (Combine 2½ cups torn fresh spinach, 3 ounces sliced lean ham, chopped, ½ cup red bell pepper strips, ½ cup shredded carrot, and 2 tablespoons fat-free Catalina dressing; toss well. [*POINTS:* 4]) **saltines,** 6 **grapes,** 1 cup
DINNER	**Rosemary Salmon** (Place a 4-ounce salmon fillet in a baking dish coated with cooking spray; drizzle with 1 tablespoon lemon juice. Sprinkle with ½ teaspoon minced fresh rosemary and a dash *each of* salt and pepper. Bake at 450° for 15 minutes or until fish flakes easily when tested with a fork. [*POINTS:* 4]) **steamed broccoli,** 1 cup **mashed cooked potato,** 1 cup, with 1 tablespoon reduced-calorie stick margarine and salt and pepper to taste	**Barbecue Chicken** (Place a 4-ounce boned, skinned chicken breast half on a broiler pan coated with cooking spray; brush with 1 tablespoon barbecue sauce. Bake at 350° for 30 minutes or until done. [*POINTS:* 3]) **frozen whole-kernel corn,** cooked, 1 cup **prepackaged coleslaw,** 1 cup, with 2 tablespoons fat-free Catalina dressing	**Rosemary Roasted Pork Tenderloin** (Rub 1 teaspoon minced fresh rosemary over 4 ounces pork tenderloin; sprinkle with salt and pepper to taste. Place on a broiler pan; bake at 400° until an instant-read thermometer registers 160° [*POINTS:* 3]) **steamed broccoli,** 1 cup **steamed carrots,** 1 cup **cooked brown rice,** ½ cup	**Cheeseburger** (Combine 4 ounces lean ground beef, a dash *each of* salt, pepper, and garlic powder; stir well. Shape into a patty; place on a broiler pan. Broil 5 minutes on each side or until done. Spread 2 teaspoons *each of* light mayonnaise and mustard on a 1½-ounce reduced-calorie wheat hamburger bun; top bottom half of bun with patty, 3 tablespoons shredded reduced-fat sharp Cheddar cheese, ¼ cup fresh spinach leaves, 2 slices tomato, and another slice of bread. [*POINTS:* 9]) **frozen French fries,** baked, 3 ounces **prepackaged coleslaw,** 1 cup, with 2 tablespoons fat-free Catalina dressing
SNACK	**fat-free milk,** 1 cup **saltines,** 6, with ¾ ounce reduced-fat sharp Cheddar cheese **tomato juice,** 1 cup	**apple pie à la mode fat-free aspartame-sweetened yogurt,** 8 ounces, with 2 tablespoons toasted wheat germ	**fat-free milk,** 1 cup **saltines,** 6, with ¾ ounce reduced-fat sharp Cheddar cheese **tomato juice,** 1 cup **gingersnaps,** 2	**fat-free milk,** 1 cup **carrot sticks,** 1 cup
POINTS	***POINTS*** for the day: 28 **Exchanges:** 7 Starch, 3 Fruit, 5½ Veg, 2 Sk Milk, 3 Very Lean Meat, 2 Med-fat Meat, 1 Fat	***POINTS*** for the day: 24 **Exchanges:** 6½ Starch, 1 Fruit, 2½ Veg, 2 Sk Milk, 6 Very Lean Meat, 1 Fat	***POINTS*** for the day: 29 **Exchanges:** 9 Starch, 1 Fruit, 7 Veg, 2 Sk Milk, 3 Lean Meat, 4 Med-fat Meat	***POINTS*** for the day: 28 **Exchanges:** 5½ Starch, 4 Fruit, 5½ Veg, 2 Sk Milk, 7 Lean Meat, 1 Med-fat Meat, 1½ Fat

	FRIDAY	SATURDAY	SUNDAY
BREAKFAST	**whole-grain frozen waffles,** 2 (4-inch), toasted, with 1 tablespoon maple syrup **fat-free milk,** 1 cup **orange juice,** ½ cup	**Banana Smoothie** (Combine 1 cup fat-free milk, 1 banana, 2 tablespoons toasted wheat germ, 1 tablespoon sugar, and 1 teaspoon vanilla extract in a blender; process until smooth. [*POINTS:* 6])	**Cinnamon Toast** (Spread 1 tablespoon reduced-calorie stick margarine, softened, over 2 slices high-fiber whole-wheat bread; sprinkle with 1 tablespoon sugar and cinnamon to taste. [*POINTS:* 5]) **fat-free milk,** 1 cup **orange juice,** ½ cup
LUNCH	**Ham Sandwich** (Spread 2 teaspoons *each of* light mayonnaise and mustard over 2 slices high-fiber whole-wheat bread; layer 3 ounces sliced lean ham, ¼ cup fresh spinach leaves, and 6 cucumber slices between bread slices. [*POINTS:* 6]) **kosher dill pickle,** 1 **carrot sticks,** 1 cup	**Veggie Burger** (Spread 2 teaspoons light mayonnaise and 1 teaspoon mustard over cut sides of 1 [1½-ounce] reduced-calorie wheat hamburger bun. Place a nonstick skillet over medium-high heat until hot. Coat 1 frozen veggie-medley-flavored fat-free veggie patty with cooking spray; cook 3 minutes on each side or until browned. Place on bun; top with ¼ cup fresh spinach leaves, 1 slice tomato, and remaining half of bun. [*POINTS:* 3]) **kosher dill pickle,** 1 **grapes,** 1 cup	**lentil soup,** 1 (19-ounce) can (such as Progresso) (*POINTS:* 3) **Spinach Salad** (Combine 1 cup torn fresh spinach, ½ cup red bell pepper strips, ¼ cup shredded carrot, and 2 tablespoons fat-free Catalina dressing; toss well. [*POINTS:* 1]) **saltines,** 6
DINNER	**cooked spaghetti,** 1 cup **bottled fresh tomato-and-basil pasta sauce,** (such as Five Brothers), 1 cup **Spinach Salad** (Combine 1 cup torn fresh spinach, ½ cup red bell pepper strips, ¼ cup shredded carrot, and 2 tablespoons fat-free blue cheese dressing; toss well. [*POINTS:* 1]) **grapes,** 1 cup	**Bourbon Glazed Ham Steak** (Coat a nonstick skillet with cooking spray; place over medium-high heat until hot. Add a 3-ounce slice of lean, boned ham; cook 2 minutes on each side or until browned. Combine 1 tablespoon bourbon, 2 teaspoons brown sugar, 2 teaspoons water, and ¼ teaspoon mustard; drizzle over ham. Cook 1 minute. [*POINTS:* 4]) **baked sweet potato,** 1 large, with 1 tablespoon brown sugar and 1½ teaspoons reduced-calorie stick margarine **green beans,** canned, 1 cup	**Buffalo Chicken** (Brown a 4-ounce skinned, boned chicken breast half in a nonstick skillet coated with cooking spray. Place in a baking dish. Combine 1 tablespoon hot sauce, 1½ teaspoons reduced-calorie stick margarine, 1 teaspoon white vinegar, and ¼ teaspoon celery seeds; drizzle over chicken. Bake at 400° for 25 minutes. Serve with 2 tablespoons fat-free blue cheese dressing. [*POINTS:* 5]) **frozen whole-kernel corn,** cooked, 1 cup **prepackaged coleslaw,** 1 cup, with 2 tablespoons fat-free Catalina dressing
SNACK	**vanilla fat-free aspartame-sweetened yogurt,** 8 ounces, with 1 apple, sliced, and 1 teaspoon brown sugar	**gingersnaps,** 2 **fat-free milk,** 1 cup	**fat-free milk,** 1 cup **saltines,** 6, with ¾-ounce reduced-fat sharp Cheddar cheese **tomato juice,** 1 cup
POINTS	*POINTS* for the day: 23 **Exchanges:** 6 Starch, 2 Fruit, 4½ Veg, 2 Sk Milk, 3 Lean Meat, ½ Fat	*POINTS* for the day: 22 **Exchanges:** 9½ Starch, 3 Fruit, 2½ Veg, 2 Sk Milk, 2 Very Lean Meat, 3 Lean Meat, 1½ Fat	*POINTS* for the day: 29 **Exchanges:** 8 Starch, 1 Fruit, 5 Veg, 2 Sk Milk, 5 Very Lean Meat, 1 Med-fat Meat, 1 Fat

179

One day's menu provides at least two servings of milk and at least five servings of fruits and/or vegetables.

	MONDAY	TUESDAY	WEDNESDAY	THURSDAY
BREAKFAST	**whole-grain frozen waffles,** 2 (4-inch), toasted, with 1 tablespoon maple syrup **orange juice,** ½ cup **fat-free milk,** 1 cup	**cooked oatmeal,** 1 cup, with 2 tablespoons raisins and 1 tablespoon brown sugar **fat-free milk,** 1 cup **orange juice,** ½ cup	**Egg-'n'-Cheese Sandwich** (Combine ½ cup egg substitute, 3 tablespoons shredded cheddar cheese, and a dash *each of* salt and pepper; stir. Cook in a small nonstick skillet over medium heat until set, stirring occasionally. Spread between 2 slices whole-wheat bread. [*POINTS:* 8]) **orange juice,** ½ cup **fat-free milk,** 1 cup	**whole-grain frozen waffles,** 2 (4-inch), toasted, with 1 tablespoon maple syrup **cantaloupe,** ¼ melon **fat-free milk,** 1 cup
LUNCH	**PB-and-Banana Sandwich** (Spread 1 tablespoon peanut butter over 1 slice whole-wheat bread; top with 1 banana, sliced. Drizzle with 1 teaspoon honey; top with 1 slice whole-wheat bread. [*POINTS:* 6]) **carrot sticks,** 1 cup **blueberry fat-free aspartame-sweetened yogurt,** 8 ounces	**Tuna Salad** (Combine 1 cup sliced romaine lettuce, 1 cup torn fresh spinach, 3 tablespoons shredded cheddar cheese, and ¼ cup *each of* sliced carrot, sliced cucumber, and sliced plum tomato; top with ½ [6-ounce] can albacore tuna in water, drained and flaked. Drizzle with 3 tablespoons fat-free Italian dressing. Reserve remaining tuna for lunch on Wednesday. [*POINTS:* 4]) **saltines,** 6 **pear,** 1	**Tuna Sandwich** (Combine ½ [6-ounce] can albacore tuna in water, drained and flaked, 1 tablespoon light mayonnaise, 1 teaspoon freeze-dried chives, and a dash of pepper; stir well. Spread over 1 slice whole-wheat bread; top with 1 romaine lettuce leaf and another slice of bread. [*POINTS:* 7]) **carrot sticks,** 1 cup **cantaloupe,** ¼ melon **vanilla fat-free aspartame-sweetened yogurt,** 8 ounces	**Black Bean-and-Chicken Pizza,** ½ (Warm remaining half of pizza from Wednesday's dinner in microwave oven. [*POINTS:* 6]) **carrot sticks,** 1 cup
DINNER	**Lemon-Dijon Fish** (Place 1 [6-ounce] orange roughy fillet in a baking dish coated with cooking spray; sprinkle with ½ teaspoon lemon juice. Bake at 400° for 12 minutes. Combine 1½ teaspoons *each of* freeze-dried chives and light mayonnaise, and ¼ teaspoon Dijon mustard; spread over fish. Bake an additional 3 minutes or until fish flakes easily when tested with a fork. [*POINTS:* 5]) **steamed fresh spinach,** 1 cup **baked potato,** 1 large, with 1 teaspoon stick margarine	**Honey Chicken** (Brush 1½ teaspoons soy sauce over both sides of a 4-ounce skinned, boned chicken breast half. Coat a small nonstick skillet with cooking spray; place over medium-high heat until hot. Add chicken; cook 5 minutes on each side or until done. Place on a plate; keep warm. Add 1 tablespoon honey and 1½ teaspoons fresh lime juice to skillet; simmer 1 minute, stirring. Pour over chicken. Sprinkle with 1 tablespoon sliced green onions. [*POINTS:* 4]) **cooked long-grain rice,** ½ cup, with 1 teaspoon margarine **steamed broccoli,** 1 cup	**Black Bean-and-Chicken Pizza,** ½ (Spread ¼ cup salsa over a 6-inch Italian cheese-flavored pizza crust [such as Boboli]; top with ½ [6-ounce] package grilled-flavored ready-to-eat skinned, boned chicken breast strips, ½ cup drained canned black beans, and 3 tablespoons shredded cheddar cheese. Bake at 450° for 10 minutes; top with 2 tablespoons sliced green onions. Cut in half; reserve half for lunch on Thursday. [*POINTS:* 6]) **green salad,** 2 cups, with 2 tablespoons fat-free Italian dressing **mango,** ½, peeled and cubed	**Pork Parmesan** (Place a 4-ounce boned center-cut pork loin chop between 2 sheets of plastic wrap; flatten to ¼-inch thickness, using a meat mallet. Combine 1½ tablespoons dry breadcrumbs and 1½ teaspoons grated Parmesan cheese in a dish. Brush chop with 1 tablespoon egg substitute; dredge in crumb mixture. Brown in a nonstick skillet coated with cooking spray. Place in a baking dish; top with ½ cup low-fat spaghetti sauce with garlic and herbs and 2 teaspoons grated Parmesan cheese. Bake at 350° for 25 minutes. [*POINTS:* 7]) **cooked spaghetti,** ½ cup **steamed broccoli,** 1 cup
SNACK	**popcorn,** 94% fat-free microwave-popped, 1 large bag	**apple pie à la mode fat-free aspartame-sweetened yogurt,** 8 ounces	**pear,** 1	**animal crackers,** 6 **fat-free milk,** 1 cup
POINTS	*POINTS* for the day: 29 **Exchanges:** 9 Starch, 3 Fruit, 3 Veg, 2 Sk Milk, 5 Very Lean Meat, ½ Hi-fat Meat, 2½ Fat	*POINTS* for the day: 22 **Exchanges:** 6 Starch, 3 Fruit, 3 Veg, 2 Sk Milk, 6 Very Lean Meat, 1 Hi-fat Meat, 1 Fat	*POINTS* for the day: 29 **Exchanges:** 6½ Starch, 4 Fruit, 3½ Veg, 2 Sk Milk, 7 Very Lean Meat, 1½ Hi-fat Meat, 1 Fat	*POINTS* for the day: 28 **Exchanges:** 8½ Starch, 1 Fruit, 3½ Veg, 2 Sk Milk, 2 Very Lean Meat, 3 Lean Meat, 1½ Hi-fat Meat

	FRIDAY	SATURDAY	SUNDAY
BREAKFAST	**cooked oatmeal,** 1 cup, with 2 table-spoons raisins and 1 tablespoon brown sugar **fat-free milk,** 1 cup **orange juice,** ½ cup	**French Toast** (Combine 2 tablespoons *each of* egg substitute and fat-free milk in a shallow dish. Dip 1 slice whole-wheat bread in mixture. Melt 1 teaspoon stick margarine in a nonstick skillet coated with cooking spray. Add bread; cook until browned and crisp, turning once. Top with 1 tablespoon maple syrup. [*POINTS:* 5]) **cantaloupe,** ¼ melon	**Cheese Omelet** (Combine ¾ cup egg substitute, 1 tablespoon *each of* freeze-dried chives and fat-free milk, and a dash *each of* salt and pepper; stir. Pour into a small nonstick skillet; place over medium heat. Cover and cook until set. Sprinkle 3 tablespoons shredded sharp cheddar cheese over omelet; fold in half. [*POINTS:* 5]) **fat-free milk,** 1 cup
LUNCH	**vegetable soup,** canned, 1½ cups **cheese toast,** 1 slice whole-wheat bread, toasted, with 3 tablespoons shredded Cheddar cheese **cantaloupe,** ¼ melon **raspberry fat-free aspartame-sweetened yogurt,** 8 ounces	**Grilled Chicken Salad** (Combine 1 cup sliced romaine lettuce, 1 cup torn fresh spinach, 3 tablespoons shredded cheddar cheese, and ¼ cup *each of* sliced carrot, sliced cucumber, and sliced plum tomato; top with ½ [6-ounce] package grilled-flavored ready-to-eat skinned, boned chicken breast strips. Drizzle with 3 tablespoons fat-free Italian dressing. [*POINTS:* 4]) **saltines,** 6 **apple,** 1 **fat-free milk,** 1 cup	**Spaghetti** (Top 1½ cups cooked spaghetti with 1 cup low-fat spaghetti sauce with garlic and herbs. Sprinkle with 1 tablespoon grated Parmesan cheese. [*POINTS:* 7]) **green salad,** 1 cup, with 1 tablespoon fat-free Italian dressing
DINNER	**Chili-Stuffed Potatoes** (Wrap a large baking potato in foil; bake at 450° for 1 hour or until done. Slit potato, and squeeze to open; fluff pulp with a fork. Spoon ½ cup canned vegetarian chili with beans, warmed, into center of pota-to; top with 3 tablespoons shredded cheddar cheese. Reserve remaining chili for dinner on Sunday. [*POINTS:* 7]) **steamed broccoli,** 1 cup	**broiled sirloin steak,** 3 ounces, topped with 3 tablespoons salsa **black beans,** ⅔ cup **steamed fresh spinach,** 1 cup	**vegetarian chili with beans, canned,** 1½ cups, topped with 3 table-spoons shredded cheddar cheese [*POINTS:* 7] **saltines,** 6 **Vanilla-Mango Yogurt** (Combine an 8-ounce carton vanilla fat-free aspar-tame-sweetened yogurt and ½ mango, peeled and cubed. [*POINTS:* 3])
SNACK	**popcorn,** 94% fat-free microwave-popped, 1 large bag	**animal crackers,** 13 **fat-free milk,** 1 cup	**popcorn,** 94% fat-free microwave-popped, 1 large bag
POINTS	*POINTS* for the day: 26 **Exchanges:** 9 Starch, 3 Fruit, 2½ Veg, 2 Sk Milk, 1 Very Lean Meat, 2 Hi-fat Meat, 1 Fat	*POINTS* for the day: 29 **Exchanges:** 6 Starch, 2 Fruit, 4 Veg, 2 Sk Milk, 4 Very Lean Meat, 3 Lean Meat, 1 Hi-fat Meat, 1 Fat	*POINTS* for the day: 28 **Exchanges:** 6½ Starch, 1 Fruit, 3 Veg, 2 Sk Milk, 2½ Very Lean Meat, 2½ Hi-fat Meat, 1 Fat

General Recipe Index

Recipes by *POINTS* Index

All recipes, including those in the Weekly Menu Planners, are listed alphabetically by title under the appropriate category. **Number of POINTS for each recipe is shown in bold.**

Acknowledgments

CONTRIBUTING PHOTOGRAPHER

Howard L. Puckett

CONTRIBUTING PHOTO STYLISTS

Melanie J. Clarke
Ashley J. Wyatt

CONTRIBUTING RECIPE DEVELOPERS

Jack Bishop
David Bonom
Leigh Ann Cox
Jim Fobel
Caroline A. Grant
Nancy Hughes
Elizabeth Tyler Luckett
Jackie Mills
Iris Crawley O'Brien
Greg Patent
Marge Perry
Victoria Abbot Riccardi
Elizabeth J. Taliaferro

EDITORIAL CONTRIBUTORS

Mindy Keyes Black
Leigh Ann Cox
Elisabeth Flynn
Jennifer Greer
Alice Lesch Kelly
Margaret Littman
Richard Mintzer
Marge Perry
Diane Quagliani
Jim Travisano
Joe Watts
Kimberly Weeks
Russell Wild
Tracey Zemitis

METRIC EQUIVALENTS

The recipes that appear in this cookbook use the standard United States method for measuring liquid and dry or solid ingredients (teaspoons, tablespoons, and cups). The information in the following charts is provided to help cooks outside the U.S. successfully use these recipes. All equivalents are approximate.

EQUIVALENTS FOR DIFFERENT TYPES OF INGREDIENTS

A standard cup measure of a dry or solid ingredient will vary in weight depending on the type of ingredient. A standard cup of liquid is the same volume for any type of liquid. Use the following chart when converting standard cup measures to grams (weight) or milliliters (volume).

Standard Cup	Fine Powder (ex. flour)	Grain (ex. rice)	Granular (ex. sugar)	Liquid Solids (ex. butter)	Liquid (ex. milk)
1	140 g	150 g	190 g	200 g	240 ml
¾	105 g	113 g	143 g	150 g	180 ml
⅔	93 g	100 g	125 g	133 g	160 ml
½	70 g	75 g	95 g	100 g	120 ml
⅓	47 g	50 g	63 g	67 g	80 ml
¼	35 g	38 g	48 g	50 g	60 ml
⅛	18 g	19 g	24 g	25 g	30 ml

DRY INGREDIENTS BY WEIGHT

(To convert ounces to grams, multiply the number of ounces by 30.)

1 oz	=	⅟₁₆ lb	=	30 g
4 oz	=	¼ lb	=	120 g
8 oz	=	½ lb	=	240 g
12 oz	=	¾ lb	=	360 g
16 oz	=	1 lb	=	480 g

LENGTH

(To convert inches to centimeters, multiply the number of inches by 2.5.)

1 in	=			=	2.5 cm			
6 in	=	½ ft		=	15 cm			
12 in	=	1 ft		=	30 cm			
36 in	=	3 ft	=	1 yd	=	90 cm		
40 in	=			=	100 cm	=	1 meter	

LIQUID INGREDIENTS BY VOLUME

¼ tsp						1 ml		
½ tsp						2 ml		
1 tsp						5 ml		
3 tsp	=	1 tbls		=	½ fl oz	=	15 ml	
		2 tbls	=	⅛ cup	=	1 fl oz	=	30 ml
		4 tbls	=	¼ cup	=	2 fl oz	=	60 ml
		5⅓ tbls	=	⅓ cup	=	3 fl oz	=	80 ml
		8 tbls	=	½ cup	=	4 fl oz	=	120 ml
		10⅔ tbls	=	⅔ cup	=	5 fl oz	=	160 ml
		12 tbls	=	¾ cup	=	6 fl oz	=	180 ml
		16 tbls	=	1 cup	=	8 fl oz	=	240 ml
1 pt	=	2 cups	=	16 fl oz	=	480 ml		
1 qt	=	4 cups	=	32 fl oz	=	960 ml		
				33 fl oz	=	1000 ml	=	1 liter

COOKING/OVEN TEMPERATURES

	Fahrenheit	Celsius	Gas Mark
Freeze Water	32° F	0° C	
Room Temperature	68° F	20° C	
Boil Water	212° F	100° C	
Bake	325° F	160° C	3
	350° F	180° C	4
	375° F	190° C	5
	400° F	200° C	6
	425° F	220° C	7
	450° F	230° C	8
Broil			Grill